The South African Society

Recent Titles in
Contributions in Ethnic Studies
Series Editor: Leonard W. Doob

The
South African
Society

Realities
and Future Prospects

HUMAN SCIENCES RESEARCH COUNCIL

CONTRIBUTIONS IN ETHNIC STUDIES, NUMBER 21

GREENWOOD PRESS
NEW YORK • WESTPORT, CONNECTICUT • LONDON

306. 0 968
S08
/ 4 6 833
Jun, 1989

Library of Congress Cataloging-in-Publication Data

The South African society.

(Contributions in ethnic studies, ISSN 0196-7088 ;
no. 21)
"Final report of the Main Committee of the HSRC
Investigation into Intergroup Relations"—Pref.
Bibliography: p.
Includes index.
1. South Africa—Social conditions—1961-
2. South Africa—Ethnic relations. I. HSRC
Investigation into Intergroup Relations. Main
Committee. II. Series.
HN801.A8S68   1987   306'.0968   86-27107
ISBN 0-313-25724-8 (lib. bdg. : alk. paper)

Library of Congress Catalog Card Number: 86-27107
ISBN: 0-313-25724-8
ISSN: 0196-7088

First published in 1987

Greenwood Press, Inc.
88 Post Road West, Westport, Connecticut 06881

Printed in the United States of America

The paper used in this book complies with the
Permanent Paper Standard issued by the National
Information Standards Organization (Z39.48-1984).

10 9 8 7 6 5 4 3 2 1

PREFACE

This is the final report of the Main Committee of the *HSRC Investigation into Intergroup Relations.*

Intergroup relations is a contentious issue both inside and outside South Africa. Inside South Africa it has not only dominated political thinking for the past several decades but has also, to a greater or lesser extent, affected the day-to-day lives of all the country's inhabitants. Outside the country's borders, the issue of intergroup relations is used as a political football in the international arena.

However, within the context of South Africa's plural society, the issue of intergroup relations offers the social scientist a unique and complex human laboratory, extending certain scientific challenges that are unequalled anywhere else in the world. If accepted, these challenges can provide a wealth of insights into intergroup relations that cannot be obtained from less complex situations.

Scholars from a spectrum of disciplines recognized the urgency and complexity of the problem posed by intergroup relations, and responded to the challenge. This report of the Main Committee is therefore not merely a scientific analysis of intergroup relations in South Africa — it represents a comprehensive interdisciplinary attempt to address the intergroup relations issue in South Africa in all its facets in a scientifically accountable way.

The *modus operandi* of the Main Committee is evident from the report, which was compiled in draft form by a number of main committee members together with other specialists, on the basis of the material collected by 13 work committees. This draft report was discussed as a whole and in detail by the Main Committee, and certain sections were revised fundamentally.

In the final report it was striven throughout to reflect different views and interpretations of the complex South African society.

All the members of the Main Committee subscribed to the broad findings of the investigation as set out in this final report.

The Main Committee trusts that the report will make a constructive contribution towards the optimal development of sound intergroup relations in South Africa.

ACKNOWLEDGEMENTS

An investigation of this nature and extent could not have been carried out without the co-operation of a great number of persons and institutions. Our sincere thanks to everyone who made a contribution, and to the following in particular:

- all the researchers and members of the work committees and the Main Committee

- universities and other institutions that allowed members of their staff to devote so much time to this undertaking

- Prof. J.H. Coetzee who got the investigation off to a good start

- Miss L. Dreyer (until July 1982), Prof. B.C. Lategan and Mr J.L. Olivier for their patience, perseverance and skill as co-ordinators, and Mmes I. Samuel (until December 1982), S.L. van der Walt (until September 1984), A.E. Pienaar and M. Marneweck for their positive support for the duration of the investigation, and

- the whole infrastructure of the HSRC which was always at the investigation's disposal, and the particular personnel for the professional services rendered.

I also wish to express my appreciation to the following persons who made the present edition possible:

- Dr Leonard W. Doob whose enthusiasm, inspiration and insight were indispensable

- Mildred Vasan, editress of *Constitutions in Ethnic Studies,* for her professional advice and support, and

- Adeline Korb for the final editing.

H.C. Marais
Chairman: HSRC Investigation into Intergroup Relations

CONTENTS

SERIES FOREWORD

Contributions in Ethnic Studies focuses upon the problems that arise when people from different cultures and with different goals come together and interact, either productively or tragically. The modes of adjustment or conflict are various, but usually one group dominates or attempts to dominate the other. Eventually, some accommodation is reached, but the process is likely to be long and, for the weaker group, painful. No one scholarly discipline monopolizes the research necesssary to comprehend these intergroup relations. The emerging analysis, therefore, is of interest to historians, social scientists, psychologists, and psychiatrists.

The acute and complex problems posed by intergroup relations in South Africa are, of course, widely known both inside and outside that country. There can be no disagreement with the view that new solutions must be uncovered and adopted if additional conflict and bloodshed are to be avoided, and if justice, however operationally defined, is eventually to be achieved. The present volume seeks to improve our understanding of South Africa and suggests "guidelines" for significant change.

The authors of this book are members of a "Main Committee," appointed by the Human Sciences Research Council in Pretoria, with the mandate to conduct research on the dynamics, structure, and future prospects of intergroup relations in South Africa. The Council, formed in 1969 by the merger of two older research organizations, is a statutory body which has undertaken, financed, and coordinated social research in that country. The majority of the Committee are Afrikaners, with one African "observer." As in the past, most but not all the cooperating scholars are also Afrikaners. The study was launched in 1981; the Committee solicited and financed 116 relevant and "directed" research "projects" by 208 South African scholars in the social sciences, economics, history, and legal studies. The nature and quality of the resulting research are evident in the monographs and articles that have appeared or are scheduled to appear. The summarizing report, the present book, was completed in March 1985 and released in an Afrikaans and English edition in July of that year. This edition by the Greenwood Press contains a number of minor changes and additions for the benefit of readers not residing in South Africa.

The book makes three contributions that can be briefly stated because they are adequately demonstrated throughout its content. In the first place, we have a clear-cut demonstration of the value of a multidisciplinary approach to the burning issue of intergroup relations. Too often we have appraisals of problems in South Africa and elsewhere from the arbitrarily restricted viewpoint of a single discipline or a headline-seeking journalist. It is therefore refreshing and enlightening to observe a frontal attack upon contemporary events in South Africa. Any wide-ranging synthesis such as the one outlined in the report necessarily omits some details and viewpoints, but any attempt to break down conventional academic preserves is stimulating to observe.

Secondly, as readers, we are able to profit from a coordinated approach to the subject, and thus to view many of the intergroup problems of South Africa in broad, yet detailed perspective. After the historical developments leading to the present situation have been briefly portrayed, we are given essential demographic facts about the country together with extrapolations into the future. In a society with "a power base traditionally dominated by whites," the "experience" of the different ethnic groups is next examined, particularly with reference to their basic cultures, their identifications, their own versions of history, and many of their current attitudes and stereotypes. In the next chapter, the economic, political, and social structure of South African society is analyzed, including references to the increase in "the number of people below the breadline in the 'homelands';" "the most striking contradictions in South Africa's group relations problems," and "institutionalized inequality."

The third and perhaps most surprising contribution of this presentation has already been illustrated in the phrases quoted in the last paragraph: the Afrikaner editors do not conceal their value judgments critical of their own nation. Although they explicitly state at the outset that evaluations and recommendations (they call them "deductions") are reserved for the last two chapters, apparently they cannot restrain themselves in the midst of the preceding scholarly sections. In the earlier chapters, for example, are references to the "need for liaison between groups at a formal and informal level," to "a long and unhappy history of exclusion from particpation in local goverment" by the "African, coloured, and Indian communities," and to the "purposeful effort [that] will have to be made to meet the exceptionally complex challenge of assisting everyone to become successfully integrated in the modern economy." On the last pages, we are told:

The conclusion reached in this report is therefore that the political ordering of inter-group relations according to the original apartheid model has reached an impasse and that constructive relations cannot be developed along these lines.

And the final two sentences of the report:

. . . The relations between groups in South Africa is a crucial matter that demands the most urgent attention. Delays in addressing the issue could have catastrophic consequences.

The book thus makes the fruits of scientific and scholarly inquiry relevant to the pending, drastic changes in South Africa. No easy panacea or political program is offered. The challenge to implement the general and specific "guidelines," however, has been sufficiently impressive to provoke an official response of government by State President P. W. Botha's office. That statement and a sampling of press comments are included in the present volume, as well as Notes (starting on page 174) that explain some of the terms or phrases not likely to be familiar to English-speaking readers. Precise references to published and unpublished research reports can be obtained by writing the Human Sciences Research Council in Pretoria.

We have here, in short, a historical document that may be viewed as a significant contribution to the future of South Africa.

Leonard W. Doob

September 1, 1986

The South African Society

CHAPTER 1

INTRODUCTION

This report is the end product of an investigation into human relations — a matter that has become increasingly topical on a national level in South Africa. The investigation was undertaken over a period of more than four years and researchers from all parts of the country participated in it on a partnership basis. The researchers represented 15 universities, the Human Sciences Research Council (HSRC) and several other organizations. The multidisciplinary approach employed involved some 20 academic disciplines.

The investigation was managed by a main committee and 13 work committees. Contracts for the execution of the research projects were entered into with approximately 100 researchers and research teams. The results and findings of the research projects were collated into 11 work committee reports and thereafter integrated into this main report.

The *HSRC Investigation into Intergroup Relations* is the third investigation to be undertaken on a co-operative basis of this nature. The preceding two large-scale co-operative research programmes were the *HSRC Investigation into Education* executed under the direction of Prof. J.P. de Lange of the Rand Afrikaans University and the *HSRC Sports Investigation* executed under the direction of Prof. G.J.L. Scholtz of Potchefstroom University. These two investigations were undertaken respectively at the request of the Cabinet and the Minister of National Education. The *HSRC Investigation into Intergroup Relations* was, however, not initiated by a request received for such research but was launched entirely on the initiative of the HSRC.

This chapter contains a concise exposition of the origin and launching of this research programme as well as of its nature and aim, the problem it addresses, the demarcation of the field concerned and the method employed in the compilation of the report. These matters are described in turn in the following paragraphs.

1

THE ORIGIN OF THE INVESTIGATION

In 1980 the first attempt was made within the framework of the *South African Plan for Research in the Human Sciences* to determine empirically research priorities in South Africa. That exercise comprised several phases in which opinion leaders of diverse ideological orientations were involved. It aimed at identifying problem areas

- that could be investigated scientifically;
- that endangered the welfare, happiness and prosperity of all the inhabitants of the country;
- for which solutions had to be found in order to improve the quality of life of every inhabitant of the country.

In this priority determination *intergroup relations* was identified as the most important problem area. On the grounds of this finding the *Research Priorities Committee* (RPC) recommended to the Council of the HSRC at the beginning of 1980 that a comprehensive investigation be conducted into this matter. The HSRC presented the merits of the proposed investigation to the Directorate for Science Planning where it was considered by the Priorities Committee together with all other applications for research funds. Upon the approval of the application the *HSRC Investigation into Intergroup Relations* (hereafter referred to as the *Investigation*) was launched at the beginning of 1981 on the basis of co-operation with the entire research community. Prof. J.H. Coetzee, professor of Anthropology at Potchefstroom University, was appointed as the first research director but he resigned in September of the same year because of poor health. He was succeeded by Dr H.C. Marais who at the time was the Director of the Institute for Research Development of the HSRC.

PREPARATORY PHASE

The Main Committee of the investigation was appointed by the Council of the HSRC during the first quarter of 1981. The members of the Main Committee were identified after extensive consultation with a wide spectrum of experts and institutions concerned with the problem of intergroup relations as well as with the aid of a seminar that was held at the HSRC on 16 February 1981.

The first meeting of the Main Committee was held on 11 May 1981. This meeting concerned itself mainly with general policy issues and appointed a work group consisting of Profs J.H. Coetzee, H.W. van der Merwe, L. Schlemmer, S.P. Cilliers, A.F. Steyn, H.G. Viljoen, S. Swart and Dr N.J. Rhoodie to undertake a preliminary demarcation of the field of investigation. This committee, in the activities of which Profs Cilliers and Viljoen were unable to participate, submitted a report to the Main Committee on 29 June 1981 which contained recommendations regarding the structure of the investigation as well as the identification of problem areas that should be investigated. The Main Committee accepted the report.

After the second meeting of the Main Committee the progress made involved changes in respect of the structure and content of the *HSRC Investigation into Intergroup Relations*. On the one hand, changes in the situations of some Main Committee members necessitated the appointment of additional members to the Main Committee. In all such cases the invitations were based on recommendations made by the Main Committee. On the other hand, the decisions taken at the Main Committee meeting of 29 June 1981 were used as the basis for the determination of the method and content of the research programme. During the course of the *Investigation* it became necessary, however, to make some adjustments of a procedural and thematic nature.

THE NATURE OF THE RESEARCH PROGRAMME

It is inconceivable that any one research institution in South Africa would be able to investigate a comprehensive problem area such as intergroup relations by means of a multidisciplinary approach without the assistance or co-operation of other institutions and individuals. It was therefore assumed from the outset that the co-operation of as many researchers as possible from the various research institutions would be required for the execution of this research programme. It was furthermore accepted that a problem area of this nature should to be approached from several theoretical, methodological and ideological perspectives. From its conceptualization onwards this research programme was regarded as a co-operative programme and it was therefore initiated, planned and executed in that manner.

The *South African Plan for Research in the Human Sciences* (SAPRHS) contains a procedure whereby investigations of this nature can be executed. The procedure described in the SAPRHS was therefore followed as closely as possible.

As stated above, the *Investigation* was launched exclusively on the initiative of the HSRC as a result of a survey of research priorities undertaken in terms of the SAPRHS and on the recommendation of the Research Priorities Committee for Human Sciences Research of the HSRC. Since this *Investigation* was not initiated and executed at the request of any interested party, it was possible to launch and execute it independently as a scientific contribution to the reflection on the issue of intergroup relations in South Africa.

3

THE PROBLEM AND AIM OF THE INVESTIGATION

Since the *Investigation* was closely associated with the aim and method of the SAPRHS, two considerations predominated in its execution from the beginning, namely

• that the aim of the investigation should be the improvement of the quality of life, in the broadest sense, of every inhabitant of the country; and

• this aim could best be achieved by means of optimum self-development, i.e. by creating opportunities for people to determine for themselves as far as possible the nature, content and realization of the quality of life.

Any attempt at improving the quality of life in South Africa must take cognisance of the reality of South African society, namely that it is complex and deeply segmented. This means that the interaction between *groups,* irrespective of the basis upon which groups are formed or classified, is a matter that is intimately related to quality of life. It is obvious that it is also the reason why the first attempt at identifying research priorities in South Africa — referred to above — clearly identified *intergroup relations* as the most important area for research.

The South African situation is such that its constituents can both promote and impede the improvement of the quality of life of its inhabitants. The impeding effect can be of such a nature that it may eventually give rise to conflict. For this reason Dr Rhoodie was requested by the Main Committee at the commencement of the *Investigation* to study and report on the phenomenon of conflict in deeply segmented societies. This report was completed at the end of 1981 (Rhoodie, 1983).

Rhoodie (1983) describes *inter alia* the following characteristics of South African society:

• Deep segmentation and complex pluralization on the basis of divisions such as culture, historical background, language and religion.

• A significant number of these divisions overlap and converge and therefore divisions such as culture, language and religion often coincide.

• Some of the divisions are related to people's basic needs for survival.

• Members of a particular group — irrespective of individual differences — are characterized by the presence or absence of largely comparable privileges.

It is characteristic of deeply segmented societies that tension is virtually endemic in them. This conclusion reached by Rhoodie should be seen against the background of the following statement made by him: *It is not specific socio-cultural and socio-psychological variables as such that generate conflict but the way in which these variables combine in a particular historical framework* (p. 163). Conceptual analyses lead to the conclusion that conflict is in fact structurally present in South African society and, if it is not regulated, it is very likely to increase in extent and intensity. It can also be concluded from the foregoing that it is almost inconceivable that a country such as South Africa will ever be completely free of tension.

As indicated above, the *Investigation* focused on the relations between segments of the population and more specifically on the potential or actual tension in those relations that can influence the improvement of the quality of life of individuals and groups in South Africa. This issue has for many years been a focal point of interest both locally and abroad. The political developments of the past few years, the renewed unrest in recent times and the intensification of foreign involvement have made the issue particularly topical. This investigation does not, therefore, pretend to be unaware of the intensive and dynamic debate and reflection taking place in South Africa at present. On the contrary, it represents an attempt by researchers from different disciplines and from all parts of the country to make a scientific contribution to the debate. It is hoped that through the publication of additional and new scientific information and perspectives a constructive contribution will be made to the handling of problems of intergroup relations in South Africa.

The *Investigation* was initiated and guided in the light of the above considerations. It was, therefore, directed at presenting a *scientifically accountable description and explanation of the nature and processes of intergroup relations in South Africa.* Attention was paid in particular to the conflict that occurs in intergroup relations or that is potentially present in these relations and an attempt was made to give an interpretation of the dynamics of conflict in that context.

The *Investigation* was launched as a *problem-oriented* research programme within the frame of reference of the SAPRHS. The Main Committee had decided at the outset that emphasis would not be given to comprehensive basic research but rather to *directed* basic research. Despite this practical and empirical orientation of the *Investigation,* no specific and politically oriented recommendations were made regarding the improvement of intergroup relations on the basis of the findings. It was considered that this field is so complex and so subject to continuous dynamic change that it would be more meaningful to distill and to present from the research undertaken those principles and guidelines for the improvement of intergroup relations that could be considered as essential conditions for the accommodation of conflict.

5

It was assumed that the principles and guidelines formulated in this report are such that they can be translated into concrete and practicable recommendations. That task will, however, require the intensive efforts of researchers and interest groups and does not fall within the ambit of the research brief as it was defined by the Main Committee.

The *Investigation* was not based on any specific political model, neither did it have a *status quo* orientation or a radical conflict approach. The orientation chosen attempted scientific fairness. However, it is not claimed that the *Investigation* was completely "neutral" or value free. The two basic premises were clearly stated at the beginning of this section. Scientific accountability was upheld as an ideal in the *Investigation* and it was required that every research report should clearly indicate the theoretical frame of reference and hypotheses adopted in it.

DEMARCATION OF THE FIELD OF INVESTIGATION

In order to render a field as wide as that of intergroup relations scientifically accessible, it was essential to specify it clearly. Besides the necessity of specifying the factors that facilitate and inhibit intergroup relations, the question regarding the meaning of the term *group* in intergroup relations was a critical one. South African society (which will be discussed in some detail in Chapter 2) includes population *categories* that have been entrenched in the juridical and political systems. For example, in census surveys and in all aspects of public life the following main population categories apply: blacks, whites, coloureds and Indians. Although there is a large measure of convergence between these categories and the ethnic and/or cultural divisions between groups, the juridical groupings do not necessarily correspond fully with reality or with the manner in which people group themselves. Explicit provision was therefore made for researchers to segment the population in other ways, depending upon their own theoretical and ideological frames of reference.

The fact that attention was focused on population categories also does not imply that the potential importance of a class perspective was not recognized. It was accepted that material interests and economic class contribute towards the establishment of social structures. On the level of perception and experience people do, however, define themselves, in the first instance, as members of a population group in a broader or more specific sense. The research also showed that population group/race/nationality are first-order interpretations, categorizations or characteristics in terms of which others are perceived.

Although particular emphasis was necessarily given to population categories in the *Investigation,* this should not be interpreted as meaning that segmentation on the basis of population category should necessarily be emphasized to the same degree in future. Since this issue will be addressed again at various places and in different contexts in this report, it will not be given further attention at this stage.

On several occasions the Main Committee considered the terminology used to identify population categories and groups since it is a matter that has many emotive and ideological elements and which often bears unexpected connotations of prejudice. After considering a submission by Prof. H.W. van der Merwe in the light of these implications, the Main Committee decided to use the terms Africans, Indians, coloureds and whites in this report to identify the four main groups of people in South Africa. This procedure does not mean that any explicit assumptions or points of departure of any interest groups in South African society were thereby either supported or ignored.

The *Investigation* and this report in particular offer a perspective on the problem of intergroup relations in *South Africa.* Throughout the research programme research undertaken abroad was taken into consideration mainly for theoretical and methodological purposes. It was accepted that although there might be many general similarities between the situation in South Africa and those in other countries, the specific configuration of factors and processes differs from country to country to such an extent that it would not be possible to do justice to a comparative study within the confines of this research programme.

As will become apparent in the course of this report, intergroup relations in certain respects constitute the building blocks of society. Consequently it is not possible to remove them from their social context and to analyze them as an abstraction. Against this background those societal areas, such as the juridical, that form frameworks within which intergroup relations are manifested, were necessarily included in the *Investigation.* The field of work of the *Investigation* was therefore for operational reasons divided into 11 subfields:

- Historical aspects including the development of intergroup relations and, especially, the role of historiography in the depiction of intergroup relations.
- Demographic facets of the South African population.
- Anthropoligical perspectives on ethnic, cultural and racial factors in intergroup and intragroup relations.
- Socio-psychological facets such as perception, attitudes, prejudice and conflict.
- The function of interpersonal communication and mass communication in intergroup relations.

- The meaning and role of religion in the relations between groups.

- Perspectives of development administration on intergroup relations in terms of, *inter alia,* development models, differential opportunities and administrative attitudes.

- Economic influences such as growth and poverty on intergroup relations as well as labour relations that reflect and influence intergroup relations.

- The juridical field which includes diverse matters such as the philosophy of law regarding groups and relations and the administration of relevant laws.

- An evaluation of constitutional, political and administrative matters.

- A sociological view of South African society and intergroup relations in general.

Two other areas common to all of the above were also identified, namely the problem of theoretical approach and methodology and the availability of bibliographical data.

A work committee was constituted for each of these areas, except the demographic area. The nature and functions of the work committees are described in the following section.

THE METHOD APPLIED IN THE INVESTIGATION

There were three levels in the management, organization and execution of the *HSRC Investigation into Intergroup Relations:* the levels of the Main Committee, work committees and contract researchers.

THE MAIN COMMITTEE

The Main Committee comprised the following members who were appointed by the HSRC in their personal capacity:

Dr H.C. Marais (Chairman)	Vice President: Human Sciences Research Council.
Prof. M. Bopape	Head: Department of Social Work, University of the North
Dr C.V. Bothma	Director: Social Planning, Department of Co-operation, Development and Education
Dr W.J. Breytenbach	Director: State Planning, Department of Constitutional Development and Planning
Prof. S.P. Cilliers	Head: Department of Sociology, University of Stellenbosch

Dr H.P. Fourie	Chief Director: Social Planning, Department of Constitutional Development and Planning
Dr J.G. Garbers	President: Human Sciences Research Council
Mr R.M. Godsell	Industrial Relations Consultant: Anglo American Corporation of SA Ltd.
Prof. W.D. Hammond-Tooke	Head: Department of Social Anthropology, University of the Witwatersrand
Prof. E. Higgins	Dean: Faculty of Social Sciences, Rhodes University
Prof. D.A. Kotzé	Head: Department of Development Administration and Politics, University of South Africa
Dr J.M. Lötter	Executive Director: Institute for Sociological and Demographic Research, Human Sciences Research Council
Mr E.B. Lubelwana (deceased)	Chairman: Community Council, Guguletu
Rev. J.J.F. Mettler	Minister of Religion, Nederduits Gereformeerde Sendingkerk, Mitchell's Plain
Prof. J.C. Moll	Dean: Faculty of Arts, University of the Orange Free State
Prof. C.J. Nel	Head: Department of Ethnology, University of the Orange Free State
Dr G.K. Nelson	Executive Director: National Institute for Personnel Research, Human Sciences Research Council
Prof. G.C. Oosthuizen	Head: Research Institute for the Study of New Religions and Independent Churches, University of Zululand. Previously attached to the Department of Religious Sciences, University of Durban-Westville
Dr K.P. Prinsloo	Executive Director: Institute for Research into Language and the Arts, Human Sciences Research Council
Prof. B.G. Ranchod	Head: Department of Private Law, University of Durban-Westville
Prof. L. Schlemmer	Director: Centre for Applied Social Sciences, University of Natal

Prof. A.F. Steyn	Head: Department of Sociology, Rand Afrikaans University
Mr G.A. Thiele	Institute for Communication Research, Human Sciences Research Council
Mr J. Tshabalala	Former mayor of Atteridgeville
Prof. H.W. van der Merwe	Director: Centre for Intergroup Studies, University of Cape Town
Dr J.D. Venter	Deputy President: Human Sciences Research Council
Prof. H.G. Viljoen	Department of Psychology, University of South Africa
Prof. H.W. Vilakazi	Department of Philosophy, University of Cape Town
Prof. M. Wiechers	Head: Department of Constitutional Law, University of South Africa
Prof. N.E. Wiehahn	Director: Department of Business Leadership, University of South Africa

Drs C.V. Bothma, W.J. Breytenbach and H.P. Fourie served on the main committee *ex officio* and as observers; their participation in decisions was therefore non-official. Prof. Vilakazi took part as an observer.

The Main Committee was responsible for the policy and management of the *Investigation* as a whole. The Council of the HSRC delegated the final responsibility for the *Investigation* to the Main Committee. The most important specific functions of the Main Committee included the following:

● Policy determination.

● Demarcation of the field and operationalization at macrolevel.

● Identification of work committees and appointment of members to these committees.

● Approval of research tenders and the identification of specific projects. In total 137 research tenders were received from the research community of which 93 were approved. At the request of the work committees a further 12 special projects were undertaken in areas in which a lack of research findings became apparent.

● The Main Committee was also responsible for the compilation of this main report, which is primarily a synthesis of the work committees reports and other reports that were specially compiled for the *Investigation* (See appendix A for a complete list). For this reason the main report only refers to the reports upon which it is based and not to other

10

specific sources that were also consulted. Owing to the very nature of the synthesis process new interpretations of the information were often required after the information had been collated in new contexts. (The method employed is described in the final section of this chapter).

The Main Committee met eight times during the course of the *Investigation*. An executive committee was appointed to deal with occasional matters as well as other matters referred to it by the Main Committee. The Executive Committee convened seven times, and the chairmen of the work committees three times.

WORK COMMITTEES

A work committee was appointed for each of the areas identified above. The primary function of the work committees was to assist the Main Committee on the meso levels and micro levels of research in specific areas. The most important specific functions of the work committees were the following:

● Description of specific research areas.

● Thematization and operationalization of specific research areas.

● Evaluation of research tenders received.

● Evaluation of research reports on completed contract projects.

● Identification of urgently needed research, identification of researchers to do the work and the evaluation of the completed research.

● Integration of the research done under the guidance of the work committees into a consolidated work committee report that was submitted to the Main Committee. The responsibility of a particular work committee for the findings, interpretations and conclusions of the *Investigation* was limited to the content of the work committee report concerned.

● An adapted method was used to generate a set of principles for spatial arrangement. The chairmen of six work committees concluded contracts with 10 experts to write concise reports in which various perspectives on the problem of spatial arrangement were highlighted from the perspective of the discipline of each of the contractors. The following disciplines were involved: law, anthropology, public administration, geography and economics. During a seminar these contributions were consolidated into a set of principles and guidelines about which the participants reached consensus.

The work committees convened several times but also attended to many matters by correspondence.

CONTRACT RESEARCHERS

Researchers were invited to undertake specific projects in the *Investigation* on a contract basis. To this end announcements regarding the programme were made in various publications, two special brochures were issued and relevant information was given to individual researchers. In all, 208 researchers were involved in projects that were executed on a contract basis, while a further 150 persons, including members of the work committees, contributed from their fields of expertise. The titles of the approved projects are given in appendix A.

PROCEDURES

The procedures followed in the *Investigation* can briefly be described as follows: Information regarding the launching of the *Investigation* was disseminated as widely as possible to the South African research community. The entire research community was also invited to participate in the research. The projects that had been operationalized by the work committees were also announced at this stage. The latter announcement contained a note stating that prospective researchers could also submit proposals regarding related research projects. The research proposals received were then evaluated and research contracts entered into with researchers for the execution of the approved project proposals.

In the execution of the research three levels were involved. Firstly, there were researchers who conducted empirical or theoretical research independently. Secondly, the HSRC undertook a multipurpose survey in which researchers could participate by, on the one hand, proposing questions and other items for inclusion in the questionnaire, and, on the other, by using the data generated by the survey for the purposes of their project reports. A third level of research concerned those researchers for whom special multipurpose surveys were undertaken on random samples of certain sections of the population. The latter surveys therefore involved only a limited number of researchers whose data gathering was collated in each questionnaire and survey.

The research infrastructure of the HSRC was available throughout to researchers who participated in the *Investigation*. This infrastructure included the following:

● A full-time information officer who established a bibliographic data bank and supplied bibliographical references.

● The services of the Opinion Survey Centre (OSC) which were used for two national and six more localized surveys.

● The Institute for Statistical Research (ISR) which was available to researchers for consultation.

- The Computer Centre at the HSRC which assisted in the analysis of empirical data.

- The Centre for Language Services which rendered editing services during various stages of the *Investigation*.

- The questionnaires as well as this report were printed by the HSRC.

The execution of the research programme entailed a significant volume of additional work for the research support services of the HSRC, particularly as requests for assistance were usually extensive and stated as urgent.

THE COMPILATION OF THIS REPORT

PROCEDURE

The preliminary findings of the various work committees were tabled for discussion and comment at a meeting of the Main Committee on 1 March 1985. Subsequently the Director of the *Investigation* and the two co-ordinators compiled a draft report that was moderated and adapted on 11 April 1985 by a work group comprising Profs S.P. Cilliers, B.C. Lategan, M. Wiechers and L. Schlemmer; Drs H.C. Marais and N.J. Rhoodie; and Mr R.M. Godsell.

The draft report that emanated from the work session was submitted on 19 April 1985 to the following persons for comment: the persons mentioned above; the chairmen of the other work committees: Profs D.A. Kotzé, J.C. Moll, B.G. Ranchod, G.C. Oosthuizen and H.G. Viljoen; as well as to the other members of the Executive Committee: Drs W.J. Breytenbach and J.G. Garbers, and Profs W.D. Hammond-Tooke and A.F. Steyn. After the incorporation of the suggested changes to the draft report, a second draft was submitted to a meeting of the Main Committee on 21-24 May 1985. This draft report was discussed as a whole and in detail and was accepted on 24 May 1985 after some final adjustments to it had been effected.

Although there are still several facets of the field that could have been researched in greater depth, it was considered important to take notice of recent developments. Since this report was intended to contribute towards the current debate on the development of constructive intergroup relations, it was decided to conclude this phase of the *Investigation* at this stage.

CONTENT OF THE REPORT

It was stated in a preceding section that the *Investigation* had been conceived and executed as a problem-oriented research programme. In view of the methodological and pragmatic demands of research of this nature, it appeared desirable to follow an inductive approach in the compilation of the report. The implication of this approach is that the most important findings are presented first (namely in Chapters 2 to 5), whereafter deductions from these findings are discussed (Chapter 6).

In the second chapter the problem addressed by the *Investigation* is specified by means of a concise description of South African society. This chapter contains what can be described as the contours of contemporary society. Chapter three presents the findings regarding the experience and perception of intergroup relations, while chapter four describes the manner in which intergroup relations are structured and institutionalized. A summarised interpretation of the preceding three chapters as well as an embracing conclusion are given in chapter five. Chapter six contains a number of deductions made from the findings and presents these in the form of preconditions for the development of constructive intergroup relations.

CHAPTER 2

GENERAL BACKGROUND TO THE PROBLEMS IN SOUTH AFRICA CONCERNING INTERGROUP RELATIONS

In this chapter the most important characteristics of South African society will be sketched in broad outline to serve as a background for the discussion of the particular findings of the *Investigation* in the following chapters. It will also attempt a delineation of the profile of South African intergroup relations.

The following paragraphs will briefly deal with the country's historical development, demography, education and training, language distribution, religious groupings, ethnic diversity, level of economic development and labour division, and, finally, the juridical, political and constitutional system. This chapter offers merely a review of the South African dispensation, and consequently only that information on which general agreement exists among scientists will be discussed.

HISTORICAL DEVELOPMENT

Intergroup relations in South Africa developed over a period of several centuries. The process was, and remains, a complex one in which individuals, groups, attitudes, values, ideologies and material interests played an important role and continue to do so. In many respects the historical process and the basic characteristics of intergroup relations in South Africa do not differ from those found elsewhere; in other respects they display elements that are unique to South African society.

The following outline of the historical development endeavours to sketch some of the more important lines of development. Owing to the vastness of the terrain — the whole history of a country — it is naturally not possible to go into detail.

15

The history of intergroup relations goes back to prehistoric times, long before the arrival of the whites. The earliest surviving inhabitants of South Africa were the San who lived a nomadic life as hunters and collectors. They were later joined by the Khoikhoi and groups speaking Bantu languages who settled in various parts of South Africa long before the arrival of the whites.

The interaction between these groups was at times characterized by conflict. The San, in particular, were ousted by the incoming Black chiefdoms. Interaction between these groups was mainly determined by economic factors, especially the acquisition and safeguarding of hunting grounds and pastures, livestock and agricultural land. There was also increasing commercial contact and, in some areas, social integration, especially between the San and Khoikhoi and between the Khoikhoi and the Bantu speakers.

The San, Khoikhoi and Black tribes were not homogeneous groups; each was in turn divided into separate communities with their own specific interests, leaders and circumstances. Between these communities there was also dynamic interaction based essentially on peaceful coexistence, but also periods of conflict as, for example, among the Khoikhoi who inhabited the Western Cape.

The settlement of the whites in South Africa had an important influence on intergroup relations. Not only did it signify the addition of a further group to the existing ones, but the whites also brought their European values and customs to Africa.

From 1652 European (white) colonial rule was established at the Cape and was gradually extended to the interior until the whole of South Africa was under colonial control. For nearly two and a half centuries South Africa (with the exception of the two Boer republics, for roughly 50 years) was under colonial rule. For economic and military reasons, first the Dutch East India Company and subsequently Britain established and maintained their authority here. Colonial control was extended to include all indigenous inhabitants so that all the groups in the region were subjected to the government at the Cape and the colonial rulers used their power and influence to try and regulate intergroup relations. This extension of authority included negotiations, treaties and military action, as was clearly illustrated by the situation on the eastern border in the 18th and

19th centuries. The establishment of colonial rule also brought foreign capital to South Africa and irrevocably linked intergroup relations to foreign interests. In due course this latter trend would become stronger.

Simultaneously with the establishment of European colonial rule, a white colonist population emerged with permanent interests in South Africa, under the control of — and at times in conflict with — the colonial power. The white colonists gradually developed a strong political consciousness and demanded greater participation in the government of the country as well as a say in the control of the new national economy. In due course a specific group, the Afrikaners, developed from the colonist population, and they, in time, developed a unique national consciousness. It was the Afrikaners — especially the Afrikaner frontier farmers — who opposed the colonial authorities and for various reasons moved away from British rule in the Cape Colony to found independent states in the interior. Afrikaner nationalism came strongly to the fore in the second half of the nineteenth century in the face of British imperialism. This led to two wars (the First and the Second Anglo-Boer Wars) between the Afrikaners and the British.

After the British occupation of the Cape in 1806, a significant number of English-speaking colonists settled in South Africa to become permanent residents of the country. Although British orientated, they soon acquired a South African (colonial) identity. They did not identify with the Afrikaners, but social and economic contact between the groups was common. Significant numbers of French and German immigrants also arrived in South Africa at an early stage of white settlement and in due course groups from numerous European countries would also find a permanent home here.

An outstanding characteristic of intergroup relations during this period was that it occurred within a typical frontier situation. The whites, in the process of expansion into the interior, came into contact with the Khoikhoi, San and Bantu-speakers. This contact was typified by competition for land (agricultural land, hunting land, pasture land) and water, and a struggle for supremacy, as was evident during the Frontier Wars of the 18th and 19th centuries. In the early phases of contact none of the groups succeeded in dominating the others. Political and social relations were fluid and all parties enjoyed equal status in the relations situation. As the whites established their authority over the indigenous communities, the latter lost their land and became subject to whites control. Labour played an increasingly important role in intergroup relations and the status of the Blacks changed from free to subordinate labourers. Reserves for the black communities were created, and these largely supplied to labour requirements of the whites.

The establishment of white authority over Africans was a process in which the colonial authorities and the white colonists united against the indigenous population. Only late in the nineteenth century was white authority indisputably established over the Africans.

African reaction to white expansion was divergent. Some groups co-operated with the whites. e.g. the Barolong; others, for example the Xhosa and Zulu, violently resisted, with the result that there was constant conflict between white and African in the border areas. African resistance to white domination was for a long time unco-ordinated and each group tried to oppose the whites on its own. The first efforts towards co-ordinated resistance only materialized late in the nineteenth century.

One of the major factors that would determine intergroup relations was the gradual growth of an assumption of white superiority and African subordination. There was a large degree of equality between whites and other groups in early Cape society. In due course, however, a legal, and especially a social, distinction was drawn between the groups so that differentiation on the basis of race and colour became a peculiarity of South African society. A wide range of factors was responsible for this, *inter alia* cultural differences, religious differences, class differences, slavery and conflict. The distinction was eventually embodied in legislation (constitutions, pass laws, labour laws, etc.).

Generally speaking the British authorities and colonists were more liberal in their attitude towards other groups than those in the Boer republics. Those groups did not have citizenship status in these republics and were not accepted as equals. Yet, although there was a considerable degree of political, social and economic differentiation between whites and other groups — which led to segregation measures and attitudes — total segregation, particularly in the field of economics, was never possible.

There was considerable social equality in early Cape society, and under these circumstances and owing to the fluid conditions of the border situation in the interior, legal marriages and numerous instances of cohabitation and miscegenation between whites and others occurred. From this miscegenation between whites, slaves (often from Asian countries), Africans, San and Khoikhoi, a group later commonly known as coloureds developed. Some of these people initially acquired equal status with the whites; the majority, however, had none and worked for whites as labourers. The coloureds have never been a homogeneous group.

In the early phases of the colonial period, before the whites occupied the interior of South Africa, there was dynamic interaction between the different African population groups. Political development, together with an increase in numbers, intensified the competition for land. This led to friction and conflict that sometimes resulted in drastic political and social changes, as, for example, during the *difaqane (mfecane)* in the early nineteenth century. The crystallizing out of a few big and powerful and a variety of smaller (e.g. the Barolong and Bataung) "tribes", was a feature of the period. The political, social and commercial relations between these communities were eventually strongly influenced by the coming of the whites.

The first Indians came to South Africa in 1860 as contract labourers for the sugar plantations in Natal, and were later followed by Indian traders. Immigration of Indians was stopped early in the 20th century. Most Indians reside in Natal and virtually all are descendants of the original settlers.

The discovery of diamonds and gold and the concomitant industrial growth brought about vast changes in South African society and in intergroup relations in the country. Africans streamed to the industrial centres in large numbers. On the one hand this caused social problems in the reserves and on the other hand it led to poor social conditions in the African residential areas of the industrial centres.

A factor that had a very real influence on intergroup relations was the strong upsurge of Afrikaner nationalism and the establishment of the political authority of the Afrikaner. This gave rise, from 1948, to the passing of a variety of acts in terms of which the ideology of apartheid ("separate development") was defined and enforced. The objective was "total" segregation between whites and others. A central part of the policy was the expansion of own areas (homelands) for the Africans within which they could express political and social rights and could eventually gain independence from South Africa as was realised in the Transkei, Bophuthatswana, Venda and Ciskei (TBVC countries). Afrikaner nationalism also effected stronger polarisation in the ranks of whites — between Afrikaans and English speaking people.

This period is characterized by increasing conflict between groups. The conflict concerned, in essence, political and economic power and social equality. The nature of the conflict was also different from that of the previous phases, namely a shift from an unco-ordinated to a more co-ordinated resistance built around organizations such as the African National Congress (ANC) and Pan Africanist Congress (PAC). However, the Africans are still not a homogeneous category — ethnicity (group interests) still plays an important role in relations between the different African groups.

The present situation is extremely volatile as increasing conflict on the one hand, and a re-evaluation of the policy of separate development on the other, have forced the whites to reassess the political dispensation.

COMPOSITION OF THE POPULATION, GROWTH AND DISTRIBUTION

A description of the population composition of the country in itself offers a clear illustration of the problems of intergroup relations. The *categories* into which the population is divided by legislation reflect a specific view of South African society. As indicated in Chapter 1, divisions such as language, culture and ethnicity often converge to form specific population groups, but even so, group boundaries remain relative. There is an implicit difference between legally defined population categories and the spontaneous group formation of people on the principle of voluntary association. In this regard reference can be made to the report of the Work Committee: Constitution and Politics: *Political co-operation within a fundamental legal order.*

When in the following discussion, the population composition is given according to official categories, this does not imply support of a specific constitutional or political model; it is done for pragmatic reasons, since this is the only form in which reliable census data are available.

Similarly, reference to the so-called TBVC countries (Transkei, Bophuthatswana, Venda and Ciskei) and national states must also not be interpreted as an indication of an acceptance a specific constitutional or ideological view. In this report the availability of the latest and most reliable statistics was the only consideration in the use of such data, and specific mention is made in each case of how the statistics were compiled.

COMPOSITION OF THE POPULATION

Constitutionally and juridically the South African population is divided into four categories, namely Asians, Africans, coloureds and whites. Numerical distribution of the population is given in Table 2.1

TABLE 2.1

COMPOSITION OF THE TOTAL SOUTH AFRICAN POPULATION: 1980 (TBVC COUNTRIES AND SELF-GOVERNING NATIONAL STATES INCLUDED)

Asians	Whites	Coloureds	Africans	Total
821 320	4 528 100	2 612 780	20 903 760	28 865 960
(2,8 %)	(15,7 %)	(9,1 %)	(72,4 %)	(100,0 %)

(*Source:* Smit *et al.*, 1983, pp. 2 and 3.)

It is clear from Table 2.1, which is based on the 1980 census, that African constitute the largest component (72 %) of the total population, followed by whites (15,7 %), coloureds (9,1 %) and Asians (2,8 %).

The population density of South Africa (TBVC countries and self-governing national states included) is 23 persons per square kilometre. However, the population density varies from 17 persons per/km² in the Republic of South Africa, to 52 persons/km² in the Transkei.

DISTRIBUTION AND REDISTRIBUTION OF THE POPULATION

In their report on the demographic aspects of intergroup relations, Smit *et al.* (1983) emphasize three trends in the population distribution pattern in South Africa:

● The presence of a few large urban concentrations,

● a denser occupation in the eastern part of the country, and,

● the numerical preponderance of certain population categories in specific geographic areas.

It is necessary to comment on each of these trends since their influence, together with other factors, on intergroup relations will be dealt with again in the next two chapters. Attention will first be paid to the urban-rural distribution. The most important particulars are given in Table 2.2 and the map (Fig. 1) may also be consulted.

TABLE 2.2

THE URBAN-RURAL DISTRIBUTION OF THE TOTAL SOUTH AFRICAN POPULATION*: 1980

Population category	Urban		Rural		Total	
	Number	%	Number	%	Number	%
Asians	743 820	90,6	77 500	9,4	821 320	100,0
Africans	6 809 660	32,6	14 094 100	67,4	20 903 760	100,0
Coloureds	2 002 300	76,6	610 480	23,4	2 612 780	100,0
Whites	4 002 000	88,4	526 100	11,6	4 528 100	100,0
Total	13 557 780	47,0	15 308 180	53,0	28 865 960	100,0

* Transkei, Bophuthatswana, Venda and Ciskei included.

It is evident from Table 2.2 that more than half of the South African population, namely 53,2 %, was urbanized by 1980. Of the four population categories, Asians (90 %) were the most urbanized followed by whites (88,4 %), coloureds (76,6 %) and Africans (32,6 %) (Smit *et al.*, 1983, p. 3).

Only 11 of the 631 formal urban settlements that can be distinguished have more than 100 000 residents. However, the informal settlements that developed around the formal settlements have not been taken into account. Moreover, the population is concentrated in four clearly distinguishable metropolitan areas: the Pretoria-Witwatersrand-Vereeniging area (PWV area), the Durban-Pinetown-Pietermaritzburg area, the Greater Cape Town area and the Port Elizabeth-Uitenhage area. These metropolitan areas, which represent only 4 % of the total area of South Africa at present accommodate (conservatively) 9,6 million people, or 53 % of the total population and this figure is expected to increase to 13 million by the year 2000.

Further analyses — not tabulated here — indicate that coloureds constitute the largest category in Greater Cape Town, Indians in Durban-Pinetown and Africans in the Port Elizabeth-Uitenhage and also in the PWV area.

Population density analyses reveal that habitation is denser in the eastern part of the country than in the western. This is particularly striking in respect of rural areas. One of the main reasons for the difference in population density between east and west is to be found in the distribution of rainfall. As precipitation gradually diminishes from east to west, so population density, except for that in river valleys with irrigation schemes, declines in the same direction.

The historical preponderance of the population was initially in the eastern part of the country, when the population was mainly dependent on agriculture. However, mining and industrial development in the northern and north-western part of the country later caused the population centre of gravity to move westwards at a rate of 0,6 km a year (Kok, 1982).

Regarding geographic focal points, the following should be mentioned: 60 % (10,1 million) of the total African population resided in the Republic of South Africa by 1980. Although 40 % of the African population resided in the national states at that stage, Smit and Kok (1981) point out that the Black population is increasingly leaving the heartland of the national states and moving closer to the borders, especially to those areas adjoining white development regions.

Eighty-five per cent of those categorized as coloureds live in the Cape Province. Increasing numbers of coloureds moved to the Transvaal, especially the PWV area, and Natal — mainly the Durban-Pietermaritzburg area — between 1970 and 1980 (Smit and Kok, 1981).

Those who are by statute categorized as Indians are mainly concentrated in Natal (80 %), where the largest percentage is found within a radius of 80 km from Durban. The concentration of Indians in Natal can mainly be attributed to legal restrictions on the movement of Indians to other provinces. These restrictions were partially lifted in 1975. This population category, too, is gradually, but increasingly, settling in the PWV area.

The white population is the most widely distributed over the entire country with the majority, namely 52 %, in the Transvaal. According to Smit et al. (1983) the Transvaal and Natal are attracting whites at the cost of the Cape and the OFS. Smit and Kok (1981) found absolute decreases in the white population in 196 magisterial districts, while 120 districts showed an increase. Decreases were particularly evident in the Cape Province (89 districts) and the Orange Free State (38 districts). The centre of gravity of the white population is thus moving in a north-easterly direction at an average rate of 2 km a year.

From the preceding review it therefore appears that there is increasing urbanization among all the population categories and that the population is concentrating in the four large metropolitan areas. The rapid growth of primary and secondary industry, in particular, is causing a systematic shift of the population to the north/north-west of the country. It also appears that gradually a more even distribution is taking place across the country.

POPULATION PROJECTIONS

When discussing the future relations between the various population categories, it is important also to take the expected population growth into account. Population growth obviously has implications for matters such as employment and unemployment, social security and social needs, political balance of power, etc. It is against this background that the following projections of population growth are given.

According to demographers such as Van Tonder and Mostert (1980, p. 1) both overestimates and underestimates in population projections are common. Their projections (see Table 2.3), which provide for both a low and a high fertility level, show that the African population's contribution to the total population will continue to increase. In contrast, the contribution of the Asians, whites and coloureds will diminish. By the year 2000 (if the premise is low fertility), 75,0 % of the total population will consist of Africans, while Asians, whites and coloureds will decrease constitute 2,8, 13,2 and 9,0 % of the total population. According to the 1980 census (Table 2.1) the total population is made up of 72,4 % Africans, 2,8 % Asians, 15,7 % whites and 9,1 % coloureds.

In 1980 the total population was 28,8 million (Table 2.1) and, according to Van Tonder and Mostert (1980) it will, by the year 2000, at a low fertility level, be 38,4 million, and 40,3 million, if the level of fertility is high.

Projections (Table 2.4) by Smit et al. (1983) shows that the metropolitan areas will probably accommodate an estimated 13 million people by the year 2000. Although there will be a slight drop in the percentual contribution of Asians, whites and Africans (at a low rate), it appears that the coloureds' share of 15,4 % in 1985 will increase to 16,6 % in the year 2000.

OTHER DEMOGRAPHIC DATA

Further demographic data — data often used as an "instant indication" of quality of life — appear in Table 2.5.

TABLE 2.3
THE PROJECTED SOUTH AFRICAN POPULATION FIGURES 1975 — 2020

Level of fertility	Year	Total population	Whites		Coloureds		Asians		Africans	
			Total	%	Total	%	Total	%	Total	%
Low level	1975	24 689 460	4 274 600	17,3	2 314 320	9,4	732 800	3,0	17 367 740	70,3
	1980	27 319 980	4 496 430	16,5	2 538 870	9,2	813 050	3,0	19 471 630	71,3
	1985	30 102 210	4 687 490	15,6	2 781 290	9,2	889 560	3,0	21 743 870	72,2
	1990	32 930 170	4 834 360	14,7	3 028 340	9,2	960 420	2,9	24 107 050	73,2
	1995	35 732 700	4 965 390	13,9	3 258 130	9,1	1 026 560	2,9	26 482 620	74,1
	2000	38 431 800	5 085 180	13,2	3 453 340	9,0	1 086 810	2,8	28 806 470	75,0
	2005	40 990 310	5 179 070	12,6	3 613 920	8,8	1 137 620	2,8	31 059 700	75,8
	2010	43 349 310	5 240 080	12,1	3 743 860	8,6	1 184 800	2,7	33 180 570	76,5
	2015	45 472 870	5 268 280	11,6	3 870 730	8,5	1 226 970	2,7	35 106 890	77,2
	2020	47 304 870	5 263 140	11,1	3 984 810	8,4	1 263 510	2,7	36 793 410	77,8
High level	1975	24 737 840	4 274 600	17,3	2 314 490	9,4	732 940	3,0	17 415 810	70,3
	1980	27 493 790	4 498 510	16,4	2 539 080	9,2	813 210	3,0	19 642 990	71,4
	1985	30 518 840	4 705 490	15,4	2 793 680	9,2	893 650	2,9	22 126 020	72,5
	1990	33 725 010	4 893 610	14,5	3 065 420	9,1	973 270	2,9	24 792 710	73,5
	1995	37 024 140	5 065 370	13,7	3 330 300	9,0	1 051 580	2,8	27 576 890	74,5
	2000	40 349 620	5 209 470	12,9	3 571 900	8,9	1 127 660	2,8	30 440 590	75,4
	2005	43 667 590	5 313 260	12,2	3 785 800	8,7	1 198 620	2,7	33 369 910	76,4
	2010	46 954 080	5 386 910	11,5	3 980 330	8,5	1 260 980	2,7	36 325 860	77,3
	2015	50 155 260	5 437 720	10,8	4 154 810	8,3	1 315 240	2,6	39 247 490	78,3
	2020	53 194 570	5 458 750	10,3	4 302 310	8,1	1 361 110	2,6	42 072 400	79,0

SUMMARY

From the preceding it is evident that the South African population (including that in the TBVC countries) at present consists of about 29 000 000 persons and that this figure will in all likelihood increase by at least 9,5 million over the next 15 years, and that the African component will make the biggest contribution to this increase.

TABLE 2.4

POSSIBLE FUTURE POPULATION OF THE METROPOLITAN AREAS: 1985-2000 (POPULATION IN THOUSANDS) *

Population category	Year			
	1985	1990	1995	2000
Asians	800	876	954	1 025
Africans: low	4 499	4 959	5 392	5 818
high	4 499	4 959	5 464	6 025
Coloureds	1 574	1 772	1 982	2 200
Whites	3 324	3 635	3 959	4 239
Total: low	10 197	11 241	12 288	13 282
high	10 197	11 241	12 361	13 488

* Smit *et al.* 1983, p. 7

Increasing urbanization of the population is largely determined by socio-economic and political factors. The various population categories gather in the urban areas where they are forced into contact with one another, at least in the work situation. Obviously this has both direct and indirect implications for the relations between the different population categories.

When the demographic trends are analyzed, it becomes clear that South Africa, as do all developing countries of the world, finds itself in a process of population redistribution that is largely the result of the interaction between population, environment and certain socio-economic and political processes.

South Africa has, within the relatively short period of less than a 100 years, moved from a traditional, self-supporting economy to a market economy, which

TABLE 2.5
DEMOGRAPHIC INDICATORS OF THE SOUTH AFRICAN POPULATION

Indicators	Asians	Whites	Coloureds	Africans
Birth rate* (1982)	25,1	16,6	30,0	38,5**
Death rate*** (1982)	5,9	8,3	9,9	11,0**
% annual growth rate (1970 — 1980)	2,7	1,8	2,4	3,0
Total fertility rate° (1980)	2,7	2,0	3,3	5,3
Life expectancy at birth (1980)	64,8**	70,3**	58,5**	57,5**
Infantile mortality°° (1982)	17,6	13,6	58,4	90,0**
Dependency ratio (1980):				
Children (< 15)°°°	61,8	42,9	65,2	70,9
Aged (> 65)+	4,3	12,1	5,1	5,4

*Birth rate: Number of births in a particular year per 1 000 of the population in the middle of that year.

**Estimates (mainly by the Institute for Sociological and Demographic Research of the HSRC).

***Death rate: Number of deaths in a particular year per 1 000 of the population in the middle of that year.

°Total fertility rate: Denotes an index indicating the total number of children that a woman will give birth to if the fertility pattern for the particular calendar year or period does not change in course of time.

°°Infantile mortality is calculated by expressing the number of deaths occuring among infants under the age of one year in a particular calendar year in relation to the number of live births in that year. The rate is expressed per 1 000 live births.

°°°Population 0 — 14/population 15 — 64 x 100.

+ Population 65 + /population 15 — 64 x 100.

has led to a dramatic shift in the distribution of the population and economic activity. Moreover, the different population categories have reacted differently to economic development stimuli, while institutional measures have greatly influenced the mobility of the different categories (Smit, *et al.*, 1983, p. 1). In the coming decades there will be striking large-scale African urbanization.

EDUCATIONAL PROVISIONS

The demand for and provision of education is taken for granted in modern society. As a rule this is associated with its role in development, economic progress in increasing the standard of living, the supply of manpower and, in particular, the significance that it has for the individual. However, education also has a socializing function which means that it cannot be seen in isolation from the society in which it exists. In a country like South Africa, with its complex population composition, great demands are made on education in respect of its task to involve the inhabitants of the country in meaningful relations. In the light of these general points of departure it is obvious that attention must be paid to education. The school and university population is discussed first, and this is followed by a discussion of inequalities in the provision of education, focus points in education and, finally, the formal structuring of education.

According to the information supplied by the Central Statistical Services, the school and university population in terms of numbers, institutions and teachers in these institutions, in 1984 was as follows (all population categories), see Table 2.6.

TABLE 2.6

SCHOOL AND UNIVERSITY POPULATION 1984

Level of education	Institutions	Pupils/ Students	Teachers
Preprimary level	1 866	148 439	8 817
Primary and secondary level			
Primary level (to std 5)	17 186	4 650 423	194 066
Secondary level		1 416 343	
Primary and secondary level			
Special schools	253	39 609	5 130
Tertiary level	98	272 519	15 666
Others	63	6 081	730
TOTAL	19 466	6 593 414	224 409

The percentage of pupils/students for the different population categories is divided as follows over the different educational levels:

TABLE 2.7

SCHOOL AND UNIVERSITY POPULATION ACCORDING TO CATEGORY

Educational level	Africans	Coloureds	Indians	Whites	Total
	%	%	%	%	%
Preprimary level	20,4	9,5	1,2	68,9	148 439(100)
Primary	70,7	13,1	3,3	12,9	4 650 423(100)
Secondary	52,3	12,6	5,8	29,3	1 416 343(100)
Primary and secondary:					
Special schools	9,2	10,1	3,5	77,1	39 609(100)
Tertiary level	19,9	6,9	7,1	66,1	272 519(100)
Other	39,9	8,4	3,8	47,8	66 081(100)
TOTAL	20,6	3,9	12,6	62,8	6 593 414(100)

From Table 2.7 it is evident that the distribution of pupils according to population category at primary school level, and to a lesser extent at secondary school level, approaches the distribution of the total number of pupils/students. This is to be expected since these two school phases usually also accommodate the compulsory school attendance period and, as compulsory school attendance for Africans and coloureds is extended, the distribution will normalize still further. The most striking differences are to be found in the non-compulsory educational phases where the African population, in particular, is underrepresented. It is also clear that the provision of special educational facilities for whites is considerably more extensive than that for the other population categories.

Although compulsory schooling for whites and Indians has been introduced in the RSA, it has not yet been fully implemented for coloureds and Africans. One result of this is that the declining birth rate in the case of Indians and whites will also lead to a drop in the number of primary and secondary school children, while in the case of coloureds (despite a decline in the birth rate) and Africans, the number of entrants at primary (and secondary) school level has not yet reached the maximum. The high birth rate (1983) among Africans (more or less 40 per 1 000 of the population) compared with, for example, that of whites (17 per 1 000 of the population) and the high percentages of pupils of compulsory school age in the African population group (1980: 26 %) contribute to the fact that the number of African pupils is growing phenomenally. This places tremendous pressure on the formal system of educational provision especially with regard to providing effective, high-quality education.

The absence of compulsory schooling and the high dropout figure have so far prevented this pressure experienced in the primary school phase, from being transferred to higher levels by the fact that only 1,96 % of African pupils who started school in 1963 completed their schooling with a schoolleaving certificate 12 years later. The corresponding figures for whites, Indians and coloureds are 58, 22, and 4 % respectively.

When formal education at all levels (primary, secondary and tertiary) is considered, the flow of pupils to the secondary and tertiary levels is considerably less favourable among Africans than among the other population categories. For example, the number of secondary school pupils — as a percentage of the total school population — was, in the case of whites 39,6 % in 1984, while the corresponding percentages for Asians, coloureds and Africans for the same year were 34,8; 22,6 and 18,4 % respectively.

The preceding figures have two implications. The first is that the *need* for non-formal education, that is education completed outside the formal education structure, in the case of Africans and coloureds over the short and the long term, will continue to differ mainly from that of the whites and the Indians and will probably be aimed at the level of compensatory and in-service training. This phenomenon is confirmed by the large percentage of the African population that is illiterate and the need for programmes to combat the problem. The other implication is contained within the first, namely that the number and percentage of Africans with no or low educational qualifications will be much higher than in the case of whites. In the age group 36 years and older, 84,1 % of Africans have a qualification lower than Std 5, while the corresponding figure for whites is only 6,5 %. The effect that improved provision of education has had on this situation is evident from the fact that, for the age group under 24 years of age, the percentage of Africans that have no educational qualifications is 32,8 as opposed to 51,8 % for those older than 25 years of age.

INEQUALITIES IN THE PROVISION OF EDUCATION

Inequalities in the provision of education to the different population groups in the RSA were identified in the HSRC Education Report *(Provision of Educa-*

tion in the RSA, 1981). This report discusses such matters as the differences in unit costs; pupil-teacher ratios; teachers' qualifications; total percentage of pupils that pass Std 10 and the percentage of pupils who obtain university entrance. (See Table 2.8).

TABLE 2.8

INEQUALITIES IN THE PROVISION OF EDUCATION

Population Category	Unit Cost 1983/84		Pupil-Teacher Ratio 1984	Teachers' Qualification		Std. 10 Results	
	Primary and Secondary	Tertiary		Prof. Unqualified	% With Std. 10	% Pass	% With University entrance
Asians	1 105	4 355	1 : 23	11,0	82,3	90,3	45,0
Africans	203	5 270	1 : 41	16,9	23,6	51,1	9,3
Coloureds	722	6 021	1 : 26	8,0	40,1	82,8	16,1
Whites	1 591	3 339	1 : 19	2,3	97	96,6	48,7

Although every positive step should be taken to eliminate the above inequalities, it is a goal that can only be fully achieved in the long term, due to financial and manpower problems.

In the HSRC Investigation into Education efforts were made to put the inequalities in education (pupil-teacher ratio, teachers' qualifications, unit costs, etc.), in perspective by calculating what it would cost the country over both the short and the long term to eliminate the inequalities. Different scenarios were developed based mainly on the pupil-teacher ratio. The calculations were based on the expenditure per pupil in white education for the 1979/80 financial year. Only two of the scenarios are used here to illustrate the extent of the cost involved. If the ideal strived for is a pupil-teacher ratio of 20:1 (as is the present case in white education), the R2 147 million spent on education in 1980 would have to be increased to R5 281 million by 1990. Taking into account inflation and changes in the value of money, this amount would probably be much greater by 1990. In real terms, however, the budget for education would have to be increased by 245 %.

Alternatively, should the target be a pupil-teacher ratio of 25:1 for all population categories by 1990, the budget would have to be increased to R4 351 million in 1990 (an increase of 210 %). The HSRC Education Report recommended that a pupil-teacher ratio of 30:1 be set as the ideal for 1990, which means that the budget will, in real terms, have to be increased by 190 % during the present decade.

FOCUS POINTS IN EDUCATION

Of considerable importance for intergroup relations, in both the medium and the long term, is a phenomenon that received prominent attention in the HSRC Education Report, namely the overemphasis on academically oriented education at the cost of technical and career-oriented education. In the field of technical and career-oriented education, the needs in the RSA have by no means been met. On the other hand the expected exponential increase in, particularly, the number of African pupils who will successfully complete more academically oriented education to the level of Std 10 over the next decade, will lead to an unprecedented situation of unemployment among relatively high-level manpower due to the irrelevance of their qualifications in terms of the requirements of the labour market. Of all pupils at secondary school level — including those who are following secondary school level courses at technical colleges and technical institutes — there are respectively only 8,0; 1,7; 2,6 and 0,8 % whites, coloureds, Indians and Africans who are following a technical or career-oriented course of study. In contrast, if the situation in developing countries can be used as a criterion, this means, on the one hand, that education will not necessarily lead to improved career opportunities and chances in life, and on the other that many pupils and their parents will probably be disappointed in their expectations of the future.

A further aspect of the unequal provision of education that is often ignored, is the much greater extent to which it favours the white pupil with access to differentiated education. The percentages given in this regard in Table 2.7 are highly significant and they indicate that this form of educational provision for, in particular, African pupils, is still woefully deficient.

FORMAL STRUCTURING OF INTERGROUP RELATIONS WITHIN THE EDUCATION CONTEXT

A distinction should be drawn between formal management structures that have been created or will be created with a view to liaison between the different education subsystems. The former matter was examined in the HSRC Investigation into Education and specific shortcomings were identified, including the following:

• Although several consulting mechanisms existed within subsystems, there were few or inadequate consulting mechanisms between the different subsystems.

• Nobody had been specifically created to effect co-ordination at national level in respect of all the subsystems.

• There were serious problems concerning the acceptability and legitimacy of the education system in the RSA.

Formal liaison mechanisms recommended in the HSRC Education Report to meet these problems, included the following:

A South African Council for Education (SACE)

This council should represent all people in South Africa and at the same time represent interested groups among the suppliers and the users of education. The Government accepted the introduction of such a council in its White Paper on the *Provision of Education in the RSA.*

A Committee of Heads of Education Departments (CHED)

Legislation has already been passed for the establishment of a committee that will represent all heads of education departments.

A statutory body for standards and examinations

An intersectoral committee has given attention to the composition and functions of a Statutory Certification Council.

Committee of Technicon Principals

The recommendation that there should be such a committee has been implemented.

Committee of University Principals (CUP)

The HSRC Education Report recommended that the present CUH be extended to include the rectors of all South African universities on an equal basis.

All these liaison bodies will function at macro-education management level and will help, at that level, to ensure co-ordinated co-operation on the planning of education across the boundaries of population categories and interest groups. The Committee of Heads of Education Departments, in particular, will be in a position to effect intergroup liaison at regional or meso level.

A further matter in respect of the abovementioned formal structures is the way in which they are accommodated constitutionally. With the definition of education as an "own affair", formal education management structures have been created for each population category. They will function independently of one another, and the abovementioned statutory liaison mechanisms will act as link between them.

LANGUAGE USE IN SOUTH AFRICA

By definition language is the major means of communication between people and it is therefore also one of the identifying characteristics of a country. In a fairly homogeneous country, language is usually not an important factor in intergroup relations, although phenomena such as dialects can complicate such relations. In a multicultural country like South Africa, however, language is potentially one of the main factors that can influence the nature, form and quality of intergroup relations.

Countries such as Belgium, Canada and Nigeria may also be mentioned in this regard. In the final analysis language is the medium by means of which people communicate with one another and form, maintain and develop mutual relations. However, the first proviso is that the people concerned should be able to understand one another. Communication problems can have an adverse effect on interpersonal understanding, optimal use of opportunities and progress in general. Language differences in a multilingual country can therefore lead to friction and even conflict between groups, — at the same time a variety of a language in a country could lead to the cultural enrichment of its people.

In view of the above considerations, a brief review of some trends in language distribution in South Africa is given below.

Although English and Afrikaans are the official languages, the 1980 census (Table 2.9) revealed that at least 24 languages are spoken in South Africa. To establish to what extent South Africans can speak the different languages, reference can be made to information obtained from a 5 % sample in the 1980 census. Table 2.10 indicates the number of people who stated that they could not speak, read or write certain languages.

34

TABLE 2.9
1980 CENSUS DATA ON HOME LANGUAGE IN THE RSA (BASED ON A 5 % SAMPLE OF THE TOTAL POPULATION)

Language	Asians	Whites	Coloureds	Africans
Afrikaans	15 500	2 581 080	2 251 860	77 320
English	698 940	1 763 220	324 360	29 120
Dutch	–	11 740	–	–
German	–	40 240	–	–
Greek	–	16 780	–	–
Italian	–	16 600	–	–
Portuguese	–	57 080	–	–
French	–	6 340	–	–
Tamil	24 720	–	–	–
Hindi	25 900	–	–	–
Telegu	4 000	–	–	–
Gujarati	25 120	–	–	–
Urdu	13 280	–	–	–
Chinese	2 700	–	–	–
Xhosa	–	–	8 440	2 870 920
Zulu	–	–	5 580	6 058 900
Swazi	–	–	1 060	649 540
Southern Ndebele	–	–	440	289 220
Northern Ndebele	–	–	100	170 120
Northern Sotho	–	–	2 440	2 429 180
Southern-Sotho	–	–	5 320	1 872 520
Tswana	–	–	9 300	1 346 360
Tsonga	–	–	1 180	886 960
Venda	–	–	40	169 700
Other	11 160	35 020	2 660	73 900
TOTAL	821 320	4 528 100	2 612 780	16 923 760

TABLE 2.10

NUMBER OF PERSONS IN THE TOTAL POPULATION (INCLUDING CHILDREN) WHO CANNOT SPEAK, READ OR WRITE AFRIKAANS, ENGLISH OR AN AFRICAN LANGUAGE

	Asians	Whites	Coloureds	Africans
Afrikaans	66,9 %	13,0 %	3,6 %	66,9 %
English	2,9 %	12,1 %	48,8 %	68,9 %
African language	89,1 %	91,8 %	95,2 %	0,2 %

It is clear from Table 2.10 that only a very small percentage of whites, Asians and coloureds have any knowledge of an African language. In turn two-thirds of the Africans indicated that they had no grasp of either English or Afrikaans. Two-thirds of the Asians indicated that they had no knowledge of Afrikaans.

Further analysis reveals that 2,2 % of Asians, 0,6 % of whites, 0,5 % of coloureds and 59,8 % of Africans could not speak, read or write either Afrikaans or English. These facts have serious implications for communication, particularly in view of the rapid rate at which Africans are becoming urbanized.

The following facts emerged in respect of urbanized Africans:

• 26,9 % of Africans over the age of 15 in white urban areas could not speak either of the official languages.

• 37,3 % of the total group of African employees could speak neither English nor Afrikaans.

It is clear from the above that many languages are spoken in South Africa. However a point that comes strongly to the fore is that many Africans, are not conversant with either official language. At the same time only a very small percentage of Asians, whites and coloureds can speak an African language.

RELIGIOUS AFFILIATIONS

Religion is one of many institutions that influences intergroup relations in a society. Society in turn also influences religion. It is often said that religion places the life of the individual in perspective and gives meaning to life.

In terms of the idealized view of religion, institutional religion should support and validate the structure of society. An analysis of the nature of religion and the proselytising endeavours of religious movements, however, indicates that religion both brings people together and divides them. Against this general background, it is necessary to determine the extent of religious belief in South Africa as well as the distribution of the various denominations. For this purpose information derived from the 1980 census that appears in the report *Religion, intergroup relations and social change in South Africa,* is given below.

Table 2.11 contains particulars of church membership in South Africa.

TABLE 2.11

CHURCH MEMBERSHIP OF THE MAIN POPULATION CATEGORIES OF THE RSA: 1980 CENSUS

Church Religion	Whites	Coloureds	Asians	Africans	Total
Ned. Gereformeerde	37,4	26,0	0,5	6,5	14,0
Gereformeerde	2,8				0,5
Ned. Hervormde	5,4				1,0
Anglican	10,1	13,5	1,1	4,7	6,5
Methodist	9,1	5,4	0,5	9,2	8,5
Presbyterian	2,8	3,7	0,1	4,1	3,7
Congregational		6,5		1,2	1,5
Lutheran		3,7	0,1	4,1	3,2
Roman Catholic	8,7	10,1	2,6	9,9	1,5
Apostolic Faith Mission	22,8	1,9		0,7	1,2
Full Gospel			2,8		0,1
Independent African		4,5		29,3	20,4
Others	12,8	15,6	4,7	6,3	8,4
Subtotal	91,8	87,0	12,5	74,1	76,6
Jewish	2,6				0,5
Hindu			62,4		2,1
Islam		6,3	18,8		1,3
Other	0,6	1,2	1,5	0,6	0,7
Subtotal	3,2	7,5	82,6	0,6	4,5
Unknown, none	5,0	5,5	4,9	25,3	18,7
TOTAL (thousands)	4 528	2 613	821	16 924	100,0

The following information, in particular in Table 2.11, is striking. Firstly, most of the world's leading religious traditions are found in South Africa, although some do not have a large following. Secondly, more than two-thirds of the population claim to be Christian. Thirdly, the single biggest religious grouping is that of the independent African churches which represent nearly 20 % of the total population. Fourthly, about one out of every five people do not belong to a specific religious group. Fifthly, virtually half of the population does not belong to one of the main Western Christian churches.

As far as the Christian churches are concerned, the Dutch Reformed family of churches is the largest, although not a structural unit. The two largest multiracial groups in South Africa are the Methodist and the Roman Catholic Church.

Analysis of religious affiliation in terms of population category reveals that Christianity predominates in all the categories except the Asian — here Hinduism has the greatest following. From information contained in the report of the Work Committee: Religion, it appears that the only grouping that is fairly well represented in all parts of the country, is that of the independent African churches. It should also be pointed out that in the rural areas there are relatively fewer people who belong to churches — some four million Africans in these areas are adherents of a traditional faith. In the urban areas five out of every six people claim church membership.

The above review should also be seen in relation to growth patterns. The report of the Work Committee: Religion indicates that proportionally the membership of a large number of churches declined, relative to the total population, between 1960 and 1980. Exceptions to this trend were the independent African Churches, which had the fastest growth and the Roman Catholic Church, which expanded among all population categories except the Asians. The category 'other Churches' also expanded, but it is difficult to determine which groupings were included, although one can deduce that non-conventional religious movements must have benefitted.

From the perspective of intergroup relations, this brief review indicates that religion is an important factor in society, and that Christianity has a large following, at least nominally. At the same time it is apparent that there are numerous divisions in the religious sphere, divisions that, to an important extent, coincide with divisions between population categories.

ETHNICITY IN SOUTH AFRICA

An analysis of the relevant scientific literature indicates that ethnicity is a social category embodying mainly the following combination of components:

- A common culture, including common values and norms
- A common language
- An awareness of group solidarity
- An awareness of a historical destiny
- Endogamy, i.e. marriages within the group and a feeling of kinship
- Concentration of the group in a specific geographic area
- A common race-semantic norm image.

(For the purpose of this and later discussions, it should be borne in mind that the concept "race" is used in its general connotation as a way of group differentiation and collective behaviour in which mainly external physical characteristics and therefore differences in biological history are of primary importance. In this sense the emphasis is therefore on the genetic and physical, not on the cultural aspects. A race and an ethnic group can therefore sometimes overlap, but this is not necessarily the case.)

The major categories used in each official population classification cannot simply be regarded as social 'groups,' each with a strong consciousness of identity. In some cases such consciousness may be present, but in others population classification may be vehemently rejected. Ethnicity and cultural identity, accordingly, have to be described independently of formal group classifications.

The concept of ethnicity cannot be approached in a categorical manner. Ethnicity, regardless of how central it may be to a group's self-experience, is a process rather than a rigid structuring of people in a population. It is a process that in the course of time, and depending on specific circumstances, can change in nature and comprehensiveness. Ethnicity is also defined in terms of the characteristics of core groups, and it cannot simply be assumed that the self-awareness of the core is typical of the wider group that can be nominally identified with the core group.

South Africa is generally regarded as a multicultural and a multi-ethnic country and consequently, against the background of the above a brief description of the phenomenon of ethnicity in South Africa is needed. In Chapter 3 ethnicity will be analyzed in terms of its inherent characteristics. What follows here is merely a broad outline of the phenomenon as it appears on the surface. Afrikaner ethnicity will be described first, followed by ethnicity among Africans, and finally ethnicity among other groups.

AFRIKANERS

Ethnicity as a significant phenomenon within the broader social context is evident among white Afrikaners. Afrikaner identity in the core groups is not based on language alone (which is shared with Afrikaans-speaking coloureds), but also on a specific Christian-national philosophy of life, a Calvinistic-based cultural heritage and awareness of a calling. This identity is also, at times, specifically linked to a particular political home or organization, although today more than one political party offers a home to Afrikaners.

Outside the Afrikaner core group, there are Afrikaans-speaking whites who, while aware of Afrikaans identity and language, accept a wider white and, indeed, a South African identity which is equally, or more, important to them.

AFRICAN ETHNICITY

Among Africans there is both strong emphasis on ethnicity and an even stronger rejection of it. There is a strong inclination in especially urban areas to reject ethnicity and to identify with the ideal of African unity and non-racialism.

In the rural areas, within the national states and among migrant labourers in urban areas, ethnicity may be manifested at two levels. "Tribal" solidarity, comes strongly to the fore; in situations of social pressure, especially in industrialized situations, and may even lead to open clashes.

As regards ethnicity in the more acceptable sense, there are varying degrees of group awareness linked to language and to historiocultural heritage and experience. This type of ethnicity has gained political stature in the national states.

Outside the national states, and in some organizations within these states that aim at identification with the broader South African concept, language identity is experienced and sometimes valued, but generally the trend is towards active identification with an inclusive black group. This more common pattern of identification does not necessarily exclude pride of language or an appreciation of traditional cultural customs, but it does seem to be the strongest group orientation among Africans at the present time. Some groups, especially since the early seventies, have exalted black identity (the so-called Black Consciousness Movement) which has developed as a reaction to white dominance.

ETHNICITY IN OTHER GROUPS

Among English-speaking whites and coloureds, ethnicity or group identity is less significant than among Afrikaners and Africans. English-speaking whites are proud of their language, but the general identification is that of being South African or a South African white.

Although some coloureds have developed a pride in being coloured in reaction to white dominance (as a parallel to or part of the Black consciousness movement) during the past decade, this orientation in no way resembles a "primordial" ethnicity. The strongest and most constant striving among coloureds is to be part of an overall South African citizenry.

There are minority groups in the country among which there is strong evidence of a conscious ethnicity. This applies particularly to Indians, Jews, Chinese and immigrant groups such as Greeks, Portuguese, and Germans. Among these groups ethnic interests are manifest in the sphere of private cultural organizations and have no link with political affiliations. In fact, the political lives of Indians, Jews and other groups all have a broad national orientation. These groups display no desire to isolate themselves socially or politically.

ECONOMIC DEVELOPMENTS AND LABOUR RELATIONS

There is no doubt that economic factors have often played a vital role in determining relations between the different population groups. Both the interdependence and the clashes between the different groups, from earliest times, can often be traced back to economic factors.

While South Africa today has a predominantly market-directed economy — as is proven by the record turnovers registered on the Johannesburg Stock Exchange — a significant portion of African farmers is still involved in a struggle for survival in a subsistence economy and many are in a transitional phase from a traditional way of life to modern industrial life. Such a change in the economic set-up makes unique demands on all the participants and often has problematical consequences for intergroup relations, especially since it concerns the satisfaction of basic needs and the realisation of opportunities.

In the labour field there is often conflict between employee and employer and between white and African employees. At the same time it is also the terrain on which there can be constructive co-operation to the benefit of all. This is where the different groups have the most contact with one another and where intergroup relations are formed and reshaped. In fact, it is not far-fetched to aver that the future development of relations depends on what happens in the work situation.

The aforegoing consideration makes it imperative to take note of specific economic realities which affect the quality of life of South Africans and also of developments in the sphere of labour relations.

ECONOMICS

The South African economy is a relative developing one that, together with those of countries such as South Koera, Brazil, the Argentine and Algeria, is classified by the World Bank as belonging to "higher middle-income countries". According to World Bank figures, South Africa's *per capita* income (measured in terms of gross domestic product) amounted to US $ 2 670 in 1982. This is slightly higher than the weighted average of US $2 490 for the group of higher middle-income countries.

Neighbouring countries such as Zimbabwe and Zambia fall in the category "lower middle-income countries" which, as a group, had a weighted average *per capita* income of US $840 in 1982.

Although the South African economy has considerable potential for development, its potential was not exploited to the full, particularly during the seventies. This was reflected in, *inter alia,* an economic growth rate that was considerably lower than that required to provide the rapidly growing population with job opportunities and a higher standard of living. From 1960 to 1970 the gross domestic product (GDP) increased by an average 6,3 % p.a. in real terms, but during the period 1970 to 1981 this figure was only 3,6 % p.a. In some years during the latter period (1975, 1976, 1977 and 1982) the GDP grew at a slower rate than the average population growth of 2,8 % p.a. during the decade from 1970 to 1980. This means that the *per capita* income dropped during those years.

Seen from a sectoral point of view, the South African economy, like those of most countries in the category of higher middle-income countries, developed through a process of industrialization. In 1980 factories contributed about 23 % to the GDP. This represented a considerable increase over the 8 % in 1911 and the 17 % in 1946. The relative increase in the contribution of factories generally went hand in hand with a decline in the importance of agriculture. The contribution of the agricultural sector to the GDP dropped from 21 % in 1911 to 13 % in 1946 to 5 % in 1983.

Foreign trade plays a vital role in the South African economy. Total imports and exports of goods and non-industrial services constituted an average 55 % of the GDP from 1981 to 1983. The composition of foreign trade is, however, not a true reflection of the structural composition of local economic activity. For example, mining contributed on average only 14 % to the GDP during 1977/78, but contributed no less than 42 % to the Republic's goods and services exports (including gold) during the same period. This means that while mining generated only 14 % of domestic income, the sector was responsible for 42 % of the country's foreign exchange earnings from the export of goods and services.

The spatial distribution of economic activity is very uneven. In 1976 52 % of industrial total net production was in the Southern Transvaal (PWV area), 12,8 % in Durban-Pinetown, 9,6 % in the Western Cape and 5,7 % in Port Elizabeth/Uitenhage. This means that about 80 % of industrial production takes place in the metropolitan areas, with the Southern Transvaal as the predominant area.

If it is borne in mind that mining plays an important role in the southern Transvaal and that the derived development generated by secondary industry in the service sector is considerable, it is understandable that economic activity is generally highly concentrated. As a result of this concentration 60 % of whites about 90 % of Asians, 55 % of coloureds and 43 % of Africans outside the national states live in the four metropolitan areas. If the low level of development in the national states is taken into account, and also the fact that only 43 % of Africans outside the national states live in the four metropoles, it is clear why there is a strong connection between the relative contribution of African population to economic activity and the spatial situation of this population category.

The division of income between the different population groups is similarly unequal. From 1917/18 to 1970 the white share in total income, according to all available studies, was always about 70 %, while that of Africans fluctuated between 18 and 23 % of the total. For the period 1970 to 1980, Natrass made estimates which show that the whites' share during this period dropped to about 60 % of total income.

According to estimates made for this investigation, the ratio of the per capita income of whites to Indians, coloureds and Africans in 1975 was 4,5; 5,8 and 12,5 respectively. An important factor in determining the per capita income is naturally the dependence ratio. The more economically inactive children and old people there are, the lower, *ceteris paribus,* the income.

Further estimates in the report of this work committee indicate that the percentage of the African population below the minimum living level has dropped from 90 % in 1960 and 80 % in 1970 to about 60 % in 1980. This level is 50 % higher than the so-called 'poverty datum line' and, according to some researchers, it includes expenditure not essential in the rural areas. The revenue

43

figures on the basis of which such analyses are made are also not very reliable. However, it must be accepted that a large percentage of the African population is indigent. On the other hand, there is no doubt that there has been a significant drop in the percentage of the very poor over the past decade.

LABOUR RELATIONS

Two of the most important labour matters are developments in the field of organized labour and unemployment. The following review deals with these two issues.

THE TRADE UNIONS

The historical development of labour relations in South Africa was determined by a series of events in which labourers, employers and the state were involved. Three periods are clearly distinguishable: the twenties with the increase in militant white trade unions; the fifties when apartheid as an ideology was formalized; and the seventies with the growth of collective consciousness among African employees. A few remarks on each of these phases will give a clearer idea of present relations.

Labour relations during the twenties were marked by the unrest of 1922, which followed efforts by the mining houses to appoint less expensive Africans in posts that had until then been regarded as "white" work by the whites. The unrest eventually led to the declaration of martial law and to military intervention.

The Industrial Conciliation Act 11 of 1924 which followed the unrest, recognized the right of whites, coloureds and Asians to bargain collectively and to strike. It also made provision for industrial councils. Features of the act were that African labourer were excluded from the bargaining machinery and that the trade union movement among Africans was declared illegal. Most of the measures embodied in the act still apply today. In 1947 legislation was proposed according to which African labourers would be granted trade union rights, but the victory of the National Party in 1948 prevented the legislation from being passed. Instead the policy of separate development was carried through in every social context and it naturally also had many implications for labour relations.

The National Party government introduced the Black Labour Relations Regulation Act 48 of 1953. In terms of this act African workers could elect representatives to work committees of which would then negotiate with employers. The Ministry of Labour could appoint officials to negotiate on behalf of African workers in industrial councils. However, African workers still did not have the right to strike. A further important development was the Industrial Conciliation Amendment Act 41 of 1959. In terms of this act new mixed trade unions were prohibited and job reservation was extended. At the same time there was also considerable activity in the field of trade union federations, in which the admission of Black trade unions was a point of contention. The efforts of the Trade Union Council of South Africa (TUCSA) in 1962 to offer a home to Black trade unions were thwarted by the amendment of its constitution in 1969, which effectively excluded Black trade unions.

A major challenge to the labour dispensation that had been established in the fifties, were the strikes in Durban during 1973 involving more than 100 000 workers. These strikes occurred at a time when the the demand for more skilled workers could not be satisfied by white labour. The Black Labour Relations Regulation Amendment Act 70 of 1973, which followed the labour unrest, gave Africans more consultation rights and was aimed at eliminating this sort of conflict. Nevertheless by 1976 there were already 26 Black trade unions with a membership of 126 000. The unrest in Soweto in 1976 contributed to the growth of Black consciousness and Black trade unions continued to expand although they had no legal status. The Government's reaction was to adapt legislation by increasing the powers of the liaison committee system to serve as an alternative for trade unions. However employers also increasingly pleaded for the legalization of trade unions.

The Wiehahn Commission was appointed in 1977 and in its report in 1979 recommended that African workers should enjoy the same trade union rights as other employees. The Government accepted most of the commission's recommendations. The first indicator of this was the Industrial Conciliation Amendment Act 94 of 1979 which not only granted trade union rights to Africans but also abolished job reservation, except that in mining. It also made provision for the National Manpower Commission and for the introduction of an industrial court. The Labour Relations Amendment Act 57 of 1981 which followed, withdrew all reference to race in the Industrial Conciliation Act and extended statutory control to unregistered trade unions. The Black Labour Relations Regulations Act was also repealed in 1981.

The trade union movement has grown over the past few years, and has changed in terms of population composition. Table 2.12 shows that membership of trade unions increased from 7,4 % of the economically active population in 1970 to 11,3 % in 1980 and to 15,5 % in 1983. At the end of 1980 the membership of trade unions covered by the Labour Relations Amendment Act amounted to 29 % of the workers who could be organized.

Table 2.13 shows the population composition of registered trade unions for the period 1969 to 1983. The growth in Black trade unions since 1980 when they could register for the first time, is striking.

TABLE 2.12

STATE OF TRADE UNIONS IN 1970 AND IN 1983

Group	Year	Number	Membership	Percentage membership
Economically active population	1970	8 114 000	603 282	7,4
	1980	9 490 000	974 977	11,3
	1983	9 996 000	1 545 822	15,5
Organizable workers	1980	5 332 000	1 545 822	29,0

(*Source:* SALDRU, July 1984 and annual report of National Manpower Commission, 1983. TBVC countries included — figures for 1983 are an estimate.)

TABLE 2.13

POPULATION COMPOSITION OF REGISTERED TRADE UNIONS 1969 TO 1983

Year	Africans	Coloureds	Whites	Total
1969	—	182 210	405 032	587 242
1975	—	271 169	382 525	653 694
1980	56 737	303 850	447 466	808 053
1981	259 582	326 794	648 029	1 054 405
1982	394 510	343 900	488 044	1 225 454
1983	469 260	330 176	474 454	1 273 890

(*Source:* Annual Reports, Department of Manpower.)

To summarize, it can be stated that in the past the whole matter of trade unions was inextricably interwoven with intergroup relations problems, and this is still the case today. The history consists largely of efforts to keep African

Figure 2.1
Unemployment trends (% of labour force) in South Africa: 1960 - 1982

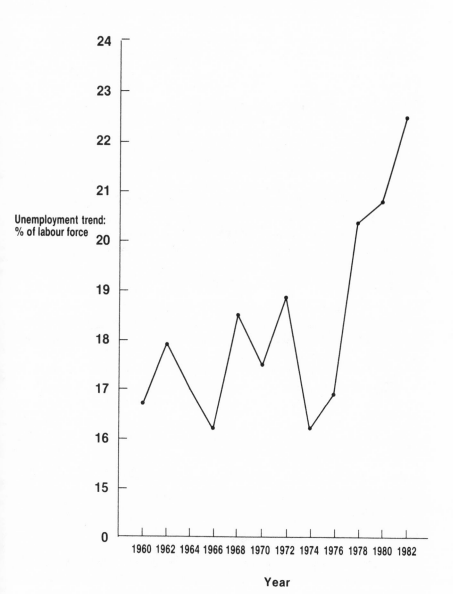

workers out of the bargaining machinery. After the normalization of labour legislation the membership of trade unions increased, there seemed to be a move towards mixed trade unions and federations, and more trade unions were prepared to operate formally within the system by applying for registration.

UNEMPLOYMENT

Observers are agreed that unemployment is one of the contributory factors to social unrest. Estimating the extent of unemployment is an extremely controversial matter. Unemployment registration figures apparently underestimate the gravity of the problem due to the fact that many unemployed have no motive to register. Surveys in which a person is classified as unemployed if he made no efforts during the previous week to find employment similarly underestimate the extent of unemployment because during certain times there is such a shortage of job opportunities that it is logical that such a person will not constantly seek employment. On the other hand, unemployment is overestimated by the assumption that unemployed persons are always looking for work. In Fig. 2.1 the estimates of Simkins (as presented by Bell) are given since they clearly indicate how unemployment increased from the mid-seventies.

JURIDICAL, POLITICAL AND CONSTITUTIONAL SYSTEM

In the final analysis intergroup relations are structured by legal and constitutional arrangements. Even if there is no differentiation between groups in a country, this must be confirmed by the country's constitution. This review will therefore be concluded with a description of legislation that concerns the relations between groups in the country, and that of the South African system of government. This is necessary because intergroup relations in South Africa are regulated by law to a greater extent than in other Western countries.

LEGAL STIPULATIONS IN RESPECT OF RELATIONS BETWEEN POPULATION CATEGORIES

Several South African acts have direct and indirect implications for intergroup relations. This review will, however, only deal with those laws which directly affect intergroup relations; they are the following:

- The Development Trust and Land Act 18 of 1936.
- The Black (Urban Areas) Consolidation Act 25 of 1945
- The Prohibition of Mixed Marriages Act 55 of 1949 and Article 16 of the Immorality Act 23 of 1957
- The Population Registration Act 30 of 1950

- The Reservation of Separate Amenities Act 49 of 1953.
- The Promotion of Black Self-government Act 46 of 1959
- The Group Areas Act 36 of 1966

The Development Trust and Land Act 18 of 1936

The specific areas that were reserved for the exclusive occupation of, and tenure by Africans, by the Black Land Act (No. 27 of 1913) were retained by this act, as were the stipulations that Africans may not own land outside the specific areas. Act No. 18 of 1936 added a further 7,25 million morgen of land to the isolated areas, known as the released area. This land was gradually acquired and added to the specific areas, but the process has still not been completed.

The Blacks (Urban Areas) Consolidation Act 25 of 1945

This act governs what is generally referred to as influx control. Articles 10 and 12 of Act 25 of 1945 contain the basic stipulations concerning influx control. Article 12 prohibits, in principle, the presence of alien Africans (African who have never had South African nationality) in the prescribed urban areas, except where special permission has been granted.

In terms of Article 10(1) a non-alien African must comply with specific stipulations before being allowed to remain in a prescribed area for longer than 72 hours. These stipulations are basically the following:

- that he has been domiciled in the area, uninterruptedly, since birth;

- that he has worked in that area for one employer without interruption for ten years, or that he has lived in the area for 15 years;

- that he/she is the legal spouse or child (under 18 years of age) of a person complying with the above requirements;

- that he has been granted permission to live in the area by a labour bureau.

The availability of housing and job opportunities is always taken into account in cases where the administrative authorities may use discretion. Up to the time of the passing of the Development of Black Communities Act (No. 4 of 1984), the 1945 act contained five stipulations whereby the removal of Africans from urban areas was regulated.

The Prohibition of Mixed Marriages Act 55 of 1949 and Article 16 of the Immorality Act 23 of 1957

This legislation prohibits marriages and sexual relations between whites and members of other population categories. In April 1985 the Government announced its intention to repeal these two acts and immediately gave instructions that no further prosecutions be instituted in terms of the acts.

The Population Registration Act 30 of 1950 and other related acts

This act makes provision for three main population categories: White, Coloured and Black. In terms of a proclamation issued by the State President in 1967, the coloured category was subdivided into seven further groups, of which Indians formed one category. Blacks were similarly subdivided into a number of ethnic groups under the Promotion of Black Self-Government Act 46 of 1959. This distinction was statutorily linked to citizenship of the independant and self-governing national states. In this regard two main categories of Blacks were created: citizens of the self-governing national states and citizens of the independent national states of Transkei, Bophuthatswana, Venda and Ciskei.

Citizenship of self-governing national states is laid down in the National States Citizenship Act (No. 26 of 1970). Under this act and the regulations proclaimed by the State President, the most important aspects of citizenship of the national states are as follows: every Black person in the Republic is a citizen of one or other of the self-governing national states. Under Act 21 of 1971 he can cast his vote above local government level. He has the rights and privileges, and he is subject to the duties, obligations and responsibilities implicit in citizenship of such self-governing areas. In this regard it must be emphasized that as far as acquiring citizenship of in the self-governing national states is concerned, the statutory categories are so wide that virtually no Black in the RSA can elude citizenship of one or another "homeland". Citizens of self-governing areas therefore in fact have two types of citizenship, their South African citizenship under the South African Citizenship Act 44 of 1949, and citizenship of one or other self-governing national state under the act of 1970.

In addition to the citizenship of independent national states that was granted to all Blacks outside the self-governing areas, there was a further statutory arrangement that in due course led to another group of Blacks being identified, namely the so-called "urban Blacks". This group includes all those Blacks who qualify for residence, under Article *10(1)(a)(b) and (c)* and the Blacks (Urban Areas) Consolidation Act (No. 25 of 1945), in the so-called urban areas on account of birth and periods of employment, and also the dependants of such Blacks.

The arrangements for citizenship of the independent national areas (which were formerly self-governing national states), follows the same classification as that laid down in the National States Citizenship Act (No. 26 of 1970), namely acquisition of citizenship by birth, domicile, language relationship, and relation-

50

ship of general identification. According to these criteria — which have been embodied in all the status acts of the independent national states — all citizens of Transkei, Bophutatswana, Venda and Ciskei have been allocated to these states on the basis of birth, descent, domicile, ethnic relationship, identification and language relationship.

The Separate Amenities Act 49 of 1953

This act makes it possible for institutions responsible for public facilities to decide whether such facilities should be reserved for use by a specific population category. There are also several provincial ordinances and municipal by-laws that regulate the use of public facilities by different population categories. The facilities affected include beaches, health services, municipal facilities and public transport.

The Promotion of Black Self-government Act 46 of 1959

This act makes provision for an increase in the competencies of local authorities created in each of the self-governing national states under the Black Authorities Act 68 of 1951. This implies the further constitutional development of the national states into self-governing units. The act deprived Blacks of the parliamentary franchise which they had had on a separate voters' role since 1936. The policy of coupling Blacks outside the national states with the to-be-formed authorities within the national states, have their origins in this act.

The Group Areas Act 36 of 1966

This act was first placed on the statute book in 1950 and makes provision for the creation of separate group areas for each of the population categories and covers
- the control of ownership of fixed property,
- the control over occupation of properties,
- the allocation of permits and exemptions from the stipulations of the act in exceptional cases.

Summary

To summarize, it herefore seems that several acts were added to the statute book with the explicit purpose of regulating relations between the different population categories. Naturally these acts cannot be seen in isolation since they constitute the formalization of a specific ideology and were aimed at creating orderly intergroup relations. It is also interesting to note that some of these acts originated before 1948. To place these acts within a broader constitutional context, a review of the South African system of government will now be given.

THE SOUTH AFRICAN SYSTEM OF GOVERNMENT

The vesting of authority in the white population category is the major feature of the South African political dispensation, and is a direct consequence of the statutory determination of population categories.

For many years only the statutorily determined white population category was directly represented in Parliament with its legislative authority over all aspects of government. Before the Republic of South Africa Constitution Act 110 of 1983 was passed, this authority was vested solely in the white Parliament. The other — concomitant — result of the establishment of white supremacy in Parliament, was that the white population category took it upon itself to dispense political and constitutional autonomy to the self-governing areas of the different African population categories. Four of these — the TBVC states — eventually became independent. It also created separate government institutions for coloureds and Indians (the Coloured Representative Council and the SA Indian Council).

The official government policy of "separate" or parallel development probably reached its constitutional and institutional zenith during the seventies with a supreme white parliament, a limited legislature for the coloureds, an advisory council for the Indians and self-governing areas for the different Black areas.

As indicated above, the institutional separation was further supported by various acts, including the Group Areas Act 36 of 1966, the Reservation of Separate Amenities Act 49 of 1953 and the Prohibition of Political Interference Act 51 of 1968, to ensure that the different population groups would reside, attend school and carry on their politics separately. (It was announced during May 1985 that this act would be repealed.)

The most important constitutional change since Union was the passing of the new Constitution Act 110 of 1983. Important constitutional changes since 1910 initially concerned the independence of the Union (i.e. the passing of the Status of the Union Act 69 of 1934 after the Statute of Westminster had been passed by the British parliament, the repeal of the right of appeal to the British Privy Council in 1950, and the eventual establishment of the Republic in 1961).

Reference can also be made to the entrenchment of white supremacy in the Parliament, first by the removal of coloured voters from the common voters' roll and later by the abolition of indirect representation of coloured population categories in Parliament.

The Constitution of 1983 signalled a significant change of direction in the political dispensation, both as regards institutional form and content. Where the

South African constitutional dispensation previously followed an adapted form of the Westminster system, the new constitution introduced an executive parliamentary head of state, separate legislative chambers for whites, coloureds and Indians, and bound Parliament, both institutionally and functionally, to the procedure of agreement of all three parliamentary chambers.

Africans at present have to exercise their political rights in the self-governing national states — they have no direct say in the South African parliament. A series of reforms are being introduced in the sphere of Black Local Authorities Act 102 of 1982 and the development boards, while new arrangements are foreseen for the orderly regulation of squatting, the granting of property rights, and the influx and mobility of qualified urban Africans across the boundaries of the fields of authority of development boards. The eventual aim is probably that Black local authorities, as they gain greater independence, will also have a greater say in the arrangement of accommodation and the influx of persons.

According to public statements, the future political and constitutional position of the African population category is enjoying the highest priority. A special cabinet committee concerned with African constitional development is busy with negotiations and discussions at all levels of government and society, as well as with the governments of the TBVC national states and the self-governing national states. On 19 April 1985 the State President extended an invitation to all opposition parties also to serve in the special cabinet committee; with one exception, all the parties reacted positively. In this connection the State President's parliamentary speech of 25 January 1985 on the incorporation of Black local authorities in the Council for the Co-ordination of Local Authority Affairs and the Regional Services Councils, must also be mentioned.

Summary

From the above it is clear how firmly the juridical and constitutional dispensation was built on the segmentation of the population on the basis of race. Despite the progress that has already been made in respect of accommodating the different population categories, South African can at present still only be described as partially democratic — a situation that contains the seeds of tension and conflict.

CONCLUSION

In the preceding discussion an outline was given of the general background against which the South African problems of intergroup relations should be seen. From the perspective of relations between different categories/groups, the following points emerge:

● South Africa is a society with a mainly indigenous population and a colonial past.

● The country has a plural composition insofar as members of different ethnic, race and/or colour groups generally do not identify with one another and they are therefore highly segmented insofar as different sectors of the population are involved in central institutions on a differential and separate basis.

● The African population group represents at least two-thirds of the total population and will in future constitute an even bigger proportion.

● There are vast educational and economic differences between, especially, the Africans and the whites.

● The country has a predominantly capitalistic system which is rapidly developing from a traditional way of life to an industrial society.

● Although the nature of the labour dispensation in the past developed parallel to the political model, the convergence changed towards the end of the seventies with the restructuring of labour relations; in general, the adjustment is taking place harmoniously.

● Intergroup relations, as they are today, have a very long past and a comparatively short history.

● The official government policy of separation that was followed until 1983 was supported by a complex collection of Acts. In this respect the present government, from 1948, distinguished itself from previous governments in the sense that it increasingly legally formalised measures and customs of segregation that were largely already in existence, and explicitly concentrated on a policy of apartheid. Insofar as certain sectors of the population are at present excluded from the central power structure, it can only be regarded as being partially democratic.

It is against this background that the findings of the research undertaken within the scope of this programme will be explained in broad outline. The main objective in this chapter was to determine which factors, given the basic points of departure of the *Investigation,* improve or reduce the quality of life. More specifically on the level of intergroup relations, it concerns the factors that generate conflict on the one hand, and that accommodate conflict on the other.

In Chapter 3 these findings will be discussed on the level of practical experience, and in Chapter 4 on the level of structuring.

CHAPTER 3

THE EXPERIENCE OF INTERGROUP RELATIONS

The most important features of South African society were discussed in Chapter 2. From this discussion it became apparent that this society is characterized by its plurality, segmentation and asymmetry. Chapters 3 and 4 deal with the additional findings of the *Investigation*. These findings illustrate and highlight some of the features identified in the previous chapter and help relate them to one another within the matrix of intergroup relations.

There is a large degree of consensus among social scientists that a meaningful distinction can be drawn between two dimensions of intergroup relations: on the one hand the experiencing of such relations, and, on the other, their structuring (compare Rhoodie, 1983 for a survey of these distinctions). *Experiencing implies the individual's involvement in, perception of and emotional reaction to intergroup relations. The structuring* of intergroup relations here refers to the formalization and institutionalization of these relations. These two dimensions constitute the themes of Chapters 3 and 4 respectively.

Chapter 3 thus deals with the individual's experiencing of and reaction to South Africa's segmented and group-differentiated society. The dynamics of the most important economic, juridical, political and constitutional structures related to political domination and social injustice will be discussed in Chapter 4. However, structures of domination and social injustice and people's experiencing of these are complementary components of basically the same social problem. For analytical purposes a distinction can be drawn between, for example, the Group Areas Act, as a structural element of the apartheid system, and people's day-to-day experience of it, but in terms of social behaviour neither has any rational significance when considered in isolation.

In this chapter the way in which people experience intergroup relations is approached from different angles. Group differentiation is briefly discussed by way of introduction, followed by an analysis of the basic dilemma of identity and identification. Identity is characterized by basic orientations according to which the individual justifies himself and his group. Religion and history constitute two of the sources of these orientations and are discussed next. Orientation in its turn is linked to mental and social processes such as perception and attitudes. The role of these processes in the experiencing of intergroup relations is considered and the chapter ends with a discussion of the role of mass communication as mediator between group and group.

IDENTITIES AND GROUP DIFFERENTIATION

GROUP DIFFERENTIATION AND INTEREST GROUPS

As indicated in the previous chapter, South African society is determined to a large extent by the particularly segmented or divided composition of the country's population. This segmentation manifests itself in a diversity of human collectivities. Historically, socially and/or legislatively this differentiation occurs on the basis of criteria that are essentially of a social nature and which can therefore not be described as being strictly 'objective'. In South Africa matters such as physical appearance, culture, religion and language figure very prominently and being generally associated with race and ethnicity, they are regarded as relatively unchangeable. In this sense race is mainly interpreted as being indicative of a person's descent and relationship to collectivities which are described in the vernacular as white/European, African, Asiatic or "mixed." Ethnicity in turn is linked to characteristics such as language and religion.

These and other basis for differentiation such as employee/employer , socialist capitalist, urban rural and Methodist versus Catholic, are not static, but are in a process of dynamic development. However, people are not quick to notice change, mainly because changes of this kind usually occur gradually over a relatively long period. Put differently: stereotypes do not change easily.

However people not only have different perceptions of others and of other groups; they also differ in their experiencing and perceptions of the South African political and social setup. As will be explained later on the basis of the findings of empirical research, these differences are determined to a large extent by the way in which people identify with their cultural and ethnic background as well as their tag.

Equally important is the way in which others categorize them and the way in which this identification manifests itself in the formation and perpetuation of interest groups.

THE FORMAL (STATUTORY) CLASSIFICATION OF GROUPS IN SOUTH AFRICA

The formal classification of South Africa's primary population categories does not always correspond with the spontaneous group differentiation prevalent in society at large. In state-administrative terms the present classification of the main population categories is based mainly on racial criteria (see Chapter 2). This classification is largely the product of a power base traditionally dominated by whites, which is probably why the present statutory classification is held in question, to say the least, by the majority of the members who do not fall within the white category. This classification is a statutory reality however and it has an important impact on intergroup relations as well on the access to South Africa's power and opportunity system by those concerned.

One of the central processes in a plural society is identification, which is multidimensional however and does not take place in a sociopolitical vacuum. For this reason identification and identity are discussed from different angles in the next pages. The following aspects will be dealt with: group differentiation and interest groups, the statutory classification of groups, ethnicity, social inequality and finally, certain problem areas.

As indicated in Chapter 2, the Population Registration Act makes provision for three main population categories, namely white, coloured and African. The coloured category is divided into seven groups by proclamation, and these include Cape Coloureds and Indians, while Africans are classified in a number of ethnic groups, e.g. Zulu, Xhosa, Swazi, Venda, Tsonga.

In most societies, groups or subgroups can be distinguished which, regardless of legal provisions, display certain social traits that do not correspond with formal group classifications. In plural societies such as that in South Africa, the task of population classification is therefore problematical. This theme is resumed later in the report. But it can be accepted that South Africa has a heterogeneous society and that, apart from the formal population classification, there is also considerable emphasis on group differences in everyday life which are not recognised as formal criteria for group differentiation. Group differentiation in South Africa must therefore be regarded as a reality, but at the same time as a very complex and dynamic phenomenon. It is also difficult to define group boundaries in a simple, one-dimensional way, as is shown by the confusion that surrounds the designation *coloured*.

GROUP DIFFERENTIATION ON THE BASIS OF ETHNICITY

For a group to qualify as an ethnicentity, it need not comply with all the above criteria, not even an awareness of group identity. In some instances of ethnic differentiation certain characteristics of ethnicity, for instance language or culture, play a more important role than in others. In addition, components of ethnicity must not be seen as absolute characteristics but rather as dimensions of the same values which means that all the members of an ethnic group need not comply with all the above criteria of the group's ethnic identity in equal or in absolute measure.

Scientists generally agree that ethnicity signifies more than a mere sociocultural heritage and that it also involves a special form of social organization with its own institutional structure. Of vital importance however, is the cultural symbolism, which focuses on common interests, and the subjective perception of an umbrella identity with a biogenetic content, as well as an historic dimension. Where racial differences are concerned, people's *perception* of a common biological history is particularly important. Today most analysts accept a shared perception of common descent (however irrational, subjective or rudimentary this may be in cognitive terms) as one of the structural factors that occurs in all real manifestations of ethnicity.

Ethnicity is, therefore, a comprehensive way of social differentiation making use a variety of identification facets (each with its own socially defined characteristics such as language, religion and race). As Nagel and Olzak (1982, p. 129) put it — *"which of those identities becomes salient at a particular moment depends upon the situational constraints and the strategic utility attached to the identity."* (quoted in Rhoodie, 1983, p. 28). Two examples illustrate this point: In Iran religion was the most strategic characteristic used as a basis for bargaining power, while it is well known what role language played in the period between World War I and World War II as a basis for the mobilization of Afrikaner-ethnic nationalism.

From the point of view of intergroup relations, an important aspect of ethnic behaviour is that one really only becomes aware of ethnicity when those concerned are mobilized as an *interest group*. It is this aspect of ethnicity which, especially in as reported American literature, is often linked to the phenomenon of social movements. It is a relatively common phenomenon that when an ethnic group is mobilized as an interest group or in a "social movement", at least one of the group's primary identities is consciously politicized to a greater or lesser extent. It is obvious that this politicizing is aimed at giving the particular ethnic group an advantage in the rivalry for scarce resources. In the USA the Black Civil Rights Movement was a good example of this process.

Ethnic differences can give rise to long-term conflict, particularly when there are also conflicting economic interests. There has often been an economic basis for conflict between different groups in South Africa. In the specific instance where ethnic and class differences coincide, there is a very strong probability of conflict.

OFFICIAL HANDLING OF ETHNICITY

From Chapter 2 it appears that South Africa's political and constitutional dispensation has always been implicitly or explicitly based on group differentiation. Under the National Party government this classification has been explicitly founded on an ethnic and racial basis. In this regard reference can be made to the juridical work committee's report *Law and justice in intergroup relations*. The official handling of group relations in South Africa raises the question whether it is based on a system of ethnic pluralism or not.

The definitions in the Population Registration (Act No. 30 of 1950) reveal that different criteria were used. Whereas Africans, for instance, were classified in terms of racial descent, coloureds were defined according to a process of conceptual elimination, namely as "a person who is not a white person or a black person". Whites on the other hand, were classified mainly on the grounds of appearance. Africans and coloureds were subdivided further on the basis of "ethnic and other" considerations. In view of the fact that different criteria were used to describe the population categories, it can be concluded that the formal sociopolitical setup was not based on purely ethnic principles. There do seem to be strong elements of Afrikaner ethnicity, but class interests and an emphasis on race also play a part. It is also evident that the formal "pluralism" embodied in government policy in respect of "black peoples" was not a purely ethnic division but rather a racially based territorially division. In this respect, too, it therefore appears that, in addition to ethnicity, other considerations such as class, territorialism and race played a role in the modern evolution of South Africa as a plural state.

One of the most important aspects of the political handling of groups and group boundaries in South Africa, is the following. A particular group, namely the whites, established ethnicity and other group differentials as the cornerstone of national policy. In this way it became the task of the state to allocate group membership to individuals and groups — for the original purpose of population registration. In due course a policy of separation resulted. In many cases the *state* literally had to decide in which category an individual should be placed. The allocation of individuals to groups was also *de facto* associated with widely divergent rights and privileges. This gave rise to a situation where groups became categories instead of voluntary groups. This point will be discussed again later.

The white government's argument in support of group differentiation is, however, only one side of the matter. The question must also be asked whether group differentiation outside the white centre of power is moulded along ethnic lines or not.

LEVELS OF IDENTIFICATION

The *Investigation* clearly showed that, whereas South Africans regard themselves as ethnic units in certain circumstances, preference is given to other group affiliations in certain other social contexts. To take the Afrikaans-speaking white as an example: From the *Investigation* it is evident that the ordinary Afrikaner does have a group identity as an Afrikaner and wishes to maintain his or her language and culture. This group consciousness is however, not exclusive in the sense that it signifies a strict delineation of the Afrikaner within the white group. In fact, the wider impression created by the empirical research is that a more comprehensive white group consciousness is stronger than the more specific Afrikaner attitude in respect of people's views on public and political matters. In view of this, one can expect the masses to deviate considerably from the attitudes of the elite. This seems to be the case with the Afrikaner. Afrikaner ethnicity as a point of departure for political mobilization is, however, a reality which clearly makes its influence felt in the political and social order in South Africa — an aspect that will be discussed again later.

The situation in general among sections of the African population group is similar to that which prevails among Afrikaans-speaking whites. A wider African group consciousness forms the nucleus around which, although not exclusively, there is particular mobilization in the bargaining for political power. In many instances this wider identification does not necessarily cancel out the narrower identification with an ethnic group and the experience and behaviour of, for instance, being Xhosa, with a specific language, system of values, norms, and customs, while the individual is also motivated to prove and to display his identity.

Without going into the finer details here, reference can be made to the report. *Communication in a divided society* for empirical confirmation in which it is stated that characteristics such as language, race and ethnicity represent some of the most important nuclei with which people identify.

60

Ethnicity is a modality which is particularly prominent within the confines of intragroup orientations such as the education of children, religious worship, close friendships. In other contexts, where other demands and criteria apply, a much less confined behavioural package is required and used. This does not mean that ethnicity does not have an effect even on this type of behaviour.

It is clear, however, is that such fields as the economy and labour, science and higher education make demands which require similar behavioural modalities from everyone. This to a considerable extent increases the incidence of overlapping between groups. The process of identification is not something static — it is a dynamic process.

Identification is part of a development process; that is why this concept is used rather than identity. In this regard reference can be made to Eisenstadt's study on the influence of modernization on group identification. He showed that Israelis in modern societal contexts have considerably more polyvalent and flexible norms, values and behavioural patterns than do those still enmeshed in a a traditional type society. The latter's 'culture' was more rigid and insular and more oriented towards specific norms for specific situations. Particularly when the phenomenon of modernization is taken into account, it seems that processes such as urbanization, contact with other groups and exposure to the culture of the masses through the mass media, could be a significant levelling mechanism. For example, it was also found in this *Investigation* that there had been a dramatic increase in the exposure of all groups to the mass media over the past ten years. In the case of the whites, coloureds and Indians, television has had the greatest impact, while in the case of Africans there has been a marked increase in the reading of newspapers and magazines. Reference can also be made to the early work of Biesheuvel, who found that young Africans incorporated typical Western values in their system of values. A condition seems to be that such groups should not remain outside the system (e.g. in the form of chronic unemployment). Under such circumstances it can even be expected that a configuration of subcultural patterns may emerge, creating an impression of reactive normlessness, at least in the opinion of the employed majority.

In view of the effects of the modernization, it can be expected that some of the more marked ethnic differences will gradually fade. In the light of the projections on urbanization mentioned in the previous chapter, it can be assumed that ethnic identification is destined to wane rather than increase, although new factors may lead to a revival of ethnicity. For example, it has been estimated that 5 % of the total population will have been urbanized by the year 2000. Although the quality of urbanization obviously varies as does also the

61

adjustments of values and norms according to time and group, it remains a phenomenon to be taken into account when deliberating on the future of ethnicity.

A fact referred to earlier, namely that the official ordering of group relations was initiated and institutionalized by whites, will now be elaborated on further. According to all empirical indications Africans, coloureds and Indians experience this policy as one of discrimination. The whites are regarded as privileged and the rest as disadvantaged (cf. *inter alia* the report of the Work Committee: Social Psychology: *The social psychology of intergroup relations*). The official system of group differentiation is responsible for this. In other words, this category regards its sociopolitical and constitutional position as a function of the official policy of the present government. A person's membership of a group therefore leads, according to this perception, to disadvantages and that is why identification with the statutorily determined group classification weakens or is denied, at least at the level of power politics. Identification with bigger and potentially stronger reference groups is one result which will be discussed in more detail below.

ETHNICITY AND POWER IN SOUTH AFRICA

Comparative studies indicate that in a plural society ethnicity is often the politically dominant group's basis of power and most important source of legitimacy. One or more primary characteristics of ethnicity, such as language and religion, usually form the basis on which such a group mobilizes and politicizes itself. The distribution of power in plural societies, and the fundamental political dividing lines which this introduces correspond largely with one or more historical, cultural and racial factors that are socially interpreted as primary indicators of ethnicity. The key role played by ethnicity in the forties to ensure the Afrikaner's political dominance in South Africa, strikingly illustrates the way in which one or more ethnic characteristics (regardless of the idiom in which the individual Afrikaner defined them) can be mobilized and politicized to enhance the bargaining power of an ethnic group. Political scientists and historians are largely agreed on this, although they may differ in respect of the objective necessity, tenability and feasibility of a policy based on ethnic division.

Taking into account the struggle for power which is inherent in South African society, the implications of another reality must be recognized, namely the fact that a significant proportion of the other population categories apparently put a very low premium on ethnicity as the nucleus for political mobilization at present. There are, however, numerous socioscientific analyses of Africa (and elsewhere) which indicate that when the distribution of power shifts from white to African, the power mobilization within African ranks tends to centre on ethnic factors. Moreover, the present mobilization around other factors such as ideology, does not mean that ethnicity does not feature prominently in the African population category. Inkatha is an example of this, whereas, in Namibia, the Ovambo basis of SWAPO is generally accepted. While it is important to take Afrikaner ethnicity into account, it is equally important to allow for the coloureds' outright rejection of coloured ethnicity as a basis for democratic reform in South Africa, as well as for the possibility that, under a different set of circumstances, ethnicity could be actualized by the Africans.

It may be argued that group identification, as an emotional reaction, for a variety of reasons could provide a most convenient refuge when a people feels itself threatened. The solidarity thus established, however, can continue long after the threat has passed, and could reach a stage where it is no longer really necessary as an adaptive process. Analysts disagree both as to whether this is now the case with Afrikaner ethnicity and also as to whether such a phenomenon could emerge among African groups.

The above does not mean that there are no strong ethnically oriented behavioural patterns in South Africa. Ethnicity is especially prevalent where it is not directly related to the policy of formal group differentiation. In the white group, for instance, there is a number of minority groups including the Greek and Portuguese communities which display strong ethnicities.

The above analysis shows that South Africa is a multi-ethnic country in which ethnicity under the Afrikaans-speaking white manifesto is accommodated by the policy of formal group institutions, but that some other groups do not wish to be accommodated on this basis at present. In this sense the question as to whether the plural community of South Africa is *mainly* an ethnic pluralism, must be answered in the negative. The group delimitations in South Africa are therefore not simple, nor are they necessarily intrinsic to groups. A number of fundamental dilemmas arise from this.

DILEMMAS

The facets of identity described above are all basically asymmetrical. Some of the most important asymmetries are the following:

● Formal classifications and differentiations that are not fully in keeping with social and political realities and subjective perceptions;

● one group that categorizes groups which in turn do not summarily accept the categories,

● the fairly common phenomenon of a revival of ethnicity in some other multicultural societies and the waning, or even denial, thereof in various groups in South Africa.

A few of the more important effects of these and other asymmetries surrounding ethnicity and identification, are the following:

Firstly ethnicity has become politicised especially since 1948 — insofar as it has become an important factor in the model for apartheid and it can no longer be used to legitimise political policies. In fact, the impression is gained that, in the past, the politicizing of ethnicity assumed the character of functional autonomy. Ethnicity for ethnicity's sake, as it was probably originally intended by Government, has for various reasons moved into the background, and political ordering has become an end in itself.

Secondly, one of the worst dilemmas in the sphere of ethnicity occurs when ethnic groups are described juridically, when such an exercise is juridically exceptionally difficult, if not impossible. In this regard the juridical work committee reached the following conclusion: . . . *this social entity (ethnicity) is too indefinite, loose, unorganized, fluid, etc. to be considered a (legal) community. Ethnic groups are therefore not valid legal entities (. . .). If it is true that an ethnic group cannot be legally defined, then it follows that no distinctions can be legally drawn between people on the basis of ethnicity.* The problem is aggravated when ethnicity is directly linked to it. In this regard the Work Committee: Juridical Aspects, found the following: *Race can never be a legally relevant ground for justified differentiation. After all, a person's physical appearance, skin colour, descent or even social affiliations cannot be said to determine the particular nature of his need for legal protection. Just as little should these details determine one's legal rights and duties (. . .) or influence one's legal status (p. 16).*

Thirdly, several groups that make their ethnicity felt in an assertive way in other plural societies, "deny" this in South Africa and identify and mobilize around other nuclei. Most individuals link their self-identity to some group or other, but quite often this could be a very passive conciliation process. A series of tension and stress factors, perhaps especially those which undermine the morale, can however create an increased need for group identification in some individuals.

The resultant "ethnicity" can be regarded as involving a limited identity since it is reactive rather than spontaneous. Elements of this process are probably present in all types of group identities in South Africa. A more explicit example of this, however, would probably be the Black Consciousness Movement of the sixties and seventies, which has now been reshaped into a more politicoideological movement. The result is that a creative force threatens to be lost, insofar as uniqueness and communality are placed in opposition rather than complementary to one another.

Another probability that must also be borne in mind is that not only psychological tension, but also social tension, and strong but frustrated, material and other interests can stimulate a self-conscious feeling of ethnicity.

ORIENTATIONS IN RESPECT OF INTERGROUP RELATIONS

Each community has a set of basic orientations explaining its *raison d'être*. These orientations offer an explanation of the individual's and the group's place among others, thereby presenting a frame of reference which, as implied in the preceding section, must *inter alia* ensure the continuity of the group. In modern society this framework is formalized, to a greater or lesser extent — the two most obvious forms of this being history and religion. History relates man and group mainly on the basis of historiocultural facts, while religion does this on the basis of values.

In the light of the above approach, it appears that these two fields could have an important formative effect on orientations in respect of intergroup relations. The most important findings regarding religion will first be discussed in terms of the report of the Work Committee : Religion : *Religion, intergroup relations and social change in South Africa,* which will be followed by a discussion of the findings of the Work Committee: Historical aspect as contained in their report *The role of historiography in intergroup relations.*

THE ROLE OF RELIGION AS ORIENTATION FRAMEWORK

It is generally accepted that religion plays a major role in South African group relations. In this regard one need only refer to the current debate on the alleged association of Afrikaans churches with apartheid, and the prominence given to the theology of liberation in debates on the relation between church and society. This opinion on the potentially important role of religion in group relations is consistent with statistical data in Chapter 2 where it is shown that all the major religions of the world are represented in South Africa and that a vast majority of the population 78 % regard themselves as Christians. From research undertaken for the *Investigation* it appears that the role of religion is considerably more complex than is generally thought, and that several of the current concepts concerning it will have to be revised. In this section attention is paid firstly to the internal functioning of religion as a psychosocial process.

This will be followed by a review of the ambivalent nature of religion, the issue of group interests, and religion as mediator and provider of common values.

Religion as psychosocial process

Religion can be analysed at least on two levels, namely in terms of its "theological" and eschatological nature thereof, or in terms of the psychosocial process underlying it. To grasp the role of religion in shaping relations in society, requires a brief analysis of its psychosocial functioning.

Considered from different socioscientific points of view (from the symbolic interactionism to the reference group approach), it can be concluded that the common norms, values, convictions and behavioural patterns that unite a religious group are represented in a set of explicit symbols. The importance of religious symbols is contained in their dual function. Firstly, the symbols express the views and feelings about reality of those concerned. This reality to a considerable extent includes the evaluation of the individual and his interrelations, and along, with this, the fundamental demand for justice. In this sense the symbols represent truth in a concentrated form. On the other hand, the symbols are associated through their use with motivating forces in an equally concentrated form. In other words, religious symbols represent an interpretative and evaluative framework, and a motivation for corresponding action. It is this interaction between determination of reality and motivation which, from the perspective of intergroup relations, is so vitally important.

Against this background the defining and motivating role which religion can play in the individual's life, reference can now be made to other dynamic functions fulfilled by religion with regard to intergroup relations.

Ambivalence: cohesion and division

From the work committee's report it appears that religion fulfils an ambivalent function in intergroup relations. Normally it would be expected that it plays a cohesive and integrating role, at least as far as adherents of the same religious tradition are concerned, if only because the content and form are the same for all within such a tradition. However, research indicates that religion can have a strong divisive effect under certain circumstances. To mention specific examples: Within certain groups, (e.g. some denominations in the Afrikaans-speaking white reformed tradition) religion is experienced as the provider of timeless values which guarantee stability in a rapidly changing world. These groups experience their position in society as relatively favourable and prefer to maintain the status quo. In such a case religion functions as a factor which counters or inhibits social change. In other groups within the same tradition, e.g. movements within the N G Sending Kerk which make use of concepts deriving from the theology of liberation, religion provides, amongst other things, an ethical ideal to which present reality should conform.

Such a perspective obviously occurs in groups and individuals who experience their situation as unfavourable or disadvantaged. In such a case religion becomes a powerful stimulus for social change.

The ambivalence become clearly visible, probably in its most severe form, in recent events in which the N G Sending Kerk accused the N G Kerk of heresy, because the latter was not prepared to dissociate itself explicitly from apartheid. This controversy in which different population categories oppose one another, illustrates how divisive the role of religion can be.

The ambivalent role of religion can also be demonstrated at another level. The countrywide multipurpose survey provided, inter alia, the following results. Regarding the involvement of religion in socio-economic issues 17,9 % whites, 19,5 % Africans, 21 % Indians and 34,9 % coloureds which placed a high premium on this aspect. In response to the suggestion that religious movements have little significance if they do not contribute to the provision of basic material needs, 52 % of the whites, 60 % of the Indians, 62 % of the coloureds and 69 % of the Africans reacted positively. From the above it therefore seems that people's views on the functional role of religion are closely related to the level of their needs. For those who experience needs at the subsistance level, the role that religion plays in the socio-economic uplifting of people is important.

The above conclusions are supported by an analysis of the role of religious movements in respect of discrimination, suppression, etc. A single example: A relatively small percentage of whites (10 %) put a high premium on structural liberation, compared with 36 % of the coloureds, 37 % of the Indians and 41 % of the Africans. Regarding the more specific aspects of the elimination of discrimination, 46 % of the whites, 67 % of the Africans, 73 % of the Indians and 74 % of the coloureds believed that religious movements should do everything possible to eliminate discrimination in society.

Empirical findings such as the above therefore confirm that whites in general regard religion as a source of stability in a changing world, while Indians, coloureds and Africans see religion as a stimulus towards the improvement of their (earthly) lot. At the same time these findings confirm the divisive role of religion.

On the other hand, many South Africans regard religion as a potentially conciliatory and cohesive factor. For example, 46 % of the whites, 57 % of the Indians, 79 % of the coloureds and 84 % of the Africans involved in the countrywide survey felt that religious movements should try to bring the different population groups together. In this regard reference can be made to interchurch discussion groups and ecumenical organizations which can, potentially or in fact, fulfil cohesive functions between groups in South Africa.

Since the divisive and cohesive role of religion is so central to the problem of intergroup relations, this matter was investigated more fully. The empirical findings clearly show that religion with regard to content, form and effect, can be divisive but also conciliatory in respect of intergroup relations.

Ambivalence: personal and communal needs

Another form of ambivalence is the contrast between personal and communal needs. From the empirical research it is clear that the spectrum of interests related to religious convictions display much variation, extending from the narrower personal sphere, via the family, the church community, the wider community to what is experienced as the total situation. Problems arise when the orientation concentrates too narrowly on any one part of this spectrum. Those whose religious orientation is aimed only at the personal sphere confine religion to a "spiritual" matter which is not integrated with that person's wider experience of reality. This leads to a withdrawal from social and political issues. At the same time there can yet be an intuitive sympathy with what more radical groups wish to achieve on the social or political terrain. One of the investigations for instance showed that in a group which could be typified as politically passive and even sceptical about the value of political action, there was nevertheless a much stronger identification with groups such as the United Democratic Front (UDF) and the SA Council of Churches (SACC) than with the Labour Party or the Progressive Federal Party (PFP). An even more telling example is the position of many African independent churches that are at present apolitical, but which, under different circumstances, could easily adopt a radical attitude due to these underlined sympathies. From this it seems that people who are apparently politically uninvolved, due to a pietistic conception of religion, nevertheless have the ability for politically radical action at a later stage.

On the other hand a survey conducted in the Cape Peninsula showed that those with a more socially involved set of beliefs had less trouble in integrating religious values at the various levels. However a problem of a different nature arose here, namely tension about the priority to be given to values at the personal and the communal level. Although religious values are regarded as important at both these levels, it appears that when a choice has to be made, preference will be given to the values at the social or national level respectively. The implication of this is that the more socially aware group is prepared to sacrifice peaceful relations at the personal level as well as the local community level and even risk suffering, if they are of the opinion that this is in the national interest.

The problem of integrating religious values at different levels is also at the root of the rift developing between church leadership and ordinary church members on a variety of issues. With regard to church leadership, matters of national interest naturally enjoy the highest priority, which is why special attention is paid to the sociopolitical implications of religious values. At local congregational level, however, individual needs are the deciding factor. The inability of the church leadership to reconcile values at these two levels, often gives rise to tension between leaders and church members and between leaders among themselves. Various examples from the recent past in, for example, the Anglican Church, the NGK and the NG Sending Kerk could be referred to in this respect. On the other hand tension also develops when the Church leadership, in the opinion of some of its members, does not give clear guidance or does not react quickly enough to change situations. An example of the result of such tension is the founding of an organization such as Reforum within the NG family of churches.

From the above it appears that South African society experiences problems at various points in its efforts to integrate religious values at the personal level with those at the sociopolitical level. In the long term this can only have an extremely adverse effect on intergroup relations in general.

Religion and group interests

The ambivalences mentioned above indicate that religion can therefore play either a constructive or conflict-generating role. The latter often occurs when religion is linked too closely with the socio-economic and political interests of a specific group at the expense of others, and especially when the particular group is in a position of power or strives to acquire power. It is important, however, to realise that this involvement in specific group interests need not have had malicious intent initially. Solidarity between men in their concrete earthly circumstances is a central theme of the Christian tradition. This is interpreted as an instruction to the religious community to identify with the suffering of others and to become a chapion for the helpless. From here it requires only a small step to give divine sanction to the needs and aspirations of a specific group.

When the boundaries of the religious group coincide with those of a specific cultural or power group, this creates a situation with obvious conflict potential.

The history of South Africa offers several examples of such a combination. During the British colonial period the interests of the British Empire and those of the expansion of the Christian faith coincided to such an extent that the British missionary effort was often seen as an integral part of the former. The close similarity between the religious values and attitudes advocated by the NGK and the basic philosophy underpinning the policy of the National Party in the time before and after its coming into power in 1948, gave rise to the typifying of an "Afrikaner civil religion". The latest example of a close relationship between religious values and group interests is the rise of Black theology, where the "Black cause" is interpreted in the light of the Biblical motif of liberation.

The link between religious values and group interests in itself carries a considerable conflict potential and is a factor which, in the present situation, has a strong influence on intergroup relations. A dramatic example of this is the rejection of apartheid as heresy by the NG Sending Kerk and subsequently by other churches and ecumenical bodies as well. A political policy is judged according to theological criteria precisely because of the theological justification offered for that policy.

The fact that South Africa is increasingly represented as a polarized society also has an effect at the religious level. The cohesive function which religion is supposed to fulfil comes under increasing pressure when people are forced to take sides in the sociopolitical debate. The mediating role of religion is no longer accepted as a matter of course. In fact, although research indicates that between 46 % and 84 % of the South African population feel that religion *should* play a conciliatory role, only 37 % believe that the church will be able to do this.

An extreme example of polarization is surely to be found in attitudes regarding the use of violence. Although there are pacifist trends among religious groups, it appears that 45 % of the Africans do not regard violence as irreconcilable with their religious views. On the one hand there are those who regard violence as permissible in maintaining the *status quo* and in the suppression of revolt. On the other hand there are those which feel that religious movements have the right to consider violence when people's basic human rights are involved. The contrast between a "just war" and a "just revolution" dramatically illustrates this conflict.

Religion and mediation

One of the most important functions of religion with regard to the relations between people and groups, is to be found on the level of mediation — an aspect regarded as a vital component of the regulation of relations by Rhoodie (1983, p. 154-156): *. . . reference can be made to the mediating role that churches, schools (. . .) can play in conflict situations. These organizations can be important catalysts in the legitimation of conflict management, for example by persuading the competing interest groups to settle their differences within the framework of mutually acceptable 'rules of play'.*

The mediating function of religion can be fulfilled at various levels such as the relationship between the personal and wider world and between ideal and reality as well as in laying down communal values.

Research has shown that religion forms an important bridge which rationally links the narrower world of personal needs with the wider world of political-social reality. In a rapidly changing situation with increasing specialization, there is a great need for such an integrating function among disadvantaged groups to find themselves and maintain themselves against other groups.

Religion should also play an important mediating role between ideal and reality. The Jewish-Christian tradition for example, is strongly future-oriented. In the past this orientation was often used as an escape route in an effort to alleviate present suffering with the promise of a glorious future. At present it is increasingly being realized that orientation towards the future need not mean that the present should be ignored, but that it should rather serve as a powerful incentive to reshape present reality in the light of this future expectation. Since it is simultaneously admitted that the present is an inperfect reality and that no instant solutions are available, religion offers an important means by which the tension between the ideal and reality can not only be tolerated, but also be linked creatively.

A close identification with shared values is of vital importance in any mediating process. Many researchers, including Adam (1985), emphasize this facet of intergroup relations. Rhoodie (1983, p. 157), for example, writes as follows: *. . . consensus can only be reached if there is compatibility of basic values . . . Obviously, the greater the frequency of commonality insofar as these values are concerned, the smaller the number of loci of conflict.*

Religion can contribute considerably towards the establishment of shared values. Unfortunately there is a lot of misunderstanding about this, which can be partially ascribed to the ambivalent role played by religion. In view of the division among denominations and the marked differences in the way in which religious principles are interpreted, there seems to be little prospect of unity among religious groups. If unity is interpreted as complete agreement in respect of the content of all creeds, there is indeed little hope that this will ever be achieved. What is overlooked, however, is that what is involved here is the articulation of religious convictions at the secondary level. For this reason the confession (at least in the Protestant tradition) can always be related to and be tested against the Bible itself. For this reason religion has the ability to relate conflicting points of view to one another in such a way that prejudices and one-sided absolutisms can be identified and be demythologised. These conflicting points of view at secondary level can be tolerated because of a communal compromise at primary level. This attachment to underlying basic values is one of the strongest forms of a cross-cutting cleavage, and religious communities figure as prominent examples of multigroup affiliations (Rhoodie: 1983, p. 148).

Common values

In the report of the Work Committee: Religion: *Religion, intergroup relations and social change in South Africa,* the work committee came to the conclusion that, despite the differences, there were also important points of agreement between a significant number of churches on the basic values that are essential for the survival of society. These values underlie human rights that can be described as the "inalienable rights that contain the minimum requirements of a worthy existence" (p. 105).

A study which considered the points of view of the following institutions, revealed considerable consensus on basic points of departure: Baptist Union, Church of the Province of South Africa, Federation of Lutheran Churches in South Africa, Methodist Church, Nederduitse Gereformeerde Kerk, Nederduitse Gereformeerde Kerk in Afrika, Nederduitse Gereformeerde Sending Kerk, Presbyterian Church of South Africa, Roman Catholic Church, SACC. The views on which agreement was noted, are the following:

- All persons can lay claim to certain basic or fundamental rights.
- These rights were granted by God to man who was created in His image and are therefore inviolable.
- Not only the individual, but the community as a community of people, has certain rights.
- A balance must be pursued between the claims and the rights of individuals and the collective rights of the community. All rights are accompanied by corresponding responsibilities and duties.

72

- A distinction can be drawn between fundamental rights and secondary rights.
- Under no circumstances may rights be withheld or suspended. Even secondary rights or privileges may not be withheld if a person (or persons) has a rightful claim to them. The distinction between rights and privileges is fluid since circumstances play such an important role in secondary rights and "privileges".
- Biblical norms that apply to human rights are charity, truth, peace, justice, liberty and human dignity. Human rights cannot be rightly understood if the full scope of a Biblical anthropology is not taken into account.
- The value of the "human rights" concept lies especially in the universal impact of this term. In the sensitive church-state relationship in South Africa, this concept could play an important role in conveying as an example to the state the socio-ethical requirements for interhuman and intergroup relations seen from religious perspective.

The foundations of a human rights perspective on the basis of these points of departure are the following:

- The right to live, which includes the right to the basic means to sustain life, ways to obtain these, protection of physical and psychic integrity, etc.
- The right to fully express one's humanity, which includes aspects such as freedom of religion, the rights to human dignity regardless of race, colour or creed, right to privacy and to the development of personal talent and ability.
- The right to life in a community with fellow humanbeings which, in its most basic form, involves the right of marriage.

However, it cannot be denied that there are also differences between religious groups. Two examples of this are the difference between the more "theological" approach of the Presbyterian Church and the more "political-practical" approach of the methodists, as well as the Presbyterian emphasis on "unity" and the NG Kerk's emphasis on diversity. These and other differences are particularly obvious when the socio-ethical implications of the rights have to be concretized.

The fact that this degree of convergence does exist at least between the religious movements identified above — and there is reason to believe that this consensus may be wider — offers a positive point of departure to the promotion of constructive relations, regardless of the differences.

Summary

From the perspective of intergroup relations it is clear that religion can indeed play an important role in creating an orientation framework and an accountability basis for the interpretation of intergroup relations. In fact, this role must not be underestimated, especially not in terms of its psychosocial dynamics. Religion potentially offers a basis to modify relations that threaten to be more conflict-oriented than constructive. A condition would however be that the ambivalent role of religion in society must be understood.

THE ROLE OF HISTORIOGRAPHY

When looking at the role of historiography in intergroup relations, one of the most typical aspects of this in South Africa is the inextricable involvement with the community from which it stems and the way in which the interests of the historian's own group are handled. In its report, *Intergroup relations as reflected in South African historiography,* the work committee reached the conclusion that despite the demands of objectivity and scientific character, historiography nevertheless reflects widely divergent *perceptions* of South African society. This gives insight into the way in which groups experience themselves and others in the South African reality. Even more important, as also stated in the reports, *The social psychology of intergroup relations* and *Communication in a divided society,* is the way in which stereotypes are consolidated and perpetuated. Moreover, perceptions are *formed* and projected into the future by the way in which historical events are interpreted and presented, especially in the school situation. Research has repeatedly confirmed that when a negative image of other groups has once been formed, it is extremely difficult to change this.

Research done by the Work Committee: Historic aspects showed that South African history revealed a fragmented picture of divergent interpretations of events in the South African past, and these were often contradictory.

These differences are not only the result of differences in interpretation, but also of different methodological points of departure. In this review the following divergent paradigms will be discussed: internal/external orientation, conflict/co-operation and class/race.

Internal-external orientation

The problem of historiography in respect of intergroup relations becomes extremely complex when it is realized that whereas at the school level history must be presented from the point of view and orientation of the pupil's own community, there must at the same time be a sympathetic and appreciative acquaintanceship with the other groups comprising South African society. The motivation for the first element is that if the principle of an own approach to history is underrated, the teaching of history can hardly assist in creating loyalty towards and identification with the pupil's own past, which remains an aspect of constructive intergroup relations. For the same reasons a negative self-image and even resistance could develop if history were presented from the viewpoint of view of a different group in which the own group is presented in an unfavourable light. The two perspectives of internal-external orientation need not necessarily clash, provided that the role, position and status of the own group is placed within the broader context of South African history. An urgent need for a comprehensive, general history of South Africa is therefore identified, a history in which the role of all groups (either ethnic groups or classes), and the interaction between the groups, are reflected in a scientifically balanced and fair way.

Different ways of presentation

The conflict potential of the different historiographic schools does not only lie in the fact that it proves the existence of different perceptions but particularly in the *way* in which the different perceptions are presented. By way of illustrating this hypothesis, the following trends can be pointed out:

• The general trend among the various historiographic schools of thought and groups is an excessive concentration on the *ethnic*. For example, for the Afrikaans-oriented historian South African history begins with the settlement of the first whites on the southern tip of Africa in 1652. The rise of the Afrikaner is seen as a struggle which from the outset concerned self-protection, self-assertion and indigenization. This process occurred in interaction with two groups in particular: the Africans and the British. In the spirit of nationalist historiography these groups, in particular, were regarded as a threat to the Afrikaner.

• British imperial and colonial historiography sees the developments in South Africa as a subsection of the vast, comprehensive history of the British Empire. In the spirit of imperialism the British extension of power was seen as a positive and essential step for the maintenance of order and economic growth. The early liberal historiography accentuates group formation, competition and conflict between the different population groups, although attempts are also made to interpret the position of Africans and coloureds in their own right and not as an appendage to the white society.

• Neo-liberal historiography, under the influence of the striving towards relevance and involvement with a view to change, and by studying prevailing controversies, purposely abandoned a nationalistic approach and emphasised human relations, socio-economic problems and the origin and development of current political problems. The neo-liberal historians' attitude towards the pre-colonial and traditional African societies is different from that of the early liberals. They do not judge these societies as being primitive and barbaric, but emphasise their social and political structures, their system of kinship, their economic system, which leads to them being described as "peasant communities" rather than livestock farmers.

• African, coloured and Indian historiography is predominantly engaged historiography in which each group's position in society is overaccentuated without placing it in the broader context. Central themes in this historiography are white exploitation, minority status, racism, discriminatory legislation and conflict.

These examples can be extended but they confirm the above trends, namely that the own group is used as the sole point of orientation in the description and explanation of historical events by all groups.

Conflict and guilt

The accent in the description of historical events is predominantly placed on conflict, while the instances of co-operation are neglected. Apart from other possible considerations, the emphasizing of conflict is related to the predominantly internal orientation of historiography already identified above. The extent to which the group forms a reference point, means that such a group is, in effect, placed *in opposition to* other groups — in reality therefore an opposing paradigm. This interpretation is also apparent from the handling of co-operation through alliances and coalitions. In the very nature of things alliances and coalitions are formed against a common opponent. Co-operation between groups to form constructive relations are almost totally neglected. It may also be added that in some approaches, *inter alia* groups in revisionist historiography, conflict is explicitly handled as an explanatory principle.

In the historiography of all groups there is sometimes strong emphasis on the problem of guilt. The focus is therefore on determining which group(s) should be held responsible for the injustices of the past. This identification of a "scapegoat" (the *English* against the Afrikaners, the *Boers* against the Africans, the *capitalists* against the working class, etc.) is probably one of the most powerful "archetypes" that strengthens group prejudice and encourages the potentially latent conflict-oriented frames of reference.

Class versus race

When studying intergroup relations, the historiographic handling of "class" is important. The radical historiographic schools make class struggle a basic explanatory factor in the analysis of the development of intergroup relations, with the result that the main analytical concept is "class", not race or ethnicity. In this way two fundamental themes are distinguished in South African history: the destruction of the sovereignty of the Africans in that they were drawn into political communities where they enjoy enferior political status; and secondly the fact that South Africa is integrated in a market economy, and that a "colonial situation'' was thus created here. One of the essential characteristics of this radical approach to historiography is the identification of the capitalist economic system as a single world system with definable suppressive and exploitive characteristics. This is emphasized as the basic cause of the special way in which South African history, specifically the relations between people in this country, developed. It is also important to point out that this approach rejects the concept *intergroup relations* as such. In this paradigm, group is narrowly interpreted as a concept which *is* a function of a capitalist conceptualization.

Summary

The report *Intergroup relations as reflected in the South African historiography* clearly shows that the way in which the past is scientifically approached and then offered to the community as a distillate, has the potential to promote rather than reduce conflict in a country such as South Africa. The ''pictures in our minds'' that history helps to form, are predominantly group-centric, guilt projecting and conflict oriented rather than co-operation-oriented. This statement must be seen against the background of the reports: *The social psychology of intergroup relations* and *Communications in a divided society.* Both reports confirm the formative influence of history as an orientation framework for pupils and students.

Comparative studies of historiography in other countries with plural populations will probably produce patterns similar to those given above. There is certainly no reason to believe that South African historiography developed in total isolation from the methodology used in other countries. Yet such analogies would not lessen the responsibility of South African historians to cooperate in the balanced interpretation of intergroup relations.

PSYCHOLOGICAL AND SOCIAL FACTORS IN INTERGROUP RELATIONS

Central to the experiencing of intergroup relations are people's perceptions of one another and of groups, their attitudes and possible prejudices and their contact with and behaviour towards others. Relations ultimately crystalize at the level of individuals. Indeed, it is the individual members of the different sections of the population who are courteous (or discourteous) towards one another, members of a trade union and employers who enter into an agreement and members of a mixed rugby team who play together. Perception, attitudes, contact and behaviour represent the bridge or connection between the individuals referred to above, and relations between groups. In fact, aspects such as ethnicity and religion, find concrete expression in perception, attitude and behaviour. There-

77

fore, given the central function fulfilled by processes such as perception, it is not surprising that most of the prognoses and directives for the promotion of constructive intergroup relations implicity or explicitly include the improvement of such relations.

As simplistic as these statements are, just as complex are the sociopsychological realities. This can be partially ascribed to the complexity of these phenomena themselves, but also to the relatively limited knowledge about them and the continuous interaction between, for example, perception, attitude and behaviour. For that reason the following review was carefully formulated, although the specific findings might appear to be unidimensional.

In this section attention will first be given to the question of how relations are perceived, then to attitudes, then to the nature of contact between members of the different population categories and, finally, to the relationship between attitude and behaviour. The findings were mainly taken from the reports, *The social psychology of intergroup relations* and *Communication in a divided society* of the Work Committees: Social Psychology and Communication respectively and, in a few cases, from other research.

Perception of relations

The concept of perception is used in a fairly broad sense here to group together facets such as awareness of, knowledge about, expectations in respect of, categorizing and the forming of impressions. In terms of this wide interpretation of perception, phenomena such as social distance, stereotyping and relative deprivation can be regarded as indicators of perception.

Social Distance

Different projects undertaken for the *Investigation* show that South Africans see themselves and the mutual relation between groups as segmented in varying degrees. For example, it was found in the multipurpose survey that members of all the population categories differentiate perceptually between groups. Each respondent was asked to give a graphic indication of where he placed the different groups in respect to himself. No suggestions were made concerning the reference framework according to which the placement had to be made. The results are represented in Figure 3.1. Although the results are fairly complex, it appears that the two white language groups regard themselves as closest to one another and Africans as being furthest away from both of them, with the Indians and coloureds about halfway between. Conversely, the three latter groups differentiate very clearly between the Afrikaans and English-speaking groups, and regard the Afrikaans-speaking white as being the furthest removed from themselves. As indicated at the beginning of the chapter and as could be expected, there is therefore more differentiation than convergence in the perceptions. At this stage it is of no real importance whether this perceptual differentiation is the result of experience, expectations or something else — the fact is that there is differentiation in perception.

The findings of various projects in which social distance was investigated in terms of situations which vary from "allowing someone into your country" to "admitting someone into your family through marriage", are in summary: Of the four population categories, coloureds and Indians are most prepared to make contact at various levels. Both groups prefer contact with English-speaking whites while coloureds are least prepared to have contact with Afrikaans-speaking whites and Africans, and the Indians are prepared to make contact with coloureds and Afrikaans-speaking whites at the same levels. Indians are much less prepared to make contact with Africans than with the other groups.

Africans are more prepared than whites, but less prepared than coloureds and Indians to accept other groups in contact situations. Africans also much prefer contact with Englishspeaking whites, while they find contact with Afrikaansspeaking whites the least acceptable option.

The two white categories accept one another almost totally at all levels of contact, but differ in the degree of acceptance of other categories, in that English-speaking whites, historically as well as currently, accept contact with other categories more readily than Afrikaansspeaking whites. Both groups find contact with Africans the least acceptable.

From comparisons of research results obtained in 1981 and 1984, it appears that there has been a gradual change in the willingness of all groups for communication at various levels. All the groups are more prepared now to have contact than was the case some years ago.

In this respect it is true that the Afrikaans-speaking white has demonstrated the least progress in the direction of greater preparedness for contact, although greater willingness has developed in the economic and the work sphere. A noteworthy point is that the Afrikaans-speaking white group is apparently less prepared to accept mixed schools now than previously. At the same time the preparedness of English-speaking whites for contact as such venues as beaches, has diminished over the past few years; venues which during this period have become increasingly to all groups.

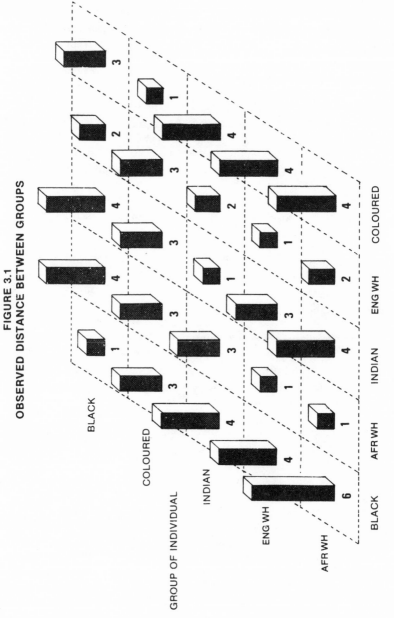

FIGURE 3.1
OBSERVED DISTANCE BETWEEN GROUPS

IN RESPECT OF

80

Research undertaken by Vergnani for the Work Committee: Social Psychology shows that coloureds and Indians have become significantly more willing to interact with one another over the past few years, also with regard to contact with Afrikaans-speaking whites. Comparable statistics for Africans are unfortunately not available, but there are theoretical grounds for assuming that this process has also occurred in their case.

Stereotypes:

As could be expected, the perceptions of *contact* with other groups are also related to the perceptions of *groups as such*. Afrikaans-speaking whites and Africans are least prepared for contact with one another, and simultaneously the stereotypes in respect of one another are also the most negative of all the groups. In contrast Indians, coloureds and Africans are more open to contact with English-speaking than with Afrikaans-speaking whites and also more positive. A graphic representation of views (stereotypes) held by various groups of themselves and of one another, is given in Fig. 3.2, and is based on research done since 1973 by the HSRC's Institute for Communication Research under the guidance of Thiele. Stereotypes are rarely changed, in fact it is safe to say that it is part of the socialising process. For example, over a period of eight years, the HSRC found only slight variations in the intensity of stereotypes, but no change in direction (that is the order in which groups are arranged). From literature on stereotypes it appears that some ethnic stereotypes have begun to assume a normative character. This normativity of the stereotypes could inhibit change in negative group perceptions. This aspect is raised again in the change and resistance to change of attitudes. Research done by the Work Committee Communication revealed, *inter alia,* that school textbooks and youth literature contain very negative stereotypes. Although there are indications that these stereotypes are also becoming less distinct in general literature, it must be remembered that older books with more negative stereotypes are still used as set books, are read and that films based on them are shown on television.

Regarding the development of stereotypes, the following considerations must also be borne in mind: Stereotypes take shape early in a child's life. Although research is not very clear on this, it is safe to assume that by the age of about 7 years, stereotypes have been internalized. Moreover, it is common knowledge that contact between children of different groups — especially whites with other groups and *vice versa* — just does not occur in practice. In fact, the education policy explicitly discourages such contact. It therefore follows that stereotypes are not the result of first-hand experience. In the socializing process the child

FIGURE 3.2
AVERAGE STEREOTYPE EVALUATIONS OF GROUPS

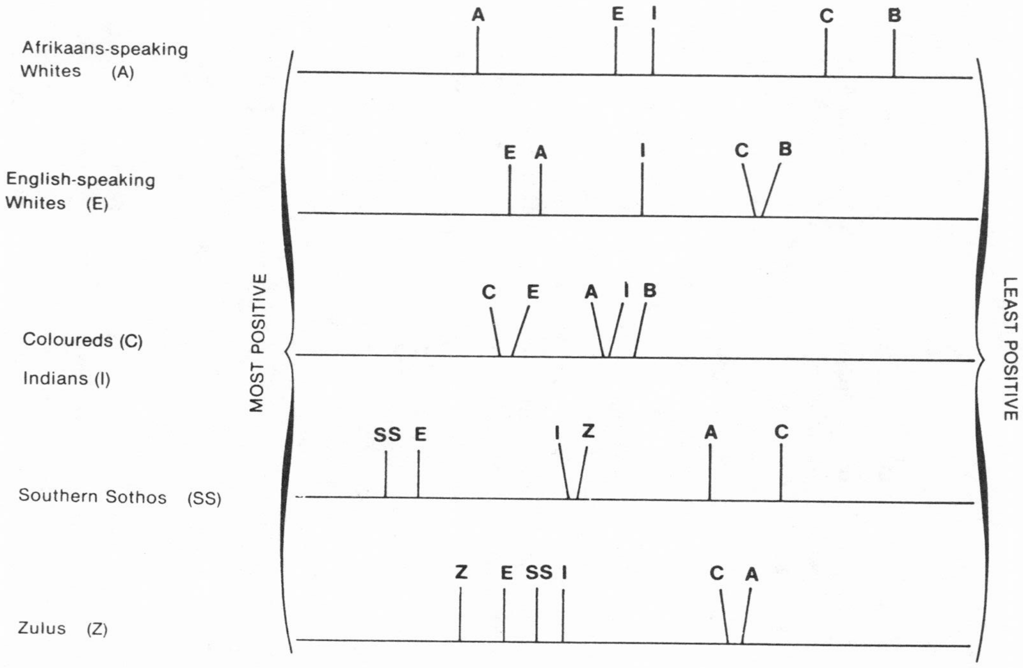
Afrikaans-speaking Whites (A)
English-speaking Whites (E)
Coloureds (C)
Indians (I)
Southern Sothos (SS)
Zulus (Z)
MOST POSITIVE
LEAST POSITIVE
A E I C B
E A I C B
C E A I B
SS E I Z A C
Z E SS I C A

Note: Blacks: B

typically undergoes merely second-hand exposure and stereotypes are formed on the basis of this.

The above can also be approached from another angle: Where groups meet one another mainly in clearly defined role situations such as that of supervisor-worker in the work place (see later), there is little opportunity to arrive at an objective, true-to-life, picture of one another as individuals. It is virtually impossible for the individual to imagine the possibility of having meaningful contact with members of such groups at more personal levels. Unfortunately, indirect channels of contact such as the media sometimes encourage this pattern of rigid stereotypes as well as the perception of relatively vast social distances.

Relative deprivation

Perceptions occur in terms of a frame of reference — a person observes something in terms of his background or environment. This fact leads to what must surely be one of the most important dynamic processes in intergroup relations, namely the observation of the relative positions of groups. The process known as relative deprivation has two facets: firstly, it points to the perceptions by people of the gap between real and anticipated satisfaction of needs; secondly, it shows that people's perception of deprivation is based on the way in which they define and evaluate their needs and the satisfying of those needs, relative to the social groups with which they identify, i.e. their *reference groups*.

The realization that American Africans utilize thirty times more of the world's natural resources per capita, than the average Pakistani is small consolation for the American African who evaluates his socio-economic position relative to his reference group, namely the middle-class "White-Anglo-Saxon-Protestant" (WASP) who lives around the corner. Well knowing what standard of living the whites maintain, South Africa's Africans feel no less deprived because — measured by objective criteria — Africans north of the Limpopo have a much lower standard of living per capita. In the multipurpose survey it was, in fact, found that 59 % of the Africans felt that their general standard of living was lower at present than it was five years ago, as opposed to 27 % of the whites, 31 % of the Indians and 33 % of the coloureds who maintained that there had been a drop in their standard of living. In other words, the vast majority of Africans experience their position as one of weakness and deterioration, although the data in Chapter 2 indicate that, regarded objectively, this is not the case.

In this regard a country-wide investigation into the quality of life — an investigation carried out in collaboration with the Centre for Applied Social Sciences at the University of Natal — provides important empirical insights. The measurement of the overall quality of life consisted of question concerning the degree of satisfaction (or otherwise) with "life as a whole", "life for Africans/whites/et cetera in South Africa" and degree of wellbeing. (Statistical analyses indicated that these questions represented reliable indices of quality of life.)

From the perspective of intergroup relations the following findings are important:

• As regards subjective experience of the quality of life, the whites were the most satisfied, followed by Indians and coloureds at more or less the same level, with Africans clearly the most dissatisfied with life. The widest chasm in the perceived satisfaction with of life is therefore between the Africans and the other groups. More than 20 % of the Africans described themselves as "very dissatisfied", while only 2 % of members of the other groups themselves as being "very dissatisfied". There is thus a wide gap in the subjective experience of life between Africans and members of other groups.

• The following circumstances, experiences subjectively, are related to global satisfaction: the ability to take care of the family; health; quality and quantity of food; the emotional effect of comparisons with other racial groups; wages and salaries; material assets; the expectation of material security in old age; the adequacy of accommodation; level of education; job opportunities and the possibility of promotion in one's career.

• The order of the above subjective circumstances was not the same for all four groups. Comparisons with other race groups, religion, job opportunities, material security of old age, happiness in the family and adequacy of accommodation were the most important factors for whites. Among coloureds promotion in the job, health, privacy in the home, the degree of protection against crime, adequacy of accommodation and the ability to care for the family were the main desiderata. For Indians family happiness, level of education, characteristics of the residential area, freedom of movement, comparisons with other racial groups and wages and salaries were the most important. Among Africans health, quality and quantity of food, the ability to take care of the family, cecurity of accommodation, level of education, the respect shown by other races and comparisons with other races were the most significant contributory factors to quality of life.

These preliminary analyses draw attention to an important characteristic of the quality of life in the context of intergroup relations. In all analyses so far made it appears that comparison of *one's own group with other racial groups* is a vital contributory factor in people's personal evaluation of the quality of their own lives. Thorough statistical analyses show that the honour and respect — or lack thereof — accorded to group membership have a significant effect on the subjective experience of everyday life.

The findings of another project undertaken for the *Investigation* also confirmed that Africans feel economically, politically and socially significantly more deprived relative to other ethnic groups than relative to their own peer groups. They also experience significantly more relative deprivation when the comparison group is white than when the groups are coloured or Indian. An important issue in this regard is that there is a significant relationship between a feeling of relative deprivation on the part of Africans in respect of their economic situation vis a vis Afrikaans-speaking people, and an increase in militancy. Since increasing contact with whites and a growing educationally sophisticated leadership mean that more and more Africans define their aspirations largely in terms of a white frame of reference, it is inevitable that these Africans will experience any restriction on equal treatment with whites as a feeling of deprivation. Africans therefore feel deprived relative to their white fellow South Africans, and not privileged relative to the citizenry of Pakistan or Ghana.

To summarise, research indicates that various factors, including rapid urbanisation, mass education and exposure to prosperous stereotypes on television have, separately and in interaction, led to two mutually dependent consequences among Africans. On the one hand, there is the feeling of being excluded and the victims of white domination — a percention which has become much more intense since Indians and coloureds gained access to the new constitutional privileges. On the other hand expectations of rapid advancement have been stimulated. This has resulted in a combination of factors that will not simply disappear of their own accord.

Attitudes

Having described how South Africans perceive one another and their mutual relations, attention will now be paid to their attitudes. This does not mean that perceptions and attitudes are independent of one another. On the contrary, it is generally accepted that there is a mutual relation between these two facets of man's psyche.

At the risk of oversimplification, the concept of attitude can be described as an orientation or disposition towards socially relevant matters. Attitudes towards people, groups and matters concerning intergroup relations can therefore be very useful indications of the prevailing intergroup climate. In the analysis of intergroup relations attitudes also serve as indicator of prejudice towards other people and groups. In the light of the conceptual considerations the Work Committee: Social Psychology compiled a very thorough review of the entire spectrum of attitude studies undertaken in South Africa so far. The review was discussed at length in the committee's report; a number of conclusions are given below.

For the purpose of this *Investigation,* systematic comparisons were made between all the social scientific investigations on the attitudes of whites undertaken over the past nearly 50 years. From these investigations it appears that the attitudes of the white groups have always been widely divergent, with English-speaking South Africans significantly more positive in their attitude towards other groups than Afrikaans-speaking South Africans. Both groups have, however, always been more negative towards Africans than towards any other group.

In view of the Afrikaner's manifestly strong identification with his own group, as reflected in this group's mobilization over the past 50 years, it is not surprising that the Afrikaner, in terms of attitude, appears to be less tolerant than his English-speaking compatriot. There is certainly enough scientific evidence for accepting that the more one isolates one's own group from other groups and identifies and mobilizes with it, the more one is inclined to make a distinction between other groups and to display negative attitudes towards them. It is obviously difficult to distinguish between cause and effect in this case, but neither is it important. What is important, however, is that the Afrikaner's striving towards the formation and delineation of and identification with the own group would inevitably lead to rejection of the other groups notwithstanding his probably well meant pronouncements that the promotion of the own cause does not signify denial and demeaning of other groups. Psychologically it would appear that man simply does not function in this way.

Africans and, to a lesser extent, also Indians and coloureds, have similarly negative attitudes towards whites. In fact, the mutual attitudes virtually mirror one another. An indication of this can be derived from the following, obviously simplified finding. On an index of ''prejudice'' that was included for the multipurpose survey, the scores could vary between a maximum positive score of 3 and a maximum negative score of 15. The mean score of Africans was 9.2 an that of Afrikaans-speaking whites 9.6. From a social psychological point of view there may be different explanationf for the various attitudes — which would at the same time involve the entire spectrum of theories — but the main conclusion is the fact that both groups reveal strong negative attitudes towards one another.

Within the framework of intergroup relations, attitudes towards violence and militancy are particularly important. Three projects undertaken in the *Investigation* paid attention to this aspect. In all three projects representative samples were used in respect of all the population categories. There was a striking similarity between the results of these projects. The outcome of the multipurpose survey can be regarded as representative on the question of whether violence was an acceptable means of achieving political aims, 63 % of the Africans, 40 % of the Indians, 37 % of the coloureds and 30 % of the whites reacted positively.

One of the other projects showed convincingly that militancy among Africans was due almost entirely to their feeling of economic deprivation.

Although, by definition, relations are comparatively stable, they are not unchangeable. The report of the Work Committee (Social-psychology) shows that there has been a slight change in the relations between all the groups over the past few years in that there is greater tolerance. This change has manifested itself in Afrikaans-speaking whites in the form of greater acceptance of the dignity of all groups. As indicated elsewhere, this change is qualified, however, in that many Afrikaans-speaking whites are still reluctant to accept other groups as their equals in contact situations, at least not according to what they say; this will be discussed in more detail later.

It is necessary to qualify the finding that attitudes have become somewhat more positive, or at least less negative in recent years. Research has shown that events such as the Soweto riots of 1976 had a negative effect on the attitudes of whites towards Africans; immediately in the case of Afrikaans-speaking whites, slightly later in the case of English-speaking whites. Particularly since unrest has occurred fairly regularly since 1976, it can be assumed that his has inhibited the development of tolerance despite other positive signs of change such as white support for the new constitutional dispensation.

On change

A very important consideration in respect of the development of attitudes, is that empirical information from the multipurpose survey indicates that the majority of the population expects that South Africa will change considerably during the next 20 years. Whites, for example, anticipate greater power sharing by all groups, specifically coloureds and Indians, but also by Africans. The other groups have similar expectations. The majority of South Africans (from 47 % of the Africans to 68 % of the coloureds) expect relations to improve within the next five years. It can therefore be assumed that there is already anticipation of a broadening of the basis of democracy.

It is important to bear in mind that even if attitudes are not yet as favourable as one would like, this does not mean that changed behaviour will not follow *once* conditions have changed. In other words, the fact that people may resist admitting someone of another group into his sports club, does not mean that they will actively refuse membership to such a person or avoid him once he is a member. When someone is actually faced with a changed situation he often reacts much less severely than his words would lead one to expect. This aspect will be discussed at greater length later.

Regarding change, it is important to note that the biggest obstacle lies in effecting the first change, however small. Lewin calls this the unfreezing phase. Subsequent changes are much easier to effect and under favourable circumstances the rate of change may even accelerate. In this regard reference can also be made to Adam's suggestion, namely that ''technocratic'' reform through the accumulation of a number of small-scale reforms, could in the end make liberation in the traditional sense of the word redundant.

Real contact between the communities

In a country like South Africa it is important to determine the extent to which there is real contact between the different population groups, particularly because original government policy was explicitly aimed at restricting contact between people of different groups only to the most essential.

According to the report of the Work Committee (Communication) *Communication in a divided society,* there is little contact between the different groups. Most of the contact occurs in structured vertical situations, the best examples being the work place (supervisor-worker) and in the commerce (e.g. shop assistant-customer). These situations are characterized by the fact that contact is limited to formal topics, that the persons concerned fulfil clearly defined roles and that the relation towards one another is pre-specified. There is little or no contact in spontaneous social situations on the basis of equal status.

Research has also shown that the degree of contact is determined by the person's own group membership and background, the population group to which the other party belongs and his views on the other group. It is therefore not possible to generalise by saying that certain groups have no contact; it can however be said that particular groups, under specific circumstances, have less contact with certain other groups.

A critical factor in the lack of contact and communication between different population groups, especially between whites and Africans, is the comparative lack of intercultural communication skills. An example of this was given in chapter 2, namely the relatively limited language ability of South Africans. South Africans often do not have the language ability to mix freely with members of other groups. Usually there are other obstacles as well, such as lack of knowledge of the other's culture. The Work Committee: Communication reached the conclusion that there was an urgent need in general for training in communication skills, but especially for people who in view of their positions continually have to liaise with people of other groups. This problem should be tackled at school level.

Consequently, if the situation is constructive at the more personal level of contact and communication, it will apply equally at the level of handling conflict. Research has indicated that ineffective communication, often even a total lack of communication, was in the past one of the main factors causing conflict to escalate into violence. Against this background it is important to determine whether there are institutions that could arbitrate in conflict situations. A thorough review has indicated that there are virtually no institutions in South Africa that could arbitrate professionally between conflicting parties. When the position abroad is analysed, it appears that such specialist arbiters are highly valued. In view of the high conflict potential in South Africa, attention should be paid to this aspect of communication.

A further important finding was that different groups do not evaluate their contact with one another in the same way. It was for instance found that whites generally evaluate their contact with other groups significantly more positively than the other groups rate their contact with whites. This matter is of critical importance particularly when it concerns contact between white officials and African civilians, as it emerged on several occasions. There were strong indications that this contact and interaction were often experienced as unpleasant by Africans. This is important in view of the fact that contact with officials is one of the few outside the work situation. Owing to the totally asymmetrical nature of the distribution of power that is inherent in the official-civilian interaction, Africans in particular, but perhaps other groups too, experience the actions of officials as indicative of the inaccessibility, lack of sympathy, etc. of the authorities and of whites. This asymmetrical perception of the satisfaction derived from contact bodes no good for the future. Because whites are unconcerned about this, or possibly unaware, or prefer to be unaware of the fact that other groups do not find the contact pleasant, they lack the motivation to effect a change in the contact patterns.

New spheres of contact for instance in the field of recreation, sport and entertainment are, however, opening up and it can therefore be expected that spontaneous and informal contact on the basis of equal status will increase. Projections of the Work Committee: Economics and Labour indicate that Africans will increasingly enter these fields in future. In view of the importance of this sport as a contact situation will be dealt with more fully.

From the report of the Work Committee: Social psychology as well as certain findings of the HSRC Sports *Investigation* (Report No. 5, 1982) it appears that there is a large degree of willingness aiming the different groups to make contact with one another on the sports field. With regard to whites, the experiencing of social distance in the sports situation differs from one type of sport to another and this also has bearing on attitudes towards non-racial sport. Whites not only have differential preference patterns in respect of the level of participation (national, provincial, club level and school sport), but divergent preferences in respect of different types of sport were also reported. There was comparatively more support for non-racial sport at national level, while non-racialism at club and school level met with considerable hardening of attitudes. In addition the intimacy in certain types of sport also had an effect on attitudes. Many people were prepared to accept mixed participation in the case of rugby/soccer, whereas much resistance was reported in the case of a sport such as swimming.

These trends did not however occur among Indians, coloureds and Africans. All three of these population groups were almost equally in favour of non-racial participation in sport regardless of the level of participation or the type of sport involved.

Obvious differences also emerged in the attitude patterns of whites on the one hand, and Indians, coloureds and Africans on the other concerning the sharing of recreational facilities. The latter three groups were again for more prepared than whites to share recreational facilities and it would appear that their perception and experiencing of social distance differ from those of whites. It may be that the experiencing of social distance is not relevant here, but rather that it concerns the claiming of rights in a society that does not allow all its members equal rights in all spheres.

The perception and experience of social distance among whites emerged strongly when non-racial recreation was at issue. The more intimate the recreational activities, the more reluctant were whites to share the facilities with other population groups. The shared use of public beaches, holiday resorts and swimming-pools was opposed much more strongly than in the sharing of public sports facities and transport.

Although whites have particular reservations regarding mixed sport and recreation — it does not occur among the other groups — this project leads one to expect that sport could become a catalyst in a situation where voluntary contact on a horizontal level could lead to constructive relations.

In summary, there is every reason to assume that contact in situations of equal status will be more satisfactory to all the parties concerned. A careful and comprehensive analysis of the literature accordingly showed that *contact as such* does not lead to a change in attitude. Consequently, the fact that there may possibly be more contact between different groups in the future does not necessarily mean that the groups will assess one another more positively. The primary condition for contact to result in more positive attitudes as that such contact must occur spontaneously, informally, between people of equal status and on a friendly basis. In this context it must again be stressed that there is very little of this type of contact, in South Africa today.

Word and deed — attitude and action

The above review of the state of the attitudes of groups towards one another gives rise to the very important question concerning the expected efforts results of these attitudes on the behaviour of groups towards one another. Put differently: Are there grounds for expecting that some South Africans will necessarily *act* negatively towards one another merely because they maintain that they do not like each other, or for example do not want to do the same type of work as another group, or see violence as a solution?

Are actions necessarily consistent with words or attitudes?

The report of the Work Committee: Social psychology clearly indicated that there is not a one to one relationship between attitudes and behaviour. Information on people's attitudes alone is totally inadequate as a basis for predicting their actions. Attitudes can, at most, indicate a psychic and social climate. Behaviour is a function of *inter alia* the following factors: experience, opportunities, abilities, motivation, models, reference groups and anticipated or real results of behaviour. This issue is particularly relevant in view of the apparently polarized negative attitudes of whites, especially Afrikaans-speaking whites, and Africans towards one another. Various investigations and theoretical analyses refer to verbal indications implying rigid and extreme attitudes. Further particulars are given in the next paragraph. There is often also a considerable gap between people's broad ideological orientations and their attitudes towards specific matters. People who, for example, normally have a conservative philosophy of life can often assume a fairly "liberal" stance in respect of specific social controversies.

One of the projects undertaken for this *Investigation* showed that nearly 25 % of the Afrikaans-speaking respondents in three predominantly conservative towns felt that the present government was moving too slowly with its perform plans, while 54 % indicated that a start should have been made years ago to improve the lot of the other groups. In the same study more than half of the Afrikaans-speaking whites agreed with the statement that increasing contact would reduce the possibility of conflict between the groups.

With the necessary caution it would be possible to deduce from the above type of findings that the basically very conservative attitude of Afrikaans-speaking

91

whites does not mean that changes in the direction of constructive and accommodating intergroup relations would necessarily be opposed. It may be assumed that the tolerance threshold of change is higher than has been indicated by attitude studies alone.

It is also important to note that where people have once reacted to one another, regardless of their previous attitudes, their attitudes are usually brought in line with their conduct. Thus: attitudes follow on and result from behaviour. This statement has very important implications for the interpretation of the South African situation — hence the earlier conclusion that voluntary intergroup contact with equality should promote good relations — but it also holds grave warnings. In recent times — especially since 1976 — South African has been characterized by a cycle of confrontation and violence particularly but not exclusively between African youths and the police. It is true that the police force consists of members of all the population categories, but it may be assumed that it is seen as being representative of the white establishment. The confrontation concerns actions and reactions and it depends on the orientation of those involved what is cause and what effect. Deeper lying causes — rejection of the *status quo* or confirmation thereof — need not be involved to arrive at the conclusion that this cycle of confrontation and violence leads and will lead to the polarization of attitudes and a genuine commitment to the necessity for destructive conflict of those concerned.

From a social psychological perspective, this is one of the most important conflict-generating factors — a vicious circle of destructive conflict.

THE ROLE OF MASS COMMUNICATION

In view of the limited extent of the intergroup contact and the negative mutual attitudes and stereotypes, attention must be paid to the role of the mass media. The question becomes even more relevant considering the increase in violence that marks intergroup relations, and the media's coverage of this.

In many parts of the world the mass media are associated one way or another with conflict between groups. Commissions of enquiry for instance into riots in the United States of America, England and South Africa, almost without exception have paid attention to the role or alleged role of the media. In fact, the so-called Steyn Commission's terms of reference specifically referred to the influence of the mass media on intergroup relations. Neither is it surprising that the question concerning the media arises since they are the single most important disseminator of information — an omnipresent watchdog.

The role of the media is discussed in detail in the report of the Work Committee: Communication: *Communication in a divided society*. For the purposes of this discussion the following facets will be dealt with: extent, coverage, access to the media, control and effects.

Extent

From a technological point of view the media in South Africa are the most highly developed in Africa. Through its infrastructure and other resources, South Africa forms part of a world chain of information dissemination. One of the results of this is that the situation between groups, the conflict, statements of leaders and sometimes those of the man in the street, are often immediately as it were, made known to the world at large, inviting a chain of reactions and counter-reactions, often before they are presented on the main news bulletin of South African television. Information is filtered by various gatekeepers which inhibit the free internal flow of information somewhat. The public is not always given an overall picture of events and developments. The phenomenon is in part also a function of the nature, representation and coverage by the South African media. Nevertheless, the comparatively large degree of freedom which the South African press enjoys makes it an important factor in the dissemination of information concerning the options, implications and effects of certain actions of government institutions, and the actions and reactions of other interest groups; it offers a forum for discussion and fulfils a watchdog function in the event of powers being exceeded.

Coverage

From the point of view of intergroup relations, the report of the Work Committee: Communication convincingly showed that the newspapers promote sectional interests in that each newspaper propagates specific ideologically based views on intergroup relations.

At the one extreme of the ideological spectrum there is the so-called alternative press which is strongly outspoken against the present white-orient government, and which openly pleads for a completely new order in South Africa. Alongside this can be placed the Black English-language press which is also extremely critical of the current dispensation and the white handling of matters, but which is more obliging or accommodating. Roughly between these two is the white English-language press which has a generally critical attitude towards the present system of intergroup relations, yet is positively appreciative of any progressive development. However this moderate English press is slightly evasive at times about the ideal way of institutionalizing intergroup relations. Closer to the conservative extreme is the Afrikaans-language press which supports the existing dispensation in varying degrees, but which explicitly argues for the greater accommodation of other groups. At the other extreme is the so-called conservative Afrikaans press which in fact pleads for a return to and total implementation of what could be described as a Verwoerdian model of intergroup relations, in other words strict apartheid in the traditional sense.

Regarding radio and television, the coverage of intergroup relations is also in fact sectional. The South African Broadcasting Corporation's (SABC) self-proclaimed intention is to promote good relations between the different population categories, but in practice this means intergroup relations as defined by the present government. Consequently there can be no question of a full and fair representation of the total spectrum of the South African situation.

From the analyses and interpretations of the particular work committee it appears that the South African reader, listener and viewer who has to rely mainly on one medium of communication, is given a one-sided view of groups, their mutual relations, policy and of alternative perspectives on policy. This gives rise to the question concerning the extent to which the public uses alternative media.

Access to the media

A very large percentage of the total population has access to the printed media, the radio and television. Consequently a larger proportion of the total South African population has access to the different media than is the case in any other country in Africa or even in all the African countries put together.

This exposure is however not distributed for the different population categories and specific media. For example it appears that the coloured population category has the widest spectrum of exposure, namely to Afrikaans and English books, the radio and television as well as the Afrikaans and English-language press and certain Black media. Then follows Afrikaans-speaking whites, who however have very little access to the Black media. The other groups have a somewhat one-sided exposure namely mainly to the English-language media, but they also have considerable exposure to the radio and television. Africans are much more exposed to the "white media" than whites are to the media aimed primarily at Africans.

It can therefore be concluded that a very wide spectrum of the South African situation is covered by the South African media in one form or another. However, since different population groups are inclined to use only specific media, they acquire relatively biased viewpoints.

The asymmetries in access to the media thus identified, are the complicated result of various factors including the language heterogeneity of the country, the level of literacy, and the availability and ideological sectional nature of the media in South Africa.

Control

The question of access to the media must also be considered within the context of control over and ownership of the media. It must therefore be pointed out that the press is totally owned by whites, although there are varying degrees of editorial freedom. In the case of the broadcasting media, the top management of the South African Broadcasting Corporation is white; despite a significant editorial input by members of other population groups and the actual control therefore rests with whites. Obviously the new constitutional dispensation has, by definition, changed this situation, but it is still too early to assess the effect that this will have.

Be that as it may, this state of affairs must be regarded as potentially conflict-generating, assesses over the long term in any case. In fact, the critical school of communication regards this issue, especially as manifested in South Africa, as the basic cause of conflict — as conflict itself. This assessment of the long-term effects of control over the media naturally does not mean that a greater say by other groups could not generate tension in the short term.

Effects of the mass media

The question of the effects of information, especially as disseminted through mass communication, must be handled circumspectly in this report. This caution is called for by the nature of the research problem, making it virtually impossible to reach simple conclusions on the effects of such institutions on society.

When considering the effects of mass communication on intergroup relations, the extent and freedom of the mass media is crucial. The comparatively large degree of freedom enjoyed by the press in South Africa makes it an important factor in the dissemination of information concerning the options, implications and effects of certain actions of the Government and other interest groups. It provides a forum for discussion and fulfils a watchdog function, in the event of certain bounds being overstepped, manipulation, etc. During the recent referendum on the new constitution the media, probably more than the politicians, informed the public about the pros and cons of the proposed system. There are empirical indications that the stereotyped representation of groups and their relations towards one another by the media is diminishing, which could contribute significantly towards the elimination of prejudices. As long as the switch from "white" politics, entertainment and sport to its "black" equivalent can be achieved by the mere turn of a switch, it must be expected that mutual influence will increase. The West German media had a similar effect on East Germany and this helped to thaw relations. "In the end, the logic of the evidence or the appeal of entertainment triumphs over ideological intent or artificially decreed divides" (Adam 1985, p. 94). But then the media must remain free.

In the regard the educational function of, particularly, radio and television must naturally also be seen as something that facilitates intergroup relations. Provided the new educational initiatives of the SABC can be implemented in a professional way *and* with the closest co-operation of the target groups, there is reason to believe that these media could make a contribution towards alleviating the educational backlog among groups.

The report of the relevant work committee disadvantaged contains fairly strong evidence that the media are successful in relaying their own agenda of priorities in the field of intergroup relations to their users. On the basis of local as well as overseas literature it appears that the media, television in particular, such things as recreational literature, do succeed at the very least in reconfirming *existing* attitudes and perceptions among the public.

The question of reinforcing existing attitudes and perceptions of intergroup relations must be seen in relation to the earlier finding that no South African medium on its own is fair in its coverage of the total South African situation. In other words, a given medium does not expose its viewers, listeners or readers to "the other side" of the question. Seen together, these two research findings signify that the motivation for dialogue between the different population categories is slight. The media user is rarely made to doubt the validity of his own points of view. This appears to be a vicious circle. The only ameliorating exceptions that appear to counter this vicious circle somewhat are the following: socially engaged Afrikaans literature, for the Afrikaans readers and the radio and television for those opposed to the *status quo*. The relatively low credibility of the SABC in the eyes of many South Africans must be taken into account, as well as the relatively high exposure of these groups to the SABC.

Investigation into riots, both in South Africa and in the rest of the world, could find no evidence that media coverage of these issues had actually instigated the violence. There are suggestions, however, that media coverage could promote the spread and possibly the intensification of such riots. It is thus extremely difficult to assess the role of the media on conflict generation. The conflict is after all already there. But, as Lord Scarman as quoted in the work committee report cautioned: "But I do urge editors and the producers to accept that there is also a responsibility to assess the likely impact on events of their own reporting of them to ensure balance in the coverage of disorder, and at all times to bear in mind that rioters, and others, in their exhibition of violence respond alarmingly to what they see (wrongly, but understandably) as the encouraging presence of the TV camera and the reporter''.

Overseas research indicates that the mass media's influence increases considerably during times of rapid sociopolitical change. The current situation in South Africa can indeed be described as one of rapid change and, for this reason, the hypothesis that the media's influence will also increase, is probably valid.

Summary

One of the most important conclusions to be drawn from this analysis of the role of the mass media in intergroup relations, is the fact that notwithstanding the potential importance of this role, there is at present very little real exchange of information on such relations. Media users are in fact not exposed to the full spectrum of the realities of the situation involving groups and their relations. Existing stereotypes are strengthened, although to a lesser extent than before, and people are not motivated to acquire more information about others. Polarization rather than dialogue must necessarily follow. It is improbable that under these circumstances people will understand the perceptions of others, appreciate their needs, or be able to form a truthful picture of: expectations and aspirations, ideals and fears, tolerance thresholds and ceilings, uniquenesses and universalities, breadth and depth of experience, and the intention of actions.

In this respect to media and not realizing their potential of actively contributing to the reduction of conflict in South Africa.

CONCLUSION

South Africans of different backgrounds experience group relations differently. Although ethnicity is an important factor, many people refuse to identify with ethnic groups because of its statutory institutionalization. Analyses of factors such as attitudes, stereotypes, communication and the ambivalent role of religion, historiography and the mass media in these show that South Africa is a divided and polarised society.

CHAPTER 4

THE STRUCTURING OF INTERGROUP RELATIONS

The preceding chapter concentrated mainly on how people experience South Africa's plural social order. By implication intergroup relations were regarded as a process of dynamic interaction between people. Any process tends to assume fixed patterns and consequently become structured. The theme of this chapter is, therefore, the human diversity and the group-differentiating pattern of South African society as it took form in specific socio-economic, administrative, juridical, political and constitutional structures through the years. Attention will also be paid to the question: to what extent can these structural components of the South African social order be regarded as functional or dysfunctional for democratic intergroup relations?

As can be deduced from the system approach and as was postulated in the previous chapter, structuring cannot be interpreted separately from experience — just as experience without structure is meaningless. The product of experience and structure will be dealt with in Chapter 5.

Naturally, not all the structures dealt with here have been institutionalized to the same extent. For example, there is apparently more 'flexibility' in respect of the shaping of intergroup relations in the economic and labour fields than in the field of politics. Put differently: the boundaries in the former sphere are not as distinct as those in the latter. The structures that will be dealt with here relate to labour and economics, education, government administration, the juridical system and, finally, to political and constitutional institutions.

ECONOMIC CONSIDERATIONS

In all communities the various groups and classes have conflicting economic interests in some respects, and mutual interests in others. In the economic sphere it is therefore not possible to eliminate a clash of interests. However, it is vitally important that interests should not conflict to such an extent that they have a destabilising effect on the economy.

Since the acceptance of the Wiehahn report much has been done to better accommodate conflict in the labour field. However, at this stage all the proposed reforms have not yet filtered through and it is therefore difficult to assess which problems are of a temporary nature and which are permanent.

In this section the economy will be dealt with first, followed by a discussion of labour affairs. Statistical data mentioned in Chapter 2 will not be repeated, although cross-reference to the data may be necessary.

THE ECONOMY

The following review of economic factors is largely derived from the report of the Work Committee : Economics and Labour. The topics will be dealt with in the following order: economic growth, employment including the informal sectors, earnings and wealth and, finally, social provision.

Economic growth

According to the Work Committee : Economics and Labour, economic growth is one of the most important determinants of future intergroup relations. This proposition is based on the undeniable connection between growth and earnings, job creation and employment and affordable social provision. From this it follows that the lower the expected and real growth rate over the next few years, the greater the economic differences between population categories will be, and the greater the chances of an intensification of conflict.

From an analysis of various projections for the next 15 years, it appears that it would be unrealistic to expect a growth rate in excess of 5 % a year. In view of this it is expected that the average growth rate will be somewhere between 3 % and 5 %, although even this may prove to be optimistic. To demonstrate the influence of the level of the growth rate, it can be pointed out that a growth rate of 3 % p.a. will mean merely a 15 % increase in real income *per capita* for all categories, as against 69 % if the average growth rate were 5 %.

However, it is not only the absolute level of growth that is important, but also its nature and how it is used. For example, the rapid growth of the sixties was mainly used to improve the whites' position, with the result that the gap in income widened still further and poverty among the other categories remained much the same. The much more modest growth of the seventies, because of different priorities, was used to narrow the income gap and reduce poverty. From this it can be inferred that the nature and use of economic growth are as important as its extent.

Employment

From the report of the Work Committee : Economics and Labour, it appears that unemployment among Africans is significantly higher than among the other groups and lowest among the whites. This pattern is the result of a complex interaction between *inter alia,* the following factors: general state of the economy, level and quality of education, capital intensive industrialization and technology, discriminatory legislation, and differential urbanization.

An average annual growth rate of 5 % is necessary — all other things being equal — to prevent a further rise in these levels of unemployment. However, should the population growth continue to expand at the present rate of about 2,6 % a year, unemployment will of necessity increase. If the present arrangements in respect of influx control remain in force, it follows that the greater proportion of these unemployed people will be concentrated in the national states. Under conditions of low economic growth, between 50 % and 54 % of the labour force, namely between 3,3 and 9,7 million people, will be unemployed by the year 2000.

The above data and projections emphasise the inevitable role that will have to be played by the non-formal sector. If the agricultural sector (characterised by increasing mechanisation and consolidation into larger units) is not restructured it will not be able to absorb more people. The non-formal sector will therefore have to grow drastically to be able to accommodate those unemployed who have nowhere else to go — especially when increasing urbanization is taken into account. This sector is not capital intensive — the creation of one job opportunity costs less than one-tenth of what it costs in the formal sector — and it also offers essential training for entrepreneurs, so that the sector should be allowed to expand with the least possible interference from government. Only if this is done can it develop to accommodate a significant percentage of the increased number of unemployed.

The conflict-generating results of unemployment for intergroup relations are numerous and very serious. A few of the most important negative effects on the relations between groups are the following:

101

• Increased mobility as a result of the search for work and the concomitant increasing disruption of the family. This problem is aggravated by influx control.

• The increased subjective feeling of helplessness and that nothing can be improved, whatever happens. Should this result in an apathetic attitude on the part of the older generation — as some of the researchers in the investigation concluded — this would mean that these adults would in any case not give dynamic and constructive guidance to the youth. There are indications that this phenomenon is now becoming manifest in the eastern Cape, where the unemployment figure is as high as 25 %. There is reason to believe that there is a direct correlation between the increase in unemployment and the probability of unrest. By definition unrest in South Africa has an intergroup connotation.

• Greater demands for social security which has in any case not reached parity between the different population categories. As will be indicated later, the pressure on financial resources to improve social amenities will continue to increase. Increasing unemployment will further aggravate the situation.

• An increase in anomic behaviour such as crime with resultant clashes with the law. This stengthens African perceptions of a cruel white system and negative white perceptions of Africans — a vicious cycle develops. In this context the data in the previous chapter should also be borne in mind.

• A greater measure of acceptance of violence as the only solution to intergroup relations problems and an increased possibility that young men will undergo military training abroad.

• Greater emphasis on the convergence of class and race, which will make the accommodation of conflict much more difficult (see Rhoodie, 1983). This is a very real possibility in view of the difference in the unemployment figure for Africans relative to the other population categories.

If the preceding serious effects of unemployment are taken into account, it follows that job creation and employment — both in the formal and the non-formal sectors — are urgent priorities, if a further escalation of conflict is to be avoided.

Earnings and poverty

In Chapter 2 a description was given of the average earnings per employed member of the various population categories. It emerged that the average income of Africans was significantly lower than that of other categories, especially the whites. According to data for 1983 the average income of Africans varied between 59 % and 65 % of that of whites in the categories from unskilled to skilled. Obviously these differences are the complex function of a great many factors.

Nevertheless, as indicated in Chapter 3, these are realities that form an important element in the phenomenon of relative deprivation.

As already indicated, the wage gap narrowed during the seventies despite a comparatively modest real growth. Although there is every reason to believe that the wage differences due to discrimination are in the process of disappearing, it will not be possible to completely eliminate wage gaps due to differential technical skills, management proficiencies and other factors. Factors which affect the productivity of employees, such as training, will be of cardinal importance in this respect. It will not be possible to wipe out differences in *per capita* income as rapidly as wage discrepancies. The economic growth rate and the concomitant growth in job opportunities and the increase in the population rate are of cardinal importance in this respect.

All this naturally does not mean that there will not be a significant increase in the number of Africans in the higher income brackets. For example, it is expected that some 750 000 people from the other population categories will be in the higher income brackets by the turn of the century. Conversely, although the proportion of poverty-stricken people in respect of the total population will decline, there will nevertheless be an increase in absolute numbers — unless the most favourable level of growth can be maintained.

The influence of the income gap on intergroup relations is very important since it is a main factor in the total convergence of class and race, which has already been identified as a strong stimulus for conflict. Relative deprivation, dealt with in Chapter 3, is naturally also heightened by the wide wage gap. It was reported in Chapter 3 that relative deprivation is the single most important factor that could explain the Africans' negative attitude towards whites as well as their empirically shown high level of militancy. Therefore: the more intense the experience of Africans that whites have a better economic deal than themselves, the more negative and militant their attitude will become. Although the correlation between objective deprivation and subjective deprivation need not be exact, it can be accepted that, at present, they largely correspond. The result of this perspective of the income gap is drastic but obvious: intensification of conflict.

Even more basic than the above considerations is the acceptance that a country should offer all its people — including disadvantaged individuals and groups — an opportunity for self-development. Should this process be left to the forces of free enterprise alone, the poor would become even more impoverished. Within the limits of the country's means, a purposeful effort will have to be made to meet the exceptionally complex challenge of assisting everyone to become successfully integrated in the modern economy. This brings the topic of social expenditure to the fore.

Social investment

What must surely be one of the greatest sources of tension in South Africa arises from the unequal provision of education, housing and health facilities from government resources. Reference need here only be made to the tension in African education and the problems flowing from the backlog in the provision of housing, the sensitivity surrounding house rent, and the squatting phenomenon. In view of the economic situation outlined above, it is evident that social security will be an increasingly important factor in the relations between groups in the future. Against this background the Work Committee : Economics and Labour made projections concerning social expenditure in fields such as health, social pensions and education. These particulars are given in Table 4.1:

TABLE 4.1

PROJECTIONS OF SOCIAL EXPENDITURE

		2000			
	1975	Presumed growth rate			
		1 % p.a.	3 % p.a.	4 % p.a.	5 % p.a.
Whites	R683	R683	R683	R683	R683
Coloureds	R270	R329	R579	R683	R683
Indians	R299	R365	R642	R683	R683
Africans	R 80	R 98	R172	R237	R329
Average					
Average (all groups)	R204	R188	R278	R337	R408

The data in this table show clearly that Africans, even under the most favourable conditions, remain behind the other categories, although it would be possible to describe the narrowing of the wage gap as dramatic if a high growth rate could be maintained. Parity would be possible if the *per capita* expenditure on whites dropped by 40 %.

Among a variety of considerations, two need to be dealt with briefly: quality of services and mobility. One of the most striking reactions from whites to the main report of the HSRC Investigation into Education, was the understanding shown for the objective of equal education provided the quality of white education was not reduced. It can be safely assumed that this standpoint can be extended to other aspects of social provision. It also indicates that the tolerance level of whites is not unlimited in respect of how far they will be prepared to contribute towards their own services so that state contributions to other categories can be increased. A very fine balance and responsible planning are needed now.

A totally different aspect of the problem must be considered here, together with an earlier finding on the improvement in the standard of living. Assuming that the social provision and general welfare improves, it is difficult to imagine that it will be possible to meet the requirements of Africans, coloureds and Indians within the present spatial arrangement defined by the Group Areas Act. The current policy in respect of group areas imposes restrictions on the extent to which the more prosperous members of these groups can realize their prosperity. Should this situation remain unchanged, the frustration among these groups will increase. It is abvious that, if people are permitted to participate in an economic dispensation, they must be allowed to share in all the benefits of such a dispensation.

Economic conditions for sound intergroup relations

Relations between the population categories in South Africa are affected strongly, both positively and negatively, by the economy. On the one hand, there is the reality of the situation which emerged from the review in Chapter 2, namely that economically, South Africa compares very favourably with other countries with a plural composition similar to South Africa's. At the same time this comparatively sophisticated economy generates tremendous tensions when placed in the context of a Third world situation. This tension is most clearly seen at the level of intergroup relations. It is therefore extremely difficult to draw up a balance sheet of the functions and dysfunctions of the economy in respect of intergroup relations, and consequently the following conclusions should be considered with the necessary circumspection.

Basically the South African economy is both strong and versatile enough to satisfy in large measure the reasonable demands of the entire population in the longer term and to ensure a reasonable quality of life for all. In this respect South Africa is in a privileged position and hope for peaceful accommodation can be pinned on the country's economic potential. The proviso is, however, that the economic potential be realised.

Economic growth is an essential condition if every reasonable need is to be satisfied. However, economic growth alone is not enough : the utilization of the growth is as important as its extent.

The most pressing need for a significant proportion of the coloured, Indian and especially the African population, is the means to satisfy basic needs. Research, such as that done by Schlemmer and Moller, shows that these people at present accept their lot, but that their attitude can in no way be interpreted as implying loyalty or satisfaction. Should significant improvements not materialize, they could be mobilized to form the vanguard against the existing dispensation in times of unrest.

There has been a striking increase in the number of free-market oriented entrepreneurs and more professional people in the ranks of Africans, coloureds and Indians, but these people must not be latently or openly thwarted since this would lead to a frustrated *bourgeoisie*. As a result of the dynamics of relative deprivation, these groups could in future come under strong pressure from members of their own groups to reject the system out of hand.

It is obvious that members of other population categories with the necessary training will increasingly have to be appointed to positions that were previously held predominantly, if not exclusively, by whites. There is reason to expect that the whites will be prepared to build constructive intergroup relations — as is indeed happening in the present dispensation.

It appears from these analyses and projections that the welfare of whites will not necessarily continue to improve. To prevent increasing conflict, a greater proportion of governmental expenditure will have to be channelled to categories other than the whites. This will, however, have to be done in such a way that whites do not come to the conclusion that the quality of their services and benefits are deteriorating, as this could promote a white backlash.

The economic system

It is evident from the above discussion that conflict between the different groups can best be contained in a market-directed economic system in which it would be possible for all groups to share in economic progress. On the one hand the socialistic model is therefore rejected. As is evident from the experience of Angola and Mozambique, the forces which create prosperity in an economy could be dealt an irreparable blow if efforts were to be made to eliminate conflict in this way. On the other hand there is the danger that if everything were to be left to the free market, the poorer groups would not adequately share in the progress with the result that labour and political unrest would eventually paralyze the economic system. The aim should be a participating market economy, that is a market economy in which all groups share in progress.

Only if all groups share in the benefits of the market economy can it be expected that allegiance to this type of economic system can be maintained. This does not imply that the economic sphere dominates the normative sphere. There is an interaction between the political, the economic, the interpretive and the normative spheres. Given the dramatic difference between the increase in the available per capita income when the economic growth rate increases from 1 % (which implies a drop in the per capita income) to 5 % (which would make it possible to achieve an increase of nearly 70 % in per capita income by the end of the century), it is obvious that success in the economic sphere is a prerequisite for significant changes in South African society.

LABOUR

The type and quality of labour and labour relations are complex functions of the economy, legislation and politics, intergroup relations, etc. Nevertheless, the labour function is important in its own right in that it is the area in which there is the most contact between the different population categories (see the report: *Communication and a divided society*). With the increasing blurring of the boundaries between First and Third World orientations, accelerated urbanization and, most importantly, with the further polarization of the labour field — on the part of both whites and Africans — labour relations, as manifest in intergroup relations, will become increasingly important in the structuring in intergroup relations.

The most important details of the present situation in respect of labour were summarized in chapter 2. They will not be repeated in this chapter, but will be interpreted from the perspective of intergroup relations and given in the form of projections. Attention will first be paid to intergroup relations in the work place, then to the role of trade unions in intergroup relations, and finally to mechanisms for conflict handling. It has already been pointed out that the labour scene, since the publication of the Wiehahn Report in 1979, has undergone drastic changes in a direction that can undoubtedly be described as constructive. It is true that the new dispensation has not yet been fully applied and that any dysfunctions that occur could be the result of transition rather than of an intrinsic problem.

The South African labour situation is basically stratified in such a way that the whites occupy the upper cadres, Indians and coloureds the next levels and Africans the lowest ranks. Exceptions do occur in some cases, but they are rare. Effectively this stratification means that whites, and to a lesser extent coloureds and Indians, occupy the positions from which instructions are issued which Africans have to carry out. Research already referred to indicates that the vertical communication channels are not satisfactory for the lower categories, especially the Africans. These findings are put into clearer perspective when Schlemmer's findings are taken into account, namely that Africans hold the view that coloureds and Indians are favoured by employers. From a different angle, an HSRC investigation by Ehlers, 1984, indicated that on average 62 % of the tradesmen questioned reported that they were not prepared to work with or under someone from another population category.

There is, however, reason to believe that the general public has a positive view of co-operation in the workplace. From the findings of the multipurpose survey undertaken for the present investigation (Table 4.2), it is clear that the vast majority of the respondents, whites to a lesser extent than the others, expressed themselves in favour of mixed work situations. White respondents did, however, reveal more reservations in this respect than members of the other three population groups. Although a large majority of the respondents held the view that the most proficient person should hold a post (Item 1), significant percentages of all four population categories, especially Africans and whites, thought that there were certain posts to which members of certain population categories should not be appointed (Item 4). The majority of each population category indicated that they were prepared to do the same work with members of other population categories at the same level (Item 2).

It appears that the majority of the respondents would be prepared to accept a position under someone of a different population category if they could find no other work. This trend came clearly to the fore among the African respondents. In contrast with the findings of Ehlers referred to above, it emerges from Table 4.2 that 61,9 % of the white respondents would find it acceptable to work with members of other population categories as equals. It should however be borne in mind that Ehlers used a specific group (namely artisans) in his study. It therefore appears from the data that the group of white respondents experienced the work situation differently than did the broader population, possibly because the trades field is one in which other population categories are increasingly entering the labour force.

TABLE 4.2

PERCEPTION CONCERNING MIXED WORK SITUATIONS (Note: For the sake of convenience the "neutral" category has been omitted)

Items	Indians		Whites		Coloureds		Africans	
	Agree	Disagree	Agree	Disagree	Agree	Disagree	Agree	Disagree
1. A job should go to the most competent person irrespective of whether that person is African, white, Indian or coloured.	90,5	2,4	70,4	20,3	95,8	1,6	93,2	2,5
2. I am not willing to do the same job on the same level as people of other population groups.	23,1	66,3	28,5	59,3	23,7	70,2	25,6	60,6
3. I will refuse to work under somebody from another population group, even if he is competent.	12,1	75,7	27,7	58,3	13,2	80,1	22,2	70,0
4. There are posts in which members of certain population groups should not be appointed.	35,4	50,7	59,6	32,2	36,6	53,2	53,4	36,4
5. As long as one's direct job supervisor is competent, he may belong to any population group.	83,6	5,8	59,1	29,1	90,9	4,3	86,7	4,8
6. If I cannot get any other job, I will accept a post under someone from another group.	76,8	7,3	65,1	21,1	84,3	8,0	84,4	8,0
7. I am prepared to work with members of other population groups as equals.	92,1	0,6	61,9	26,0	93,8	2,2	94,8	2,3

Findings such as the above indicate that the workplace is a very sensitive terrain for intergroup relations. This sensitivity increases in times of economic "cooling" and political "heat", such as those prevailing in the country at present. The importance of this can hardly be overestimated; several researchers have pointed out thet the appointment of coloureds and Indians to supervisory positions over Africans is interpreted by the latter as proof that an African employee never gives orders and never rises above the others. As a result Africans also do not have the opportunity to experience work from the supervisor's point of view.

The fact that everyone in the work situation has to work together on a common task regardless of population category suggests that the workplace may be one of the most important, if not the most important, meeting places for the different population categories. In this regard the results of empirical investigations also give cause for cautious optimism. The extent to which common interests are articulated and the rigid stratification changes to a merit-based system, will have a bearing on this optimism. Every employer has the important task of promoting the interpersonal skills of all his employees by means of in-service training courses and incentives. To reduce conflict on the factory floor, merit will have to become the decisive factor in promotion and thorough training in the handling of intergroup relations will have to be an integral part of every employee's expertise. A state can create the overarching structures, but the onus is on the employer to create and maintain a climate of mutual trust and respect among the various segments of the labour force.

The trade unions

The Wiehahn report represents important changes in the thinking on labour matters. The acceptance by Government of the majority of the recommendations concerning labour affairs has meant that colour as such should no longer play a role in labour relations. Theoretically, at least, these steps mean that henceforth only matters inherent in the employer-employee relationship should play a role in negotiations. The fact that trade unions are increasingly prepared to settle disputes within the system and in an institutionalized manner, can be regarded as a step forward on the road towards constructive intergroup relations.

As indicated in Chapter 2, legal recognition of African trade unions at the end of the seventies led to a significant increase in the growth and activities of African trade unions. Apart from the closing of ranks among some whites — which meant virtual polarization — the struggle to recruit members intensified. This competition for members sometimes resulted in apparently unexpected provocation, wildcat strikes, inflexibility in negotiations, etc., — all of which tend to promote polarization among groups. In some respects this situation will probably continue for some time since, according to projections made by the Work Committee : Economics and Labour, the growth of African trade unions will increase sharply within the next 15 years (it is expected that membership will treble). African trade union membership has already increased by 86 % since 1979. According to projections there is no reason to expect that competition between trade unions will disappear. Where the chief concern is for larger membership, the potential for conflict will increase — outside the institutionalized system as well. This also applies where trade unions are not all equally well organized and professionally managed. The work committee summarized the situation as follows: "Conflict is inherent in any industrial society. South Africa cannot escape centuries of racial polarization (. . .) without periods of disruptive conflict" (p. 4).

Another factor that should be taken into account is that trade unions for artisans are traditionally white, while industrial trade unions are becoming increasingly Black oriented. This division holds very real risks for group polarization.

Over the past decade South Africa experienced an increase in the number of annual strikes. However analyses indicate that the loss of man-days due to strikes is still considerably less in South Africa that in industrialized countries.

These results indicate that despite all the uncertainties that accompanied the recognition of trade unions these were resolved fairly harmoniously during the first five years. There are more indications that Black trade unions are using the new mechanisms for settling disputes — mechanisms to which they have had access since 1979 — even though they are doing so conditionally. It must however be accepted that these trade unions will not summarily accept the *bona fides* of a system that they did not help to create. There are however indications that the trade unions are now having a formative influence on the structures in this system.

A dispensation in which Africans for so long had no bargaining powers cannot be completely changed overnight — this includes employer attitudes. There is still too much resistance to accepting the full consequences of the new dispensation. In this regard both the analyses of the work committee and those of individual researchers seem to indicate that the Government continues to feature too largely as a party in the conflict. As long as labour conflict is not totally privatized, as is the case in the USA, the Government will too often be seen as interfering in favour of the employer. As a result the legitimacy of industrial councils and industrial courts is sometimes questioned. The observation in particular that the Industrial Court has so far not given clear guidance or specific verdicts on the question of unfair labour practices, has had an adverse effect on confidence in labour reform.

Conflict in the labour sphere is usually characterized by phases of uncertainty and lack of continuity and such is not necessarily an example of an exact and predictable closed system. However, should the conflict degenerate into chaos, constructive intergroup relations become impossible and the conflict will take a course from which neither of the parties can benefit. Healthy conflict can easily turn into destructive conflict, but it seems as if the limit has not yet been exceeded. At the same time many analyses indicate that attempts are being made to politicize the trade unions. At present they form the only channel through which the Africans within the RSA can exert any meaningful pressure on both the public and the private sector. As long as Africans are effectively excluded from significant decision making, the trade unions will have a potentially political character. This could certainly increase the conflict potential in the country.

The Work Committee : Economics and Labour summarized the situation in respect of mechanisms for handling conflict in the labour field as follows: *If these challenges regarding institutionalization of industrial conflict cannot be satisfactorily attended to, then managerial power will not be legitimised into authority and workers' power will not be consolidated or channelled through the functioning of the union. Disorder will then become the characteristic of the work place by the year 2000.*

International influences on labour relations

As a result of the open character of foreign trade, which is for example equal to almost 50 % of South Africa's gross domestic product, foreign powers can be expected to exert an influence on labour relations in this country. Both the Sullivan Code and the present debate on disinvestment are clear examples of such influence. International contact is increasing, not only at managerial level, but also at the level of the organized trade union movement (as for example with the International Trade Secretariat). Despite the usefulness of contacts of this nature, particularly as far as the exchange of skills is concerned, it is well-known that solutions that are successful in one country do not necessarily yield positive results in another — for the simple reason that circumstances differ from one country to another. Although it is at this stage difficult to determine the precise effect that international forces will have on intergroup relations in South Africa, it is quite clear that an effect of some kind can be expected.

Summary

In certain respects the field of labour relations can be regarded as a testing ground for a new dispensation in intergroup relations in South Africa. As such it will naturally be subject to problems and uncertainties but, labour relations have great potential as a growth point for the formation of constructive intergroup relations, although it remains a field fraught with uncertainties. Seen from the perspective of intergroup relations, the following factors are currently the most important:

Co-operation at the micro level of the factory floor must be promoted through sensitizing, training and fairpractice.

The relative lack of experience on the part of trade unions regarding organization and negotiation methods, as well as employers' lack of expertise in the latter respect, need to be rectified through training.

Employers tend to be reluctant to accept the full consequences of the new labour dispensation.

The Government is too deeply involved in labour disputes and consequently such disputes should perhaps be privatized. This would mean that the disputes should be handled in another context and that the legitimacy of the negotiating machinery would not come under suspicion.

ECONOMIC FORCES AND LABOUR FORCES : A CONCLUSION

This review indicates that the strongest conflict-accommodating forces in the South African economy are probably to be found in the Government's efforts to allow all groups to share in the benefits of a market-oriented economy. The embourgeoisement of large numbers of the working class could form part of a political and economic reform process initiated from the top with the expectation that the benefits accruing from this will increasingly become accessible to all Africans. This would lessen the need for destructive action.

In the labour field, the future role of trade unions and employer organizations could develop into a catalyst for constructive intergroup relations, if trade unions are allowed to participate in the actual bargaining process. However, if the business sector becomes too closely associated with the Government, it could have the opposite effect.

113

Regardless of other considerations, the economy and labour can only play a constructive role if the economy continues to grow. A constructive urbanization policy is also needed. The mobility of African labourers must no longer be artificially inhibited, and the integrated nature of the South African economy must be accepted in any ordering of intergroup relations.

EDUCATION

Education is at present at the very centre of problems of intergroup relations in South Africa. Various recent statements by ministers bluntly indicate that, as far as the present government is concerned, separate schools for the different population categories is a non-negotiable matter. As will be shown later, education is also the only institution in respect of which there is statutory differentiation between Afrikaans-speaking and English-speaking whites. In the African communities schools have been the focus of political protest and unrest since 1976. Against this background the following matters will be discussed: organizational principles, the role of education in intergroup relations and growth points.

STRUCTURAL ASPECTS OF THE PROVISION OF EDUCATION

It was evident from the review in chapter 2 that the provision of education in the RSA is characterized by the closed nature of the system, the high premium placed on academically-oriented education and the concomitant underemphasis of technical and career-oriented education. Although high-quality education is provided for whites and Indians, and serious efforts are being made with increasing success to raise the standard of African and coloured education to the same level, the closed nature of the education system means that education in all the subsystems is marked by inherent shortcomings. One of the most important of these is the restriction on the movement of pupils between the different educational institutions and constraints on the direction of study within specific educational institutions. The mobility of pupils between the formal education system and non-formal education is mostly on a hit-and-miss basis, and has so far received little attention. This was specifically identified in the HSRC Education Report as a problem that required urgent attention.

The excessive emphasis on academically oriented education at the expense of technical and career-oriented education has its historical origins in the colonial era when education systems that were irrelevant for developing countries were held up as the ideal, and were imposed upon them. This led to unrealistic educational expectations on the one hand and also proclaimed academically oriented education as the type of education to be pursued. In contrast the demand for technically and technologically trained people has increased in the RSA, a demand which could not be met. Although the same prejudiced attitude towards technical and career-oriented education occurs among whites, careers in this field are mainly practised by whites, as is apparent from the fact that 78 % of the natural scientists, 99 % of the engineers, 91 % of the technicians and 12 % of the artisans and apprentices in 1979 were whites. Despite some improvement in this regard, the interest among Africans in technical and career-oriented education is still totally inadequate in view of the country's manpower needs and career opportunities.

PRINCIPLES FOR THE PROVISION OF EDUCATION

While the education scene in the RSA has been characterized by parallel, unequal educational facilities for whites, Asians, coloureds and Africans, with few, if any, contact points for realizing comparable systems for providing education, the HSRC Education Report formulated a number of principles — which were accepted by the Government in the White Paper on the Provision of Education in South Africa — to serve as a basis for all education in the RSA. These principles have already been included in legislation and describe the basic point of departure as one in which equal educational opportunities and standards, regardless of race, colour, creed or sex, will be the Government's objective. The complete set of principles as embodied in the General Educational Affairs Act 76 of 1984 is as follows:

● Equal opportunities for education, including equal standards in education, for every inhabitant, irrespective of race, colour, creed or sex, shall be the purposeful endeavour of the State.

● Education shall afford positive recognition of what is common as well as what is diverse in the religious and cultural way of life and the languages of the inhabitants.

● Education shall give positive recognition to the freedom of choice of the individual, parents and organizations in society.

● The provision of education shall be directed in an educationally responsible manner to meet the needs of the individual as well as those of society and economic development, and shall, inter alia, take into consideration the manpower needs of the country.

● Education shall endeavour to achieve a positive relationship between the formal, non-formal and informal aspects of education in the school, society and family.

● The provision of formal education shall be a responsibility of the State provided that the individual, parents and organized society shall have a shared responsibility, choice and voice in this matter.

- The private sector and the State shall have a shared responsibility for the provision of non-formal education.

- Provision shall be made for the establishment and state subsidization of private education within the system of educational provision.

- In the provision of education the processes of centralization and decentralization shall be reconciled organizationally and functionally.

- The professional status of the teacher and lecturer shall be recognized.

- Effective provision of education shall be based on continuing research.

On the basis of these principles and other recommendations of the HSRC Education Report that have been accepted by the Government and incorporated in the White Paper on the Provision of Education, a start was made in 1981 to create mechanisms for introducing an improved education system. Not only was the education budget as a percentage of the total budget increased still further (1984/85: 16,8 %), but the R4 200 million spent on education in 1984/85 for the first time exceeded that spent on defence (15 %). In addition, the budget of the Department of Education and Training during this fiscal year doubled in comparison with 1981/82. A start was also made with the creation of mechanisms for laying down standards (Statutory Certification Council) and for placing liaison mechanisms between the different subsystems on a firmer basis.

THE ROLE OF EDUCATION IN INTERGROUP RELATIONS

It is well that the South African system for providing education has always been characterized by segregated subsystems each of which provides for the educational needs of a specific population category. This segregation extends vertically through all levels of education from separate management systems to separate schools for whites, Asians, coloureds and Africans at the local or school level. In the White Paper on the Provision of Education, the Government's policy was reiterated and it was also formalized in the new constitutional dispensation in the definition of education as an "own affair". In the organizational and administrative (management) structure, provision is made for co-operation by means of various statutory bodies, such as the Committee of Education Departmental Heads, the SA Council for Education, the Central Statutory Certification Board, the Advisory Council for Universities and Technikons, and the Committee of University Principals. In addition further contact points were created by permitting specific tertiary education institutions and certain private schools to accept students and pupils from different population categories under prescribed conditions.

116

The segregated formal education dispensation, embedded in a segregated society, together with other institutions in society, contributes to the deep segmentation of South African society, including education itself. Education therefore does not contribute to intersocial, intercultural, interreligious and intersport activities, in fact its influence is in the opposite direction.

As regards non-formal education, the situation is different in that its different forms (training, compensatory education, literacy programmes, etc.) are classified as "general affairs" insofar as a state or public control function is concerned. To the extent that non-formal education is the exclusive prerogative of the private sector and is aimed at the learning requirements of adults, it is exempt from the ideological prescriptions of the State. In this context non-formal education is a potentially valuable laboratory for practising positive relations in the intergroup context. The situation is, however, much more complex than it appears at first glance. For example, the training of apprentices — mainly youths and young adults — is the responsibility of the Department of Manpower and is therefore a "general affair", while training centres for adults are under the control of the different administrations for education and culture and as such are "own affairs" for each population category (Indians, coloureds, whites). The recently released report on the training of artisans in fact recommends that adult training centres should also fall under the Department of Manpower so as to end divided control over the training of artisans.

The social dilemma contained in segmented formal education is aggravated by the inequality in the provision of education referred to in Chapter 2. While Africans place a high premium on education as a means to social mobility, they experience the education offered to them as being inferior, they question its standard and compare it with the impact and quality of white education. For various understandable reasons African education has not yet succeeded in providing the same individual, social and economic advantages for the African that white education provides for the white student. This phenomenon contributes to the estrangement, both academic and socio-economic, between the African and the white pupil within a system where unequal, separate education is maintained.

Taking into account the declared and statutorily determined organization of formal education as an "own affair" which has to find expression within separate subsystems in the different population categories, it is obvious that equal educational opportunities and standards are a prerequisite if education is to serve as a medium by means of which the different population categories will develop greater understanding of one another.

The role that education can play in intergroup relations will therefore be co-determined by the rate at which, and the visibility with which, obvious inequalities in the provision of education for the different population categories can be eliminated. At the same time studies elsewhere in the world indicate that the expansion of education and the eradication of inequalities in this regard must be accompanied by corresponding access to economic and political opportunities. Should this not be the case, structural friction in the society will necessarily be aggravated.

To summarize: education is at present statutorily organized, is not specifically aimed at effecting positive intergroup relations and whatever contact does take place is sporadic and isolated. The present policy is aimed at the creation of universal norms and standards (scholastic and financial) by the Department of National Education but, in practice, education is the responsibility of the separate education departments for "own affairs" for the main population categories. The contents of the curricula also do not pay specific attention to inculcating positive intergroup relations.

GROWTH POINTS

Despite its general aim of promoting positive intergroup relations the educational scene in the RSA represents a complex kaleidoscope of structures, organizations and events that have an impeding effect on such relations. On the one hand there are the formal structures that have been created to facilitate intergroup liaison and on the other there are the inequalities in the provision of education and the visibility of the unequal and separate educational dispensation which is the most readily observed and experienced aspect of pupils' own educational experience. It therefore seems as if determined efforts will have to be made to elevate the mechanisms built into the system for intergroup liaison to a level where they can be more readily observed and experienced by the pupils. Constructive relations between population categories can only be effected if pupils can meet one another across the boundaries of separate structures at *all* levels of education.

The following suggestion could possibly assist the creation of constructive points of contact:

It is a recognized fact that education is a matter close to the heart of the parents of all population categories. Reaction to the HSRC Education Report, by way of written comment and by way of standpoints taken at seminars, conferences and congresses after the report was released, again emphasized this important point. This report, and numerous recent studies, consequently stressed the importance of community involvement in education. The foundation of a new *Afrikaner* Parent Association in the Transvaal reflects this need of parents to be more meaningfully involved in education. In the African communities there is concern about the estrangement of parents and their children which contributes to the school unrest that has had wide repercussions in these communities and appears to be uncontrollable. However, the development of positive intergroup relations requires that such parent associations should extend their hand across the boundaries of population categories, culture and language to create a forum for discussion where matters of common interest can be discussed. Despite the differences there are enough common facets in education for meaningful dialogue.

Such dialogue has already commenced and is apparently being used to considerable mutual benefit. An example is the teachers' associations. The representatives of the umbrella teachers' associations of the various population categories have for some time been meeting periodically to discuss matters of mutual interest. The basis on which these discussions are arranged could possibly also serve as model for parent associations or parent groups. In respect of both parent and teachers' associations it is, however, essential that the dialogue, started at national level, should eventually filter through to local level where such meetings could have maximum impact on intergroup relations by making a special contribution to a better understanding of one another's problems and points of view.

The HSRC Education Report recommended the establishment of co-operative educational service centres at national and regional level with a view to making optimum use of the services of scarce and highly trained auxiliary personnel, while the cost of such services could also be substantially reduced. Identified shortcomings in education which led to this recommendation, are the grave shortage of professional personnel; the fact that some educational institutions have numerous school clinics while others have none; and the lack of co-ordination between existing services. Should such educational service centres be open to students from all population categories, pressing problems in, for example, African and coloured education would be alleviated and it would also be possible to create a contact point for intergroup liaison.

The statement has been made that contemporary formal education has become so expensive that the Government can no longer afford it. This applies not only to developing countries, but also to developed countries such as the USA with its strong economy. Norms for buildings, premises and facilities for education in South Africa are such that it has become difficult to base the provision of educational facilities on them. If these norms have to be observed in the layout of new townships in future, city and town planning and development during the next decade and longer will be presented with serious space problems.

This problem is naturally much more complicated in the planning and development of African residential areas. The present phenomenon of urbanization with the concomitant depopulation of the rural areas and, in particular, the shift of the population to specific growth points in the country also means that educational facilities in some areas are unused or underused, while other areas experience overuse of facilities. A related matter is the unequal division of facilities as a result of which over and underuse of scarce and expensive educational facilities are not uncommon.

In terms of the promotion of intergroup relations, the question is whether a basis can be created on which the sharing of expensive facilities whould become possible. Although such sharing should probably, in the first instance, be investigated within the group context, the relevant question for the theme under discussion here is whether it would be possible to effect such sharing between groups that have and those that do not have. What is quite clear is that this question will only be addressed when the parent-teacher associations of the different population categories, but particularly the parent associations, are prepared to meet one another to discuss the matter. In the meantime in the layout of new residential areas the norms that apply to educational facilities will require serious reconsideration.

Instruction in and the learning and use of specific languages have always been sensitive issues in the South African educational setup. This was again evident in the polemic that developed around the choice and the level of implementation of the medium of education other than the mother tongue in African schools. Despite the sound arguments in favour of mother-tongue instruction, at least until the end of the basic educational phase, African parents, teachers and educationists have always, for understandable reasons, advocated an early switch to one of the official languages as the medium of education. It is obvious that here — from an intergroup relations point of view — there is considerable potential for tension, resistance and misunderstanding. What is also important is that the quality of African education cannot and will not improve before these problems have been thoroughly discussed and solutions found. One implication is that the existing expertise in white education can and should be used to enhance the proficiency level of African education in the languages involved.

Linked with the preceding, the question arises as to what extent the expertise in white education can by used in African education to create simultaneously opportunities for intergroup liaison and extend positive relations. The problem of the availability of qualified teachers of Mathematics, Natural Science and Chemistry and white education remains a very real one; in African education, however, the situation is critical since only a very small percentage of African teachers have the necessary qualifications in these subjects. Sporadic efforts are being made in the bigger centres to muster the available expertise in white education (secondary and tertiary) so as to assist selected African teachers by means of in-service training course. The question is whether this method could be used more often, and once again it seems as if contact at local level between teachers from the different population categories would be a prerequisite for such a development.

The RSA is once again experiencing extensive school riots in the African communities. The Van der Walt Commission of Enquiry into these riots has completed its activities, but the findings have not yet been published. It can, however, be accepted that a variety of related and interdependent factors have played a role, including the inequalities in the provision of education for the different population categories. In 1984 HSRC's Institute for Sociological and Demographic Research (ISODEM), by means of a random survey among urban Africans in the PWV area, found that educational problems, including school boycotts, were the third most important problem with which Africans in the area had to cope (with a considerably lower percentage incidence of 5,7 % of the respondents as compared with the most important problem, namely economic pressure, which was mentioned by 64,0 % of the respondents). As regards the perceptions of school boycotts by this group, 56,3 % held the view that it was wrong of African pupils to boycott their schools: this probably indicates a generation gap between the older and the younger respondents since a larger percentage (76,6 %) of the older Africans (over 40 years) held this view. It is also significant that 27,5 % (the highest percentage) of the respondents felt that diverse (white) government institutions and leaders were responsible for the boycotts.

What is abundantly clear from these data is that there were differences of opinion within the particular African community about the merit of the boycotts and the persons or institutions that should bear the blame for them. It is also clear that the older generation of Africans adopted a more moderate attitude and that they were in fact faced with a dilemma in respect of their relations with the youth. The need for liaison between groups at a formal and an informal level was confirmed — liaison by means of which the sources of frustation can be brought into the open so that joint solutions can be sought.

121

The HSRC Education Report formulated a programme for achieving equal quality education for all the inhabitants of the RSA. A *first* policy guideline was the progressive provision of adequate means for making it possible for each and every individual to acquire the essential minimum of knowledge, skills and values. Among other proposals was the introduction of general compulsory school attendance, coupled with "free" education for a certain number of years. The *second* policy guideline was that no person should be excluded from the available educational opportunities from which he/she could benefit on educationally irrelevant grounds. The main implication here is that there will have to be clarity about the methods (and rate) that will have to be applied to eliminate restrictions on access to, and provision, of educational facilities based purely on race or colour discrimination.

The *third* policy guideline was that the provision of equal opportunities to all clients of education should be recognized and maintained as a priority. The implication here is that there will have to be clarity about the *model* that will be used for determining quality benefits, and naturally such a model will have to be determined according to feasible criteria in terms of the available manpower and funds. The *fourth* and *final* policy guideline stated that irrelevant inequalities in the provision of education should be eliminated. This implies that such inequalities must be identified and eliminated as far as this is possible, given the restrictions of manpower and funds.

These recommendations are not only aimed at a more just education dispensation, but their implementation should also bring about better intergroup relations.

DEVELOPMENT AND CONTACT BETWEEN GROUPS

The field investigated by the Work Committee: Developmental Aspects is one of the most sensitive areas as regards both conflict potential and the creation of sound relations between South Africa's diverse communities. It is here where the actual contact is made between administration and population, between official and citizen. In the following discussion attention will first be paid to approaches to development, then to administrative matters and finally to urban local government.

DEVELOPMENT STRATEGIES

At the risk of total oversimplification, it is necessary to linger a while on the most important element of the two main views regarding development. Different inequalities in South African society were identified earlier in this report.

122

A few of the most important are the inequality in prosperity, education, social provision, the geographically uneven development of the country, poverty in the national states, the unique nature of a transitional economy, etc. In these respects South Africa has both of a developed nucleus and an underdeveloped periphery. Theories on development should therefore be regarded as a background against which the potential role of development can be put in perspective.

The *modernization approach* suggests that poverty can be dealt with by economic growth, especially industrialization. This means that capital, technology, etc., must flow from the developed nucleus to the underdeveloped periphery to put the latter on the road to development. An analogous process takes place within the underdeveloped area because it is the nucleus of that area which benefits first before the effects filter through to the periphery.

The *dependency* approach explains the process the other way around, namely that the nucleus, in fact, parasitizes labour and resources from the periphery for the former's selfish benefit. In this way the periphery becomes dependent on the nucleus and autonomous development is disturbed and eventually destroyed. In this perspective decentralization is seen simply as an attempt to acquire the periphery's resources even more efficiently. According to this view, development can only be measured in terms of the acquisition of economic and political sovereignty. These theorists maintain that socialism offers the only system within which such development can take place.

The dependency school therefore argues that the non-capitalistic mode of production in South Africa was purposely retained to serve the interests of capitalism. An alliance of mining and agricultural capital originally created the African reserves with this end in view. These areas were too small to be self-reliant and they therefore had to fall back on migrant labour. They provided the labour force for the capitalist economy and simultaneously kept state expenditure on welfare services, housing, pensions and social services low, as migrant labourers and other inhabitants had to be self-reliant in this respect. The policy of separate development carried this "strategy" further, and the independence school attributes the economic growth in South Africa after 1948 to this also. The growth of capital intensive industries made the transfer of Africans to the reserves necessary. With the accompanying drop in productivity in the reserves, the segregationist policy was strengthened and this was followed by the decentralization of industries to the reserves.

The academic status of the above point of view is not relevant to those who regard themselves as part of the underdeveloped periphery. The terminology of the dependency school has, however, achieved wide acceptance and offers a plausible explanation for the South African policy of separate development.

On the other hand the proponents of the modernization approach accepted that the development of the Black areas would follow more or less the same road as that of the Western capitalist countries. To prevent African exploitation by white entrepreneurs and capital forces, restrictions were placed on whites in respect of investment in African areas. The state would act as guardian for the development of Africans, but such development would only take place in the national states. However the modernization school also has a liberal wing which believes that African development would follow the same course as that of the whites, but that it would only be successful if the measures that restricted the Africans were repealed.

The official approach to development therefore links up with the modernization theory, while the radical opposition is strongly inspired by the dependency approach. Moderate Africans and coloureds in South Africa are modernization oriented, although there is some support for the dependency view. The Government and its radical opponents therefore represent two different diagnoses of and therapies for the same situation. The resultant polarizing effects and the comcomitant generation of conflict are obvious. In fact these differences lie at the root of the South African dilemma.

Development strategies assume the existence of an underdeveloped sector of society that must be enabled to reach the same level as other sectors. In South Africa the combination of First World and Third World elements is a reality, with all the forms of inequality that go with this. Obviously it is the dominant group in such a situation that takes the initiative in respect of development on the assumption that its values and standards are the norm by which development should be measured, and towards which other groups should strive. This means that paternalism is virtually built into the system. Research shows that this attitude is evident in the administrative system in South Africa and that it remained the general pattern even after the national states became independent. This trend has been aggravated by white attempts to determine development priorities in the absence of joint decision making.

A lack of cultural awareness among white officials and development agents means that development programmes are formulated that do not take the culture of the Africans into account. This contributes to social disruption, antagonism and conflict. On the other hand, it is clear that an increasing number of Africans desire full incorporation in Western type societies and espouse Western goals and values.

The Government's development policy, and especially the rate at which it was implemented, evoked different reactions from Africans, coloureds and Indians and their leaders. The fragmented strategy was applied in Transkei in particular: "Take what you can get and use it in order to get what you want." There were different forms of pragmatism, all of them aimed at enjoying the benefits of government policy without any real acceptance of the underlying ideology. Others purposely used conflict as a strategy, while the most extreme stand was taken by individuals and organizations such as AZAPO and the UDF, which advocate radical and sometimes revolutionary action.

The development strategy that has been followed, and the nature of the South African policy, constitute a dilemma in various respects. It is estimated that development assistance to the national states amounts to about R2 500 000 000 a year. South African opposition parties are generally highly critical of this. Yet recipients are also sometimes very critical of the development strategies and aid, although they themselves derive the advantages from it. The resulting dissonance is conflict-generating in its own right. However this dilemma seems to be inherent in development problems throughout the world.

SEPARATE DEVELOPMENT AND DEVELOPMENT

The confidence crisis caused by administrative measures, as a result of which all government actions are regarded with suspicion and distrust, is just as important as the development policy itself when it comes to conflict potential.

To what extent has the policy been successful in achieving development objectives? Although difficult, in answering this question a distinction would have to be drawn between the results of the political policy, on the one hand, and the development policy on the other.

From analyses in the report of the Work Committee: Development Aspect: *Balanced development in South Africa,* it appears that whatever the answer may be (see the development philosophies referred to earlier), it would have to be strongly qualified. To quote only two examples: While there has been a striking narrowing of the wage gap between Africans and whites over the past 12 years, the number of people living below the breadline in the "homelands" has increased. Although the governments concerned are given real opportunities to develop political and administrative structures, they simultaneously have become estranged from the urban Africans (in this regard see also the report of the Work Committee: Constitution and Politics: *Political co-operation within a fundamental juridical order.)*

In the evaluation it is difficult to compare real development with that in other countries in the Third World; something which *is* necessary at a given stage. In what follows, brief reference will be made only to the effect of two measures: the Group Areas Act and influx control.

According to research undertaken in the Western Cape, the two measures that have most adversely affected sound intergroup relations were the enforcement of the Group Areas Act and the Africans (. . .) 25 of 1945 influx control. The Theron Report has pointed out the incalculable and irreparable harm caused by removals under the Group Areas Act. The disruption of the community and the emotional effect of these measures make every further removal a potential source of conflict. At the same time the measures influenced intergroup relations in a wide field. To quote a concrete example: From data collected it appears that the Group Areas Act made the biggest contribution to the radicalization of theological standpoints in the NG Sendingkerk. It was the biggest single factor leading to the *status confessionis* and the Belhar Confession of 1982.

Influx control is the other explosive measure that can rapidly lead to serious conflict. Examples from the recent past tragically illustrate this point. Much more could be said on several facets of this act in the light of data obtained from the work committee report and other research. Apart from the urban implications, it also became the means for the removal of large numbers of Africans in the rural areas to the national states. Recent changes in the enforcement of the act are potentially positive.

ADMINISTRATIVE ASPECTS

In respect of the administration of development, there are three mutually dependent factors that adversely affect intergroup relations, namely incomplete localization, administrative attitudes and style of communication and lack of participation. In the self-governing and independent national states most of the posts have been indigenized, except in the case of highly professional and technical posts because of a lack of trained manpower. Differentiation in the conditions of service of different categories of officers are also a source of tension. Should seconded officials also maintain some form of social apartheid, this naturally aggravates matters.

In the development of Black areas, the functional model is employed in most cases. According to this model each department is responsible for its own development programme and activities. Co-ordination is central and mainly of a political nature, while there is little, if any, horizontal liaison at local level. The danger that such a form of development is not sensitive enough for local needs, with all the comcomitant human problems, is obvious. Communication in this model is also vertical, and mainly from above to below. There is therefore little opportunity for public participation when needs are determined, in planning, decision making and evaluation. The involvement of the very people whose development is at stake is thus minimal.

Development according to this pattern cannot in the long term contribute much to the improvement of intergroup relations. In fact, it contains considerable potential for generating conflict as has been revealed in a few substantial research projects conducted in this field. The most striking dysfunctional trait is that it has a (vertical) downward character which means that communication is largely bureacratic, paternalistic and lacks local co-ordination.

LOCAL GOVERNMENT

Participation in local government leaves much to be desired. In the national states there are, in the rural areas, tribal authorities consisting of chiefs, headmen and traditional counsellors. They help to maintain law and order in the tribal area, collect certain monies and are responsible for providing local services. Public interest in their activities is minimal and the more modern section of the African communities do not regard them as fully respresentative of all interests in the communities concerned. Their activities are mainly aimed at aspects of law and order while local services are at a comparatively low level.

Urban local government in the national states and elsewhere differs vastly. In the national states it is in an elementary stage of development, consisting generally only of advisory councils. Outside the national states rapid progress has been made in this respect over the past few years, and a number of full-fledged municipal councils have been established. Coloureds and Indians are still dependent however on management committees that function under the wing of white local authorities. Full-fledged municipalities have been created in one coloured and in four Indian residential areas.

African, coloured and Indian communities have a long and unhappy history of exclusion from participation in local government and, as a result of this, there is a growing spirit of confrontation with white local authorities and administrations (now development) boards, as well as resistance to efforts made by the authorities to create new, improved, but still separate, structures. The exclusion of African, coloured and Indian groups in the past from participation in local government has led to a shortage of trained personnel among these population categories, while financial sources must also be found to provide equal municipal services for them. The lack of funds and personnel create unique intergroup relations problems.

Opposition has been expressed from the ranks of coloured and Indian groups to the proposed system of local government as contained in the Regional Services Councils Act 109 of 1985. This opposition is based on the fact that the proposed system is still based on group differentiation.

There is also opposition from the ranks of white local authorities since they see a loss of "autonomy" in the transfer of so-called "hard services" to regional services councils. They also fear that the financing of the new African municipal councils could encroach upon their own potential sources of income, and that the financing of the regional services councils could effect a redistribution of revenue to the residential areas of the other population categories. Although the proposed system is based on group differentiation, some regard it as a more attractive alternative to either group dominance within an undifferentiated system, or totally separate local authorities.

Among the Africans there are also misgivings about new development at the local government level. The main problems here are the trusteeship of the administration (development) boards and the extremely unsatisfactory relations between these institutions and the African local authorities. Also important are the political legitimacy problems of the African local authorities, who are often seen as unrepresentative of the people. This latter problem was slightly alleviated by the inclusion, early in 1985, of representatives of African local authorities on the Council for Co-ordination of Local Authority Affairs, and the announcement of the intention to effect liaison between African local authorities and regional services councils. The standpoint of African opponents of this system of local government is that it is, perhaps, a welcome development, but that it is not a solution for the political problem of Africans outside the national states, makes it a target in the present unrest. There are therefore misgivings in each of the four population categories about their participation in the proposed local authority system. Although there is considerable potential for intergroup conflict, there is also hope for the peaceful resolution of these problems as each category's reservations and problems are relatively distinctive.

There are two specific reasons why it is exceptionally difficult to evaluate the influence of development administration on intergroup relations. Firstly the premises of the two basic philosophies of development are irreconcilable, so that what would be regarded as an advantage from one point of view would be regarded as the exact opposite from the other. Secondly, South African development policy is a direct result of the policy of apartheid, which hardly makes it possible to assess the one without the other.

In view of the above complications, the following conclusions should be seen as an attempt nevertheless to assess the role of development in intergroup relations.

● The nature of the South African situation means that, regardless of the internal policy followed, intensive development inputs are essential.

● Thus far development policy can be described as being of a mixed nature, although its link with the apartheid makes it suspect. The different points of reference, namely development and separation, contribute to tensions in intergroup relations.

● Judged purely by the extent of funds channelled to development, the efforts up to now cannot summarily be written off as a shirking of responsibilities, or ill intent. Moreover the strategy employed, has led to the development of administrative and other infrastructures that have the potential to support development in a positive way in future, if they are regarded purely from a development point of view.

● The fact that the development policy is a direct offshoot of apartheid policy places the biggest restriction on its potential value. In this regard it can be accepted without any doubt that actions such as removals and influx control will eliminate any positive results of a development approach, at least from a intergroup relations point of view.

JURIDICAL ASPECTS

Control measures in a society can vary from completely informal to fully formal. The law respresents the most formalized form of control measures by means of which legal privileges, rights and juridical obligations are determined, in other words it determines the limits and conditions for the operationalization of intergroup relations without specifying the nature, content and direction of such relations — in fact the rules according to which relations become reality. One of the local points of the law is the regulation and defusing of conflict situations in which parties differ from one another because of, for example, mutually exclusive interests, divergent approaches to self-realization, etc. This type of conflict occurs in all societies. The law cannot eliminate the causes of conflict, but it can regulate them. The facets of life that are covered by the law are actually a political matter, and that is why what is regulated by law in one country, will often be controlled administratively or even informally in another.

In the light of these general remarks on the important place of the law in society, it is clear that the law is one of the most central facets in a society insofar as in the final analysis it is the law that provides the individual's final guarantee and that is why it is also central to problems of intergroup relations.

South Africa has already built up a tradition of legal regulation of intergroup relations; examples of important acts in this regard were identified in Chapter 2 and were briefly described. From that review it appeared that the law is indeed drastic and that it tends to restrict certain groups, Africans in particular, more than others. These specific acts will not be discussed again in this chapter. From the analysis of the Work Committee: Juridical Aspects it appeared that some of the acts in one or more respects, e.g. content, enforcement and results, did not fully ensure equal treatment for all population categories. One example will suffice: The Group Areas Act 36 of 1966 is concerned with the ownership of fixed property and the control of the occupation of land, buildings and properties. At first glance the act does not appear to discriminate between population categories. However an analysis of its enforcement indicates that it is discriminatory in that, up to the end of 1982, the following number of families had been removed in terms of legislation: coloureds 81 948; Indians 39 485 and whites 2 285. In the case of traders that were moved, the figures are as follows: whites 54, coloureds 180 and Indians 2 507. If it is considered that every removal was accompanied by deprivation, the extent of the results of the enforcement of this act becomes clear. In this regard reference can be made to the report of the Theron Commission.

That the law creates specific dilemmas, became apparent from the analysis in chapter 3 where it was shown that the identification of groups is very problematical since ethnicity and race are, in reality, concepts that cannot be handled by law. In fact, the conclusion can be reached that the juridical handling of identity is at the root of intergroup relations problems.

While security legislation is not intended to regulate intergroup relations, the Work Committee : Juridical Aspects gave attention to it because the enforcement of the Internal Security Act 74 of 1982 and related legislation has implications for race relations in South Africa.

The need to maintain order in a society where the potential for violent conflict is high, and the duty of the government to provide security for its citizens, justify the granting of the extra-ordinary powers found in security legislation. While the legislation makes no reference to race, in practice it has been largely employed to deal with persons and organizations engaged in extra-parliamentary opposition to the government's racial policies.

In evaluating security legislation and its impact on intergroup relations, the Committee found that the suppression of non-violent opposition by the use of this legislation has not reduced conflict in our society.

Given the wide spectrum of acts in terms of which intergroup relations are regulated in this country,and also the juridical problem of the handling of identity, this chapter will deal with the following matters: the fundamental values with which a just legal order should comply, criminal law, law enforcement, access to the law, administration of justice and international law.

FUNDAMENTAL VALUES

In the report of the Work Committee : Juridical Aspects : *Law and justice and intergroup relations,* the work committee dealt first with the identification of the essential conditions with which a just legal order must comply for optimum regulation of conflict in society. For this purpose an analysis was made of the values basic to the Roman-Dutch and English legal traditions. The importance of these principles is that they simultaneously represent a group of criteria against which the entire juridical system with all its constituent parts can be tested. The fundamental point of departure in this regard is the "rule of law" concept, according to which the following requirements for a just legal order were formulated.

A just legal order recognizes and respects the uniqueness or distinctiveness of all the various facets of being human. For example, the law cannot prescribe what it "good" art, the "right" religion, the "best" business principles or what suitable ethical norms are or should be.

The law should authoritatively provide for the accommodation of a variety of structurally unique societal institutions by recognizing, respecting and protecting the authority and freedom of each of these (non-state) institutions to handle their own unique affairs in the realization of their own unique functions. This means that the *de facto* powerful state, whose function it is to maintain law and order, should not monopolize the "own affairs" of non-state institutions or try to run them or prescribe how they should be run. The State's task is to delineate the juridical spheres of competency and the legal obligations of society's institutions towards one another and towards individual legal subjects and to officially settle any disputes that may arise from such delineation.

A legal order and its institutions should be fair, that is they should leave scope for the individualized application of legal norms (formulated in general terms and which, given their unique nature, apply in general) in concrete situations — especially the ones that do not occur generally. The discretion of those who enforce the law should therefore be primarily directed toward correlating that which is right (not necessarily according to the letter, but also the spirit of the law) with the demands of the concrete situation. Proper discretion is neither predetermined by law neither is it purely arbitrary.

A just legal order avoids mere formalities. Legal norms and the legal order are not ends in themselves, but means to an end. Their authority — and fairness — are therefore not found in their (outward) form, but should rather be sought in their basic regulatory task and purpose. This truth is ignored when laws are interpreted solely literally.

A just legal order does not discriminate. From what was said in Chapter 2, this guideline indicates that realistic differentiation on *ethnic grounds* is hardly possible since ethnic groups cannot be described in legal terms, and that — due to the essentially generalizing nature of legal norms — *racial differentiation* always have a discriminating effect.

Legal norms should apply with certainty and all those to whom they apply should be able to grasp them. Legal rules and the law should be clearly formulated and easily accessible. The right of legal representation is a phenomenon of the application of this criterion. It is no longer possible for John Citizen to "know all the laws", and his knowledge of the law is therefore mainly acquired via either an independent professional expert or (and this fact must not be overlooked) officials and officers in the employ of the executive and legal authority in the state.

A legal order should engender and promote respect for the different procedures and legal remedies for which it provides — i.e., to summarize, for "the ways of the law" — among both subjects and authorities (and persons in authority) This is the *requirement for legality* which, if properly respected, contributes to keeping the channels for orderly interpersonal relations in society "open" and ensures that they are correctly and properly used. The law provides these channels also in its capacity as regulator of conflict in society.

A legal order should provide for the impartial settling of disputes. According to the sixth guideline above, specific rules are required in the regulation of a person's rights. However provision should also be made for these rights to be tried — and this requires impartial and independent courts.

The above guidelines, which emanate directly from the South African legal tradition, offer a basis for an equitable legal system. Such a basis is a guarantee to the citizens of the country of equality before the law, protection by the law and access to the law, regardless of the government of the day. In this respect it is a powerful guarantee for the development of constructive intergroup rela tions. The recent repeal of the Prohibition of Mixed Marriages Act and Article 16 of the Immorality Act, No. 23 of 1957, is in full agreement with the implications of these guidelines.

ADMINISTRATION OF JUSTICE

It was indicated in Chapter 2 and also above, that the legal definition of group identity is highly complex but it further appears that this definition in all the relevant acts is not uniform. This state of affairs naturally leads to the possibility of confusion, diminished access to the law and other hampering effects. Especially since the matter of population categorization is already so sensitive, this situation must be regarded as being potentially conflict generating.

Related to the above, it appears that there are also numerous race-oriented crimes on the statute-book. In fact, is seems as if many regulations that could have been handled administratively, have been criminalized. In this regard the work committee arrived at the conclusion that this group of acts is extraordinarily complex and in essence discriminatory in that an offence is based on the status of the offender (therefore race of population category) and not on the damage done. It should be clear that harmonious intergroup relations and the legitimacy of the law are not promoted in this way. One of the most obvious results of this state of affairs is to be found in the high South African crime and prisons statistics.

LAW ENFORCEMENT AGENCIES

It is very difficult to determine the intrinsic role of law enforcement officials in the promotion or troubling of intergroup relations since methods have not yet been devised to establish whether people think of the law itself or of its enforcement. There are as yet no sophisticated measuring and analytical techniques to distinguish the various effects of the two factors.

There is absolutely no doubt that law enforcement is a highly sensitive matter. Indeed, for many people it is their first contact with an abstract system that is supposed to be just and impartial. Absolute professionalism in human relations should be the criterion. Mention has been made elsewhere in this report of the fact that law enforcement officials play a key role in the sphere of intergroup relations — a role that has dual relevance. On the one hand the person who enforces the law represents a group, and it is virtually unavoidable that his actions will be regarded as reflecting the interests of that group. On the other hand he also represents a system or institution and his actions — which may be perceived as intolerant — can bring legitimacy of the system or institution into question.

133

The preceding considerations should be seen in the light of the exceptionally high number of prosecutions and the large prison population in South Africa. The potential effect on the population could be considerable.

ACCESS TO THE LAW

Seen from the public's point view, access to the law represents the *possibility* of having recourse to the law. Access to the law can assume three forms, namely knowledge, means and trust. Especially in a country like South Africa where there are sections of the population with varying cultural backgrounds, different levels of education, etc., it is in any case difficult to bring about equal access to the law. Research undertaken for the Investigation showed that whites for various reasons have, in terms of all three definitions, easier access to the law than Africans. This finding is related to the following theme and will be expanded upon.

ADMINISTRATION OF JUSTICE

The work committee investigated three facets of the administration of justice: the perception of the administration of justice, communication in court and its effect on intergroup relations. These three facets, and some others that have already been discussed, are naturally dependent on one another and the following discussion should therefore be viewed against this background.

As could be expected from the results of research on perception discussed in the previous chapter, whites and Africans differ virtually diametrically in their evaluation of the administration of justice and related matters. Empirical research has established that factors such as sex and age also influence the perception of various matters, but that the population category of the respondent is the single most important influence. For example, whites had the most positive impression of South African law and Africans the most negative, with coloureds and Indians about midway between these two extremes. The same patterns emerged in respect of obeying the law and the perception of the police and the administration of justice.

Highly innovative research was also done on communication in court. Structural analyses of the dialogue of coloureds in court revealed that their evidence is often poorly structured and difficult to understand in terms of standard procedures and could therefore be judged as potentially unreliable. On the grounds of these results it was concluded that coloureds were less able to structure their evidence according to coherent narratives than were whites.

In essence the above concerns typical problems in intercultural communication and the so-called attribution process. Tremendous responsibility is placed on the shoulders of the officials concerned to be sensitive, and to take specific cultural traits into account when evaluating evidence. Special training is required for this.

One way of alleviating the problem would naturally be to use interpreters. Unfortunately research indicates that this approach is also not totally successful. In a study that focused on the unrepresented accused it emerged that interpretation and translation were often stopped at critical stages. This occurs especially when procedures and arrangements have to be discussed. For example it was found that in only 39 % of cases, where postponement was granted, were the reasons for this translated for the accused. In only 12 % of the cases where bail was applied for, were the reasons for the court's decision translated for the accused.

The above cannot be attributed to poorly trained interpreters as exceptional care is taken in the training of court interpreters. It is nevertheless clear that such cases do not promote confidence in the legal system and therefore also do not promote good intergroup relations.

The cited empirical studies again stress the complexity of many facets of the multicultural population of South Africa. Problems such as the above occur in virtually every sphere of society. What makes the juridical incidents so very important are the drastic results that could ensue for the accused. And even more important: in a stable country the law should be the surest guarantee for justice. It is obvious that the perception of a person will be influenced if he gets the impression that he "cannot get through" or that there is no understanding for his case.

INTERNATIONAL LAW

It was stated in Chapter 3 that, typically, perception takes place within a framework or against a certain background. In recent times there have been indications that South African law is being judged against the background of international law. In fact, news items that implicitly or explicitly deal with the topic are common. It is therefore to be expected that those sections of the population that believe they are being prejudiced by the system will compare South African law to international law and that they will see the latter as the ideal.

Research cited in the report of the Work Committee: Juridical Aspects emphasizes the question of human rights in international law. Human rights are contained in inter alia the European Convention of Human Rights, 1950; and the American Convention of Human Rights of 1970. These and other conventions include the basic ideas of the well-known Universal Declaration of Human Rights in 1948. Generally speaking, the basic aspects of this declaration are today accepted as rules of international common law. One of these rules is the prohibition of racial discrimination.

There are obviously different arguments and views about some of the content of and motives behind international law. What *is* certain, is that it is used as a criterion by which South Africa and its laws are measured — locally as well as abroad. It seems as if South Africa will not be able to continue avoiding this judgement.

SUMMARY

Intergroup relations and the law are interwoven in some aspects because the official arrangement of these relations in the country is based on the statutory categorization of the entire population. It was established in the previous chapter that this categorization cannot, in important respects, contain both the dynamics and the complexity of identity. This must be regarded as one of the basic dilemmas of intergroup relations.

Various aspects of the law can be evaluated according to a number of guidelines derived from the South African legal tradition. Such an evaluation shows that the law in several respects currently does not fully comply with all these criteria. This applies to some acts, portions of criminal law, law enforcement as perceived by some people, access to the law and elements of the administration of justice.

The conflict-regulating function of the law cannot be disputed, especially not in the field of intergroup relations. In fact, there is little doubt that the law could become one of the initiators of constructive intergroup relations provided that the guidelines given in this chapter are used as a touchstone. If this were done the present conflict-generating factors could be eliminated. Unless all South Africans accept the legal system, intergroup relations will come under increasing pressure.

THE CONSTITUTION AND POLITICS

A country's constitution provides a political framework within which its inhabitants should be able to achieve selfregulation, while it simultaneously reflects how those in power feel about the way in which intergroup relations in a country should be ordered. South Africa is no exception to this. The fact that the country has over the past few years experienced constitutional changes that essentially revolve around the problems of intergroup relations means that due account should be taken of political influences. It was in this light that the balance sheet of the influences as stated in the report of the Work Committee: Constition and Politics: *Political co-operation within a fundamental legal order* was compiled. The nature of the constitutional arrangements was dealt with in Chapter 2, and will not be repeated here.

This section will first evaluate government initiatives from the viewpoint of intergroup relations; this will be followed by a discussion of some anomalies, and the section will conclude with a summarized perspective.

AN EVALUATION OF GOVERNMENT INITIATIVES

All indications are that the Government has latterly been more "open" in respect of constructive dialogue than ever before. As was pointed out in the report of the Work Committee: Constitution and Politics there was real devolution of power with the introduction of ethnically based self-government areas, and this, despite all its negative aspects has developed into an important catalyst for reform.

It would be one-sided, and even dishonest to aver that no attempts have been made in South Africa over the years to put intergroup relations on a sounder basis and thereby reduce conflict. Probably the most radical development in the overall arrangement of intergroup relations was the introduction of ethnic self-governing areas, the establishment of their own governments for these areas and the eventual independence of Bophuthatswana, Transkei, Ciskei and Venda. Notwithstanding the obvious shortcomings and obstacles inherent in this large-scale devolution of power, it cannot be denied that the national states and the independent TBVC states have become permanent elements in the broader South African dispensation and that they have made important contributions towards the improvement of intergroup relations. (Some of the most serious problems are fragmented boundaries, unconsolidated areas, inadequate manpower and infrastructure, poor economies and lack of revenue, severe poverty, inadequate government services, little management experience and ostracism by the international community and international organizations).

These states, with their African governments have, to a greater or lesser extent, succeeded in establishing multiracial communities within which members of the different South African population categories live and work together and share education. Bophuthatswana, in addition, has an entrenched human rights declaration as part of its constitution and has whites in its government. The above factors must be recognized as independent and valuable contributions to the improvement of intergroup relations. Reference can also be made to the establishment of sophisticated government structures, specific democratic traditions, regular elections and the expansion of modern administrations. The introduction of umbrella institutions for consultations with the RSA, and the provision of, especially, higher education institutions should be seen as the positive results of the drastic devolution of power.

Both the specific content and the manner of implementation of the concept of decentralization and devolution of power to self-governing areas and independent states are, however, such that they are in danger of being completely discredited as a political method for arranging intergroup relations. Some of the major problems in this regard are the South African insistence on total independence for all the areas, the one-sided and broadly based allocation of citizenship of these areas to all African population groups (with the inherent risk of total loss of South African citizenship as happened in the case of TBVC nationals) and the further possibility that these areas and states could be used as dumping-grounds for Africans from the Republic. Such ideological and political overtaxing of the system holds the danger that the entire homeland policy could develop into an obstacle rather than be one of the most important means for ordering constructive intergroup relations.

The greater flexibility on the part of Government (mentioned earlier) also applies to the dysfunctions mentioned above. During the debate on his budget vote in April 1985 the State President indicated that the loss of RSA nationality need not necessarily follows when a self-governing national state becomes independent. This indicates a significant adjustment of policy which nevertheless still retains the principles of devolution coupled with regional autonomy. Since the latter two matters are regarded as desirable in terms of South African realities, South Africa's political system could develop more clearly defined federal traits. This could be more acceptable to a greater proportion of the African population, particularly since the present citizenship arrangements, which all Africans regard as an impediment to sounder intergroup relations, could be adapted in this way.

A second and generally favourable development in the ordering of intergroup relations in the recent past, has been the acceptance and implementation of the new 1983 Constitution, irrespective of the shortcomings and deficiencies that have still to be dealt with. The positive side of the new constitution is simply that other population categories, namely the coloureds and the Indians, have for the first time been offered the opportunity of direct participation in the central government. Regardless of how qualified this participation may be, the new constitutional dispensation is a major political breakthrough in that it has partially lifted the colour bar in the South African system of central government.

This breakthrough is of extreme importance in South Africa politics, and also for intergroup relations, since it has made possible the development of a form of government and political processes that are more accommodating. Giving the Indian and coloured communities some say has certainly heralded a new era of government. This peaceful, democratizing measure, probably more than any other reform, has stimulated optimism in respect of future constitutional and political change.

The fact that this major initiative was so strongly supported by the white electorate in a referendum is a very positive indication of a change in white attitudes. If it is further taken into account that the constitution is generally regarded as being start and not the end of constitutional reform, it is surely not out of place to expect continued reform efforts.

The above evaluation should also be seen against the background of the statement in chapter 3, namely that one of the major problems in the dynamics of change is to set the process in motion. That chapter mentioned a thawing phase. The new constitution itself and support for the constitution in the referendum indicate that circumstances have changed irrevocably in South Africa.

The "openness" to dialogue on the part of Government was recently confirmed by the creation of an open forum to which everyone who rejected violence as a means for change and was prepared to participate constructively was invited. Adam (1985, p. 121) consequently disagrees with Davidson's statement that "nothing has been officially proposed, or even discussed, that could in any way improve the social and political situation of the Africans". Adam holds the contrary to be true. The critical question is how far the Government is prepared to go in this dialogue.

A further development that should not be ignored is that there has been an easing of tension in the relations between South Africa and its neighbouring states. Adam (1985, p. 116) points out that the frontline states have been increasingly neutralized as a threat in the military sense of the word. This change of attitude was underscored by the 'Nkomati Accord. This means that expectation among opponents of the Government of "liberation" by external forces has been considerably reduced. The apparent inability of groups such as the external wing of the ANC to make significant military progress could mean that they will take a more realistic view of internal possibilities for political reform.

At the same time the diplomatic successes in respect of the frontline states signify that an important prop in the "total onslaught" argument has become less secure. There are indications that South Africa, for a variety of reasons, is at present fairly low on Moscow's priority list. The external threat played a role in the introduction of internal reform, but now that this factor has changed, the insistence on further reform could diminish. However it would be better to use the current more favourable climate to continue essential constitutional reforms.

It would probably be in the interest of all parties concerned with the future of South Africa if the first move in the direction of dialogue were not be held in public. Furthermore, there will be little hope of progress if those carrying on the dialogue are not interested in real change, but merely use the dialogue for propaganda reasons.

ANOMALIES

Seen from a constitutional point of view the present political dispensation contains a number of important anomalies. Although the 1983 Constitution effected some positive changes in this situation (these will be discussed later), important anomalies still exist.

One of the most striking anomalies must surely be that the legislator tried, by law, to place all the different population groups, except the whites, in different statutory categories according to ethnic descent, kinship, cultural identification or other physical factors (cf. Chapters 2 and 3). Whites however were not classified in this manner despite the fact that they had clearly identifiable characteristics (cf. Chapters 2 and 3). (The only statutory difference regarding the Afrikaans- and English-speaking groups was that some provincial educational ordinances prescribe that white scholars, up to and including Standard 8, must be instructed in their mother tongue. This distinction is, however, not transferred to any form of state institution). This probably contains one of the most striking contradictions in South Africa's group relations problems. As shown in Chapter 3 the fact that this statutory process of group classification for coloureds, Indians and Africans was completely in the hands of the white legislator and had been devised by the white government, was a transparent display of white power manipulation in relation to the other groups and one of the most striking contradictions in South African group relations problems.

In this regard it is essential to remember that the political and constitutional institutions of a society largely reflect the distribution of power within that society. These institutions together provide the power structure of a society. Since power is one of the key resources in any society it is self-evident that people in diverse organizational contexts will compete for access to this. In many deeply-segmented societies this competition often leads to asymmetric distribution of power and therefore to structures of political dominance. Drastic changes in these structures can usually only occur if there is far-reaching reorganization of the society's power institutions — especially concerning people's access and recruitment to central authorities. In brief, structured social inequality never occurs in a political vacuum. In the final analysis drastic changes in this asymmetrical opportunity system can only be effected through political channels.

Another complicating result of the classification of statutory African ethnic groups and the concomitant division into separate Black states (regardless of whether they are independent Black states or self-governing national states) is the distinction between Black South African citizens and former Black South African citizens and their descendants. As indicated earlier, there are strong indications, for example in the form of statements by the State President, that this matter is being reconsidered.

A further dilemma is to be found in the: statutory classification of population groups which also found expression in party politics, especially in the form of the Prohibition of Political Interference Act, No. 31 of 1968. This Act finally formalized the government policy that members of particular population groups may not be members of political parties of other racial groups and also that they may not actively support or influence one another. Although this Act to some extent has not been strictly enforced, and the Cabinet is once more considering it, it resulted in proclaimed objectives of white opposition parties opposing this political division. This compulsory division provided coloured, Indian and African political parties with an incentive towards common political objectives and policy. The foundation of the Black Alliance is an example of this joining of forces. The policy of selfgoverning African areas also led to the formation of more specifically "homeland-oriented" political parties which rejected the Government's power in these states and tried to gain electoral support among the citizens. Most striking is the growth during times when political separation reigned supreme — growth of African parties outside parliament and also of resistance groups such as the Black Consciousness Movement. On the other hand it is remarkable that, at a stage when government policy granted greater recognition to group co-operation in government appointments, strong white opposition came to the fore leading to the formation of new white political opposition parties.

SUMMARY

In the preceding review of the constitutional and political aspects of intergroup relations developments in this field were evaluated. This review must be seen together with the description of the constitutional dispensation in chapter 2 as well as the explanation of the South African juridical system. When everything is taken into account, it may be stated that the original design for separate development cannot be fully implemented and that many of the supposed advantages for the population categories concerned did not materialize in any case. The process also created many frustrations and a great deal of polarization which will for a very long time continue to hamper the real development of constructive relations.

The Work Committee for Constitution and Politics came to the conclusion that the new constitution undoubtedly means a change of direction. In the short term this change does not necessarily imply a drastic turn-about, but the fact remains that a different course offering new opportunities is envisaged.

FINAL PERSPECTIVE

It cannot be denied that South Africa contains a variety of population groups. Different verdicts can be passed on the effect of the mainly one-sided dispensation. On the one hand it can be maintained that the statutory classification, in so far as it rests on the state of reality and the view of the government of the day, cosntitutes the only basis on which peaceful and constructive group relations and state institutions can be built. In other words, according to this view it was absolutely essential for the legislator to give statutory form to the plural nature of South African society and to structure it in that manner before any durable and permanent structures for co-operation could be built.

On the other hand it can be averred that the vast institutionalization and socio-economic enforcement of group separation based on statutory classification of people in population categories, in reality descridited the historical and spon-teneous bases of ethnicity. This caused political polarization, bureaucratic control and official rigidity, and created so much suspicion and uncertainty that group relations in South Africa became a permanent source of conflict. This matter was taken to such extremes that any future policy that is designed to identify groups, minorities in particular, and a desire to protect them, will be hailed with mistrust and even active resistance.

The present pattern of defferentiation of interest groups in South Africa is undeniably, and probably the major source of conflict in South Africa. Statutory group classification by the white parliament and the large-scale institutionalization of group differentiation has so far increased the conflict potential in may respects. This conflict potential was enhanced by the empirically confirmed fact that group differentiation led to material and non-material harm to some of the groups, regardless of whether this was intentional or not, or whether it could have been foreseen or not. This, however, does not mean that there have not been any attempts recent years to control and even defuse such conflict potential.

Democratic intergroup accommodation in deeply-segmented societies is, however, difficult to reconcile with an asynmetrical distribution of power which gives one segment an unjustifiable competitive advantage over other interest groups. Critics of government policy argue that this policy evolved from a system of political monopoly. This monopoly traditionally benefited the white, particularly the Afrikaner, and continues to motivate "outside groups" to wage the battle for social and economic equality mainly in the political arena. Any attempt to move away from South Africa's structures of social inequality and political dominance will therefore have to involve a redivision of political decision-making power in any way or another.

It is obvious from this research that politicaland economic stability and social order are prerequisities for viable reform. In this sense social order which does not signify maintenance of the *status quo,* is both a result of and a prerequisite for reform. Several indicators of political, social and economic forces were found to indicate a moderately favourable climate for the development of constructive relations. The search for a democratic and stable social order in which all South Africans can achieve their basic aspirations is, however, not yet over. The backlog which Indians, coloureds and Blacks have built up in so many fields is, in this respect a historical force with considerable negative effect.

Although whites seem to be more receptive to change and in light democratic reform, increased expectations and protest behaviour it is understandable why Blacks will not interpret the repeal of the Prohibition of Mixed Marriages Act and Section 16 of the Immorality Act as a concession, but rather as redress for a fundamental injustice. The repeal of this and other discriminatory measures will probably not reduce the rate or lower the level of social, economic and, especially, political aspirations, nor retard them. On the contrary, the opposite can be expected.

In South Africa reform will inevitably be inconvenient for whites. However, the current Investigation found that due to increasing pragmatism Whites are

143

starting to take up the challenge. On the other hand there are also indications that some leaders of the other groups are beginning to understand the whites' dilemmas in the "farewell" to apartheid. The conditions for the expansion of constructive group relations well be dealt with in the final chapter.

CHAPTER 5

EVALUATION

This *Investigation* was in essence an attempt to analyze the most pressing issue in South Africa, intergroup relations, and to ascertain in what direction these relations were developing. To this end the preceding chapters offered a review and analysis of the most important facets of the problem — the contours of intergroup relations as it were. An evaluation of the present situation and of possible future developments require that these facets be brought into relation with each other and the underlying and fundamental processes be distilled from them. A scientific evaluation rather than merely the identification of symptoms should then be possible.

This chapter is thus concerned with the integration and interpretation of those facets of intergroup relations dealt with earlier; at the same time it offers a tentative explanation of the underlying causes and determinants of intergroup conflict in South Africa. In the next chapter perspectives based on the findings of the *Investigation* will be given on the development of constructive intergroup relations. The following themes are discussed in the present chapter: fundamental realities, four core problems in intergroup relations, a potentially destructive configuration and the relation between conflict and change.

FUNDAMENTAL REALITIES

In the preceding three chapters some realities of the South African situation were outlined which must be taken into account in any attempt to understand the problem of intergroup relations in this country. On the basis of the findings in Chapters 2, 3 and 4 South African society can be represented in different ways. The present pattern of relations between the various groups is the result of the interaction of a large number of factors over a relatively long period of time, which makes it virtually impossible at times to distinguish between action and reaction. For the purpose of this general summary of the problem area, the development of South African society over the years may be sketched as follows.

From its colonial origins South Africa eventually developed into a politically independent state with jurisdiction over a gegraphical area inhabited by a markedly heterogeneous population. White colonists from Western Europe settled here and in time (particularly in the case of the ancestors of the white Afrikaners) developed a sense of common destiny, ethnicity in other words, to which in due course political expression was given in the form of a predominantly white political orientation in general and an exclusive Afrikaner nationalist movement in particular. This political movement led to the structuring of the political system in such a way as to entrench the identity and interests of whites. This was done by establishing a segmented institutional structure based on race and colour as the formal markers of identity. Thus the different categories of the population were involved differentially on the basis of these ascriptive physical markers of ethnicity in the central institutions of the social system.

Along with this, the cultural heritages introduced into the social system by the different components of the heterogeneous population varied from those normally associated with traditional cultures to those associated with present western civilization.

Under the circumstances set out above, the hierarchical ordering of society adopted a distinctly layered character coinciding with the differential involvement of the different elements of the population in the central institutions on the basis of the formal markers of ethnicity. This stratal character was underlined by the development of an expanding industrial economy initiated and still controlled by the predominantly western oriented whites.

The South African social order therefore stemmed from a formal institutional structure that was aimed at entrenching the ethnic group identity and interests of the white component of the population and particularly those of the Afrikaner element in the population. White ethnicity was politicized by stressing group interests, thus assuming that there would necessarily be conflict of interests between different ethnic groups competing for resources within the same territory. In essence this point of view stemmed from a conflict perspective in terms of which race and colour as markers of ethnicity were the basis for the structuring of South African society. Maintaining such an order therefore required continuing political mobilization of ethnicity and hence white dominance.

In the development of this sociopolitical order a contradiction arose as a consequence of the prevailing value system. On the one hand deepseated religious values as well as common law traditions and democratic principles called for equal rights for all individual members of society. On the other hand, however, the preservation of the ethnic identity of white Afrikaners required the emphasiz-

146

ing of the differences between members and non-members of this ethnic group insofar as their involvement in the social dispensation was concerned. This clash of value orientations gave rise to a legitimacy crisis involving the whole sociopolitical system.

Attempts at resolving this crisis were made at the religious level in the development of what could be described as a civil variant of Afrikaner-Calvinist protestantism, at the legal level in the replacement of the principle of the rule of law by the principle of legalism, and at the political level by the reordering of the formal political structure explicitly on the basis of ethnicity. The results of the *Investigation* indicate that these and other measures did not succeed in reducing the tensions in the sociopolitical order although they did in large measure insulate the whites and particularly the white Afrikaners from experiencing the effects of these structural tensions. This, however, merely served to intensify the other groups' experience of the tensions. A grave credibility crisis thus developed that led increasingly to the use of force as the only basis for maintaining social order.

When considering the complex nature of intergroup relations in South Africa, as outlined macro-analytically above, one almost inevitably reaches the conclusion that these relations are deteriorating into conflict that cannot be resolved through the normal channels. This conflict currently manifests itself mainly, but not exclusively, in the rivalry between the primary politically and economically relevant interest groups that have sprung from the country's plural population composition. Furthermore, relatively drastic and potentially farreaching changes are occurring in South African society which in turn are generating widespread structural stress, tensions and even conflict as the whites, confronted by the realities of a burgeoning black bargaining power, make adjustments in the direction of co-operative and accommodative group relations and accordingly a more democratic social order.

CORE PROBLEMS IN INTERGROUP RELATIONS

The particularization of the problems regarding intergroup relations outlined above, calls for the interpretation of the findings in this report in more specific terms. When the findings of the preceding three chapters are read together, four specific problems emerge which are basic to the relations situation, viz. the handling of diversity, the individual and his group association, institutionalized inequality and, finally, isolation and insulation.

HANDLING OF DIVERSITY

In Chapter 2 reasons were advanced as to why ethnicity as experienced subjectively by people, deviates in important respects from the ideal type ethnicity as described in scientific literature. Ideal types are actually found only in the core group, and not in the wider set of that group. In other words, a particular ethnic group consists of members who in varying degrees comply with some of the typical characteristics of that group. But ethnicity is nevertheless a social reality that cannot be denied or argued away.

In Chapter 3 it was indicated that from a juridical point of view ethnicity is an almost unmanageable concept/category for the determining of group boundaries. Simultaneously it was found that from the same point of view race is an irrelevant concept as a basis for differentiation. In the ordering of intergroup relations in South Africa, a dynamic phenomenon whose boundaries are sometimes difficult to determine even by social scientists, has thus been elevated to the level of a juridical factor. The current analyses indicate that what is of concern here is not just ethnicity but also race. In terms of the ordering of intergroup relations people are therefore ascriptively categorized in particular social positions; the decisive criteria of differentiation are characteristics such as descent, somatic appearance and ethnic factors such as language.

Historically the whites unilaterally institutionalized ethnicity and related characteristics as political and constitutional criteria. In the implementation of the policy, at least, it benefitted the whites in the short and medium term, while the other groups were prejudiced in at least the short term and in their view, and according to all external indications, would be increasingly prejudiced. Because the group membership of a person defined for instance as a coloured is determined by birth, he is — within the South African context — burdened from the outset with certain characteristics — even a physical stamp — that are interpreted by the dominant white group as the deciding indicators of "being coloured", with all the negative status implications and social disqualifications associated with this classification. Thus the individual coloured inherits an inferior position in this society and accordingly fewer opportunities.

Africans, coloureds and Indians do not deny the reality of group differentiation in a plural society. What they object to, however, is the way in which the group membership of individuals is ascriptively and statutorily enforced by a politically dominant group that regards group differentiation as a basis for the unequal opportunities, power, etc. For these members of South African society it is only too clear that white ethnicity in terms of rights and privileges means something quite different to, say, African ethnicity. The African communities in particular began to believe that, whereas white and especially Afrikaner ethnicity was a cornerstone of white political hegemony, African ethnicity was a factor that prevented Africans from utilizing their most effective weapon, namely their collective numerical superiority, to improve their economic and political bargaining positions. The potential tensions between traditional and urban leaders were a further complicating factor.

The policy of unilaterally assigning ethnic and related differences as determinants for institutionalized separation and segregation had the effect of hamstringing the potentially positive and creative power inherent in ethnicity.

THE INDIVIDUAL AND HIS GROUP ASSOCIATION

A basic problem in any plural society is that concerning the relative interests of the individual and the group. Plurality per definition refers to the multiplicity of groups, although in the final instance it is the individual who reaps the benefits and/or disadvantages of a particular sociopolitical dispensation. This was one of the reasons why the experiencing of intergroup relations was looked into in some detail in Chapter 3. In South Africa attention was increasingly placed, statutorily, on the group in the sense that individuals were forced to view their interests in the context of particular groups.

In Chapter 3 it was indicated that the tension between individual and group in South Africa stemmed from the tendency to categorize people. The upshot was that not only do whites think of Indians, for instance, in terms of a category rather than as individuals, but that Indians likewise regard whites as a group that as such discriminates against other groups.

Because of the overwhelming emphasis placed on the category rather than the individual, neither the reasoning behind nor the results of the ordering of intergroup relations in South Africa are observed and appreciated at the personal level. Coloureds and Indians, but particularly Africans, argue that they inevitably become the victims of discrimination because they are ascriptively classified in groups that as such are relegated to an inferior position in society. They therefore reason that in their capacity as *individual South African citizens* they have a claim to *individual human rights*. This placing of the individual at the centre of the human rights issue is strongly endorsed by leaders of these groups. In terms of this approach any social issue in the final instance can be reduced to its individual human elements. Consequently, even if a group is discriminated against on the basis of ascriptive criteria, in the end it remains the individual who has to suffer the practical consequences of social inequality.

149

Reference was made earlier to the finding that the implementation of apartheid has always been more advantageous to the white population group than to the other groups. At the same time there can be little doubt that an ordering of intergroup relations that does not ensure equal opportunities for everyone, will not be readily accepted by the disadvantaged groups. The findings in chapter 2 as well as the analysis in Chapter 4 indicate that neither in daily life does separateness mean equality nor, from a historical perspective, has it succeeded in bringing about equality. The research shows that Africans, coloureds and Indians experience the current statutory group differentiation as a serious restriction on their social and economic mobility. Structured social inequality almost always means a greater or lesser degree of restriction on the opportunities for upward mobility across class or ethnic barriers of persons lower in the hierarchy. In this sense restrictions on people's mobility across hierarchical ranks will create a state of conflict whose intensity will tend to vary according to the extent to which the dominant ranks restrict people's opportunities in life by arbitrarily blocking their upward socio-economic mobility. According to the literature by far the greatest conflict potential exists where lower social positions are arbitrarily and categorically assigned to particular persons on the basis of particular characteristics that are socially defined as indices or criteria of social status.

The implications of inequality for intergroup relations are that when people see how relatively well others are living while regarding themselves as relatively deprived, they will relate the observed (and objective) differences directly to the way in which, on various occasions, they have been excluded from the opportunity system in South Africa. In Chapters 3 and 4 research was referred to which confirmed the existence of the phenomenon of relative deprivation. The historical development of intergroup relations in South Africa actually presents a classic example of relative deprivation, a phenomenon that is in the present circumstances accompanied by increasing militancy.

The third core problem therefore lies in the fact that segregation and separateness are manifestly associated with inequality, although all inequality does not necessarily stem from segregation. Indeed, it would be easy to show that some historical instances of inequality have become less obvious over the past few decades (as in the case of wages and salaries) without this, having had a marked effect on the association of separateness with inequality. The subjective acceptance of this association almost invariably gives rise to strained relations and, as indicated, may even precede potentially serious conflict.

ISOLATION AND INSULATION

The policy of separate development pursued since 1948 alienated groups from one another in that it reduced the opportunities for spontaneous and close contact between them — i.e. contact between individual members of groups. Separation thus also meant personal isolation for the members of the different groups in this country. It can be shown that a lack of contact can give rise to mistrust and suspicion between groups, ultimately leading to what can be described as vicarious or indirect perspectives of one another. None of the above can be conducive to good human relations and can in fact lead to insulation, with one group not knowing what another group thinks, feels or experiences.

It could be argued that contact and communication occur in the work place and in commerce. The view held in this report, however, is that contact in formal situations does not help people become acquainted at the personal or individual level — a necessary condition for constructive human relations. The mediating role of the mass media does not resolve the problem either because of the media's tendency to generalize and thus to categorize and stereotype.

The fourth core problem therefore lies in the fact that South African society is characterized by people who have become isolated from one another. South Africans have consequently forfeited the opportunity to perceive one another not only as members of conventional categories but also as individuals with personal needs and aspirations, fears and hopes and divergent and common characteristics and interests.

A DESTRUCTIVE CONFIGURATION

The preceding macro-analytical perspective on South African society and the particular core problems in intergroup relations discussed above, point to a configuration of factors that could have a potentially destructive effect on intergroup relations in the country. Few social systems have a greater conflict potential than a group-differentiated configuration in which the political dominance of a particular ethnic or cultural segment of the population over a subordinate segment forms a dividing line that runs parallel with a socio-economic divide stratifying the two segments into a higher and lower class position respectively. And this is precisely what the matrix of intergroup relations in South Africa amounts to: Whites normally have a higher status along with more rights and privileges than the other groups, particularly the Africans who are relegated to the lowest position in the hierarchy. The divisions between ethnic groups and classes converge in large measure. People who belong to a particular ethnic or colour group can simultaneously be described as a particular class and have either less or more influence in the central political system than other groups. Differences were historically accommodated by a strategy of separation, although at the same time inequality was confirmed. The individual was as such unable to free himself from his group connection and thus became a victim of his group membership. Simultaneously association between the groups was restricted to the bare minimum.

Experts agree that even major economic and other inequalities have little political effect when they cut across other group boundaries. However when economic, social and cultural divisions coincide, the potential for serious conflict increases vastly mainly because the groups (strata or categories or even individuals) have no shared interests or loyalties. The four core problems that were identified in the *Investigation* confirm very clearly that the course of intergroup relations in South Africa necessarily had to result in such a convergence of cleavages. This could only have been averted had it been possible to develop the country into totally separate and economically viable geo-political units — something which has evidently not been achieved and is obviously not feasible.

Empirical evidence indicates that peaceful intergroup accommodation in deeply segmented societies is promoted to the extent that socio-economic strata cut across basic group cleavages such as culture, ethnicity, religion, language and race. Because this type of crosscutting alliance promotes the development of common loyalties, multiple group attachments and common interests, it reduces the likelihood of certain cleavages becoming so politicized and mobilized that confrontation ensues between the groups concerned over a wide front. At the same time such crosscutting alliances facilitate the development of common lifestyles which, owing to their assimilative effect, tend to promote accommodative and co-operative behaviour without which democratic intergroup accommodation is not possible.

Conflict management is promoted to the extent that the rival interest groups agree on the fundamental norms and values according to which society should be ordered. In particular there has to be consensus on the institutional framework within which decisions are reached on people's access to the opportunities offered by society. Such consensus can only be achieved on the basis of compatibility of basic values. Dissensus in the sense that the legitimacy of the state's institutional structures is challenged or rejected, tends to inhibit conflict management. If the differentiated interest groups believe that their vital interests are incompatible and irreconcilable, consensual accommodation will be difficult to achieve. Consensus on norms and values also implies certain common objectives that transcend the particularistic objectives of the respective interest groups.

Fundamental norms and values apart, it is surprising how consensus on bread-and-butter issues can help facilitate conflict management. In their day-to-day lives people are seldom swayed by ideological considerations to make certain choices. In this sense group-oriented interest should not be confused with ideological orientations.

From Chapters 3 and 4 it can be concluded that the sharing of political power is not only a crucial determinant of intergroup relations in South Africa, but also that a broadening of the democratic base of the current power structure is a prerequisite for the development of a stable social order. It is a fact that the majority of Africans and large percentages of coloureds an Indians reject the legitimacy of the current political dispensation. These people regard themselves as outside the system, a sentiment echoed in the political credos of various African, coloured and Indian organizations operating outside the current power structures, and thus precluding their dispute with the system from being handled through the conventional institutions for conflict accommodation. In a certain sense this may be seen as a boomeranging of the original separation idea in that it was originally believed that each group should have its own institutions, but now that this has not happened, these groupings do not accept the present "white" institutions as legitimate either.

From Chapters 2 and 4 it is clear that clashes in the economic sphere often lie at the root of conflict between the different groups. At the same time, however, it is obviously in everyone's interests that economic growth and stability be maintained. During the past decade there has been significant reform in the labour field, with the groups other than white sharing increasingly in the benefits of the South African economy. Inequalities in the field of social welfare have also been reduced. A condition for stability and progress in the economic field, and accordingly for accommodation in the political and normative sphere, is that all groups should share increasingly in South Africa's economic prosperity.

THE RECIPROCAL RELATION BETWEEN CONFLICT AND CHANGE

The analyses in Chapters 2, 3 and 4 indicate in various respects the need for reform in the South African social system. On the one hand there is the expectation that changes in the form of greater accommodation are likely to occur within the next few years, while on the other hand there are, for instance, the extensive reforms in the labour field that have already been effected. Even more important is the new constitutional dispensation which government spokesmen themselves say does not mark the end of reform but rather the beginning. There is every reason to believe, however, that reform in South Africa will not be painless and without conflict. In this connection the rapidly rising expectations in African, coloured and Indian ranks will become a crucial variable in the reform process.

There is considerable empirical evidence to show that reforms during periods of rapidly rising expectations tend to stimulate conflict rather than inhibit it. This is clearly illustrated by the sharp division between factions within population categories, the emergence of new action groups, the increase in unrest, etc. The same phenomenon occurred in the USA, for instance, where a radical democratization of the position of blacks coupled with a significant liberalization of white attitudes towards blacks did not prevent the riots that erupted in more than a hundred American cities during the sixties. In South Africa it can likewise be expected that changes — regardless of whether they are described as normalization or reform — will give rise to instability and make extraordinary demands on the evolving conflict-accommodating institutions.

This is sure to be the case unless all groups can be given the assurance that aspirations not yet fulfilled or interests that are threatened will not be overlooked in the further reform process. *Optimal* confidence in the reform process should therefore be encouraged. In this respect the symbolism in the communication process that accompanies reform will play a very important role.

The fact that the unrest and conflict that accompanies reform can often be related to a lack of confidence in the process, also indicates that there is no simple or direct relation between the current unrest in black residential areas and recent policy adjustments.

No reorientation of intergroup relations in South Africa can possibly occur in a vacuum, as all facets of life are involved in such a process. And indeed the analyses in Chapter 4 showed that not only is political reform under way but, in the context of rapid urbanization, also educational reform, economic improvement and change in the field of labour relations. The fact that reform is occurring in a rapidly modernizing society is bound to have a marked impact on the nature, intensity and extent of the reform — and particularly on people's reactions to it. In modern times rapid social and economic growth as such has often led to political instability and hence increased tension between groups in complex plural societies. Modernization, particularly in the context of rapid urban industrial development, gives rise to new disputes that can be politicized — a trend that is evident in South Africa at present. Industrialization, modernization and sociopolitical development will have to keep pace with one another in order to prevent the potentially uncontrollable escalation of conflict.

154

CONCLUSION

This research programme in which the perspectives of various social sciences were dealt with, clearly spells out the realities of intergroup relations in South Africa. Not only was an in-depth study made of the realities that had crystallized out historically in the social order, but the forces of change that herald the realities of the future were also looked into. The vast mass of information obtained, emits certain clear signals, some arousing more hopeful and others less hopeful expectations regarding the future of human relations in South Africa. Whether the message will be one of hope or despair will however also depend on how each individual South African expects to be affected by the changes: the one's hope may be the other's despair; what some regard as a movement towards a more democratic society, may signify the road to anarchy to others; reforms regarded by some as too many and too sudden, may be considered as too few and too late by others; what some regard as fundamental reforms, others may regard as regression, and still others as superficial cosmetic change.

The key issue is whether the forces active in society are sufficient to ensure, separately and collectively, that South Africa will develop a stable social order with an inescapable but manageable minimum of social disruption and conflict. A social order is called for in which firstly, individual human rights and the rightful interests of spontaneously developed groups will be reconciled democratically; in which secondly, equal civil rights will be guaranteed to all South Africans irrespective of race, class, creed, ethnic group, language and culture; and in which thirdly, each individual will enjoy equal opportunities to improve the quality of his life optimally.

From all the information gleaned from a variety of sources in the course of this *Investigation,* one indisputable fact emerged: there will not be much consolation for those who are under the illusion that the transition from an apartheid society to a broader democratically oriented social order will occur virtually overnight and without a hitch, or that the whites have such control over their own destiny that they can dictate the rate, direction and nature of change according to their own need, and as a matter of fact not for those either who simply assume that uncontrolled violence will lead to the ideal society.

Judging by the balance of the historical forces presently determining the rate and direction of change in South Africa, it appears that there are various factors that may be regarded as conducive to the establishment of a democratic social order. Positive forces identified during the *Investigation* relate particularly to current reform initiatives aimed at the repeal (or initially at least the relieving) of offensive discriminatory measures; the recognition of the residential rights of Africans who for all practical purposes reside permanently in the RSA; the Government's growing willingness to enter into dialogue with black leaders on the accommodation of the political aspirations of Africans; recognition of the right of Africans to be involved at the highest level of government in decision making regarding their own interest; the irreversible accommodation of Africans, coloureds and Indians in the South African economy; the increasing general upward mobility of Africans, coloureds and Indians; a growing willingness among whites to accept Africans as full-fledged South African citizens; the new constitutional dispensation that circumvented the traditional South African "colour line", and the increase in crosscutting interests and associations that cut across the "colour line" and thus promote common interests and values.

Throughout the *Investigation* an attempt was made to follow a scientifically fair approach in which all scholarly orientations and everyone's interests were recognized. Against this background it must be concluded that the plans of particular white governments in the past for the ordering of intergroup relations have not been (could not be) fully realized, and accordingly that the *status quo* cannot be maintained. At the same time, however, it would be incorrect to infer from this that alternative policies proposed in the past would therefore necessarily have succeeded. More important though is the finding that attitudes have changed; that there are signs of a greater willingness among people of different groups to join forces and face the challenges together, and that the future belongs to those who geniunely wish to make a contribution that will serve everyone's best interests. The next and final chapter provides some leads as to the course that should be followed.

CHAPTER 6

FUNDAMENTAL PREREQUISITES FOR CONSTRUCTIVE INTERGROUP RELATIONS

The foregoing evaluation of intergroup relations has confirmed that serious tensions are hampering these relations in South African society, both with regard to the experiencing of intergroup relations and the inherent conflict-generating structures in the social order. It was shown that certain historical forces, and the human realities in South Africa, have given rise to a legitimacy crisis concerning the ordering of intergroup relations. Earlier attempts at resolving this crisis merely resulted in the whites becoming insulated from the tensions and constraints, thereby increasing the severity of the conflict. In the course of the *Investigation* four specific relations problems were identified that lie at the root of this conflict. These issues concern the elevation and *institutionalization of ethnicity* and related characteristics to the extreme that the individual is compelled to order his life within prescribed group contexts, while there are obvious *inequalities* involved in such group allocation and people eventually become *isolated and insulated* from one another.

The analyses in this report underscore the fact that, if this situation is allowed to develop further, it will become increasingly difficult to transform conflict constructively. In Chapter 5 indications were indeed found of growth points on which constructive relations could be established. This does not mean however that the solutions to South Africa's intergroup problems are either obvious or simple to implement. On the contrary, this *Investigation* has shown clearly that South Africa is a complexly segmented country in which, as a result of a variety of internal as well as external factors, intergroup relations have developed over a lengthy period to arrive at their present form. Passive acceptance of an historical determinism, according to which developments inevitably follow a particular course should, however not be inferred from this. Both the report in general and this chapter in particular in fact reflect the conviction that history will be determined by those who are willing to allow intergroup relations in South Africa to develop on a rational and democratic basis.

In this chapter certain general premises concerning the achievement of constructive intergroup relations will be dealt with first, after which fundamental prerequisities for the social system as a whole and the operationalization of these prerequisities in societal subsystems will be discussed.

ON THE ROAD TO CONSTRUCTIVE INTERGROUP RELATIONS

In any society, but especially in a plural society, the central problem is how to prevent the striving after a variety of individual and group objectives from leading to continuous strife and intergroup conflict. It is also important to ensure that the achievement of individual and group objectives will also take into account the need to maintain and promote constructive and co-operative relations with others. Particularly important in this regard is the function of the government and of society in maintaining norms in terms of which constructive intergroup relations can be developed. At the one extreme there is the type of government that, regardless of the convictions of the members or groups of society, forces a social order upon them and which therefore is not seen as legitimate. At the other extreme there is the government that uses the common values prevalent in society as the basis of the social order. Such common values can exist, despite differences in cultural values and other group interests and/or sections of the population.

Most social scientists agree that the peaceful coexistence of people in a segmented society such as that in South Africa can be promoted according to the extent that they share certain norms in respect of co-operative relations. Such common norms are based, at a more general level, on shared value orientations. At this general normative level conciliation and accommodation are particularly important, since they also protect the right of groups to have their own outlook on life.

An overriding conclusion of this report is that a shared value system must be promoted with a view to achieving the goals of constructive human relations. The central question therefore is whether there is sufficient consensus among South Africans regarding a desirable social order to enable these shared value orientations to serve as a basis for common set of norms. The results of this *Investigation* indicate that this is in fact potentially the case insofar as (a) general religious values are subscribed to, with recognition and protection of freedom of religion and worship (see Work Committee : Religion); (b) recognize the importance of civil rights in terms of common law (see Work Committee : Juridical aspects); (c), recognize the individual's right to economic freedom (see Work

Committee : Economy and labour); (d) recognize the right to democratic participation in decision making (see Work Committee : Race, ethnicity and culture). The effect of the acceptance of these generally binding values will be enhanced if they can be coupled with other binding factors such as common interests, interdependence and an identification with the South African socio-political order, thus presupposing a common loyalty and common symbols.

In view of the above perspective of society the following shared experiences and perceptions were identified as a basis for constructive intergroup relations:

- Common experience of and resistance to any form of colonialization
- Inclusion and participation in the same economic system
- Widespread realization of economic interdependence
- A fair amount of common ground in language usage
- Sufficient space and resources to ensure everyone of a reasonable standard of living
- Relatively sophisticated infrastructures in the public and private sectors, for instance the public service, education, health services, mass media, transport
- A general rejection of violence and an equally general acceptance of peaceful negotiation as a means of settling differences.

Against this background and looking towards the development and promotion of constructive human relations, it is true to say that the future has already begun for South Africa. In any discussion of presumed development and change it is of vital importance to determine whether meaningful change has in fact begun, or whether no move at all has been made. From the findings of different work committees as indicated in Chapters 3 and 4, it appears that a process of change in South Africa has indeed begun. The trade union movement, for instance, signals a completely different labour dispensation and is already making its presence felt, while the rapid urbanization of Africans is already in progress. Change is not something that will happen only in the distant future. Above all there is an observable change in people's views regarding intergroup relations, including a greater willingness to accept such things as the repeal of discriminatory race laws. In any discussion on the move towards constructive intergroup relations it should be borne in mind that a variety of forces are already active in this regard. In this sense the future is less unknown than is generally thought.

PREREQUISITES FOR CONSTRUCTIVE INTERGROUP RELATIONS

When considering the promotion of constructive intergroup relations, it is necessary first to specify what conditions the social system as a whole must comply with in order to ensure such relations. In the introduction to this chapter it was stated that constructive relations must be based on a common system of values, a precondition for which is the existence or development of a conciliation-oriented conception of social order which is shared by as many members of the population as possible.

A particularly important implication of the search for a common value system is the problem of *individualism* versus *group orientation*. As a social being the individual always functions in a group context in order to satisfy his needs, but this does not mean that the individual's needs and the objectives of the group always coincide. The main aim, however, remains the optimal fulfilment of the individual's needs. As a result of the development *inter alia* of these needs and aspirations it is essential that the individual should have freedom of movement between groups and be able to change his membership and affiliations. However, when the individual's group membership is determined on the basis of such characteristics as ethnicity or race, equal opportunity for the optimal fulfilment of needs no longer exist — as was clearly shown by the inequalities mentioned in Chapter 2. The basic problem in a plural society therefore revolves around the accommodation of everyone's rights, privileges and security at an individual as well as group level. In this process the relation between the individual's experiencing of his position in society, and the structuring of intergroup relations should also be taken into account, and the structuring, which is necessary in any society, should be done in as positive and constructive a manner as possible.

In a relatively homogeneous society all that is required is the protection of the individual's interests. The present research has shown that in South Africa provision has been made for group interests at the expense of individual interests. Where group interests do not fully correspond with those of the individual, and likewise where all individuals do not identify equally strongly with a group, as was indeed indicated in Chapter 3, it necessarily follows that the individual can be discriminated against in relation to others in the group unless his interests are explicitly protected. The recognition of individual interests can indeed be regarded as a fundamental condition for dynamic and voluntary group identification. By the same token the recognition of individual interests does not mean the denial of group interests. The research findings underline the need for equal recognition to be given to both individual and group.

The above approach is closely related to the view that groups, even when voluntarily formed, already by the mere fact of their existence have an influence on other people and groups. This furthermore means that when a change occurs in one group, for instance a drastic change in the level of prosperity, this will have a systematic effect on the other groups. From another point of view this also means that the different levels or segments of the social system are mutually dependent: government presupposes opposition; citizenry has meaning only in relation to government, etc.

Group recognition, however, has a negative connotation for many people in South Africa because the statutory discrimination still largely present in South Africa is *inter alia* linked to group recognition and unequal opportunities. Consequently a legal measure such as the Group Areas Act which in itself is not necessarily discriminatory, in terms of the allocation of a scarce resource nevertheless has a discriminatory effect within the broader sociopolitical dispensation. An important precondition for group recognition in South Africa should therefore be the introduction of equal opportunities for all, and the removal of group-based discrimination. A further requirement would be that group recognition should not lead to group domination of any nature whatsoever in the political system.

Differences between people and groups are not denied in the above analysis but, as confirmed by various of the work committees, the socio-ethical prescription regarding every individual's right to equal treatment in the allocation of collective benefits as well as before the law is hereby recognized. It was evident from the research that despite *bona fide* intentions the goal of "separate but equal" simply cannot be achieved. To the extent that this basic requirement is not complied with, it is just not practically possible to guarantee everyone's rights, privileges and security at both individual and group level — thus making the chances of reducing polarization in intergroup relations very slight.

Research also showed that social identification can operate at more than one level, and that identification at the ethnic level does not exclude the possibility of identification with a broader South African order. But when the aim is wider involvement and inclusion at a higher level of identification, attention must also be paid to a common loyalty, which immediately gives rise to the question of shared symbols: Society as a whole will necessarily have to decide on a set of common symbols in order to accomplish involvement. This matter gains in importance when it is remembered that, to those groups currently excluded from participation, many of the existing symbols represent exclusion rather than inclusion.

Achieving a balance between individual and group interests in general terms requires a social system that allows for all members of the population to realize their reasonable aspirations within a democratic framework, with full recognition of the human dignity of all its members.

In a plural society achievement of the above ideals will depend upon the following *basic requirements* which should be read in relation to one another:

- Freedom of association with other individuals and groups, which includes the right to non-association. In other words, according to this basic precondition group formation should be the result of voluntary association, while at the same time the right of a group thus formed to decide itself who should have access to the group should also be recognised.

- The right to participate in decision-making processes in the public arena.

- Equal opportunities for the realization of every individual's potential.

- Legitimization, i.e. the establishment of public institutions that are worthy of trust and acceptance.

- The recognition of the human dignity of all members of society.

- In view of the plural character of South African society, the recognition and observance of group identity.

These six requirements should furthermore be tested against two overriding criteria, namely

- that all essential change should occur in a co-operative and constructive, i.e. non-violent way, and
- that development should be carried out within the parameters of what is economically feasible.

These requirements were not randomly determined. From the research results of the different work committees referred to in Chapters 3 and 4, it appears that such conditions can count on wide support and are in fact endorsed by important sections of the population.

The application of these requirements to the different fields of South African society implies *inter alia* the following:

- The political order should enable everyone domiciled within the area of jurisdiction of a given political subsystem to participate in one way or another in the decision-making process at local, regional and national level.

- The economic system should make provision for growth and development in order to provide for the reasonable needs of a growing and modernizing society. The system should also offer equal opportunities for everyone.

- The social system should enable people to maintain personal, family and community relationships.

- The juridical system should make provision for the restitution and protection of juridical values in terms of common law.

- The religious system should make provision for the establishment and application of generaly valid religious values.

162

- The education system should make provision for the establishment and propagation of common values.

- The communication system should make provision for freedom of information dissemination among all components of the social system.

In the light of these general objectives it can now be indicated briefly how these basic conditions could be realized in the different fields of society. A more comprehensive treatment of these conditions can be found in the work committee reports. The various fields will be discussed in the same order as above.

FIELD OF POLITICS

- Politically and constitutionally intergroup relations in South Africa must be given expression within a democratic framework and secured within a fundamental legal order. This condition presupposes an underlying faith and confidence in the principles of democracy and in the ability of such a system to accommodate and protect the interests of groups, as it is only through sustained faith and vision that the processes of negotiation and consensus can maintain momentum and possible revolutionary action be averted.

- The conditions for a participating democracy within a fundamental legal system presuppose, on the one hand, the establishment of a system which by means of participation, representation and joint authority offers all citizens the right to realize their political claims and aspirations. On the other hand, a legal system is presupposed that provides assurances on protection and safety at a deeper level than the normal rivalry between different political groups and actors. Such a participating democracy secured within a fundamental legal order cannot yet be realized in South Africa, since the majority of the population have not yet had the opportunity to realize their political aspirations and the legal order is as yet unentrenched. Full participation in political deliberation is currently still inhibited, or even prohibited in various ways, and is hampered to such an extent by a system of population registration that free political association and voluntary handling of own interests are not possible. These factors thwart the prospects for a participating democracy and should be reconsidered.

- The present system of government is based on the separation of group interests into "own" and "general" affairs. This policy of separation rests on the assumption that the different races or colour groups in themselves and predeterminedly are the propagators of particular interests and claims. In the light of the analyses in this chapter the stressing of deliberation and consensus and the protection of own affairs and interests will increasingly occur on a basis of voluntary association (and the implied possibility of forming political alliances). To ensure community autonomy and to give political meaning and content to the principle of group accommodation on the bases of consensus and protection of identity, the greatest possible degree of devolution of authority to regional and local levels will have to be accomplished.

• It is not the aim of this report to prescribe what system of government would be the most appropriate for South Africa's plural society, for the very reason that this should be the product of deliberation and negotiation between all the population categories. In this regard attention can only be directed at a number of pitfalls that may inhibit the establishment of a participating democracy, namely the entrenchment and centralization of power, the exclusion of recognized political leaders from the negotiating processes, the propagation of a system where winner takes all and the retention of institutions which, on the basis of race and colour discrimination, are regarded and experienced as inferior and subordinate. In brief, democratization in South Africa calls for a willingness to co-operate and compromise in all fields of society.

ECONOMICS AND LABOUR

In the economic sphere there are four interrelated objectives that must be achieved in order to reduce conflict and promote collective interests, namely the effective combating of poverty, the achievement of the highest possible economic growth rate, the granting of economic opportunities to all groups and classes, and the accommodation of workers' claims. These objectives can only be achieved in a climate of greater political equality. The following guidelines are provided for achieving these objectives:

• Since South Africa is not a very wealthy country, continuing economic growth is essential. In order to promote constructive intergroup relations, this growth must lead to greater equality at both individual and group level.

• In view of the above, access to key economic resources should not be determined by ascriptive group membership.

• The complete removal of statutory job reservation should be regarded as a matter of urgency. The effective equalization of educational opportunities will facilitate equal access to skills. In this regard the private sector (both employers and trade unions) should ensure that all workers have access to skilled supervisory, technical and management positions. To achieve this a change in organizational structure will be required.

• Access to capital: While the opening of some central business districts to all race groups has been widely welcomed, all economic restrictions should be abolished. The Group Areas Act should not be used to regulate the occupation of industrial and commercial land.

• Access to land: Apart from the deregulation of the economic use of urban land, the economic activities of members of other groups in white rural areas (and *vice versa*) should also be deregulated.

• Since the large-scale formal sector of the economy is unlikely to expand rapidly enought to absorb all job seekers, the small-scale non-formal sector should be offered every opportunity to create jobs for these people — this calls for the complete deregulation of this sector.

In view of the extent of poverty in South Africa, social and preventive health services should be developed and large public work schemes (for instance housing schemes) instituted.

Since it was accepted in this report that the interdependence of the different groups is a feature of South African society, it follows that the development of all these groups is an important prerequisite for constructive intergroup relations. Consequently it is essential that consensus be reached by all those concerned on specific development objectives. At the same time the dependence of one group on another should be avoided so that each group can develop its human potential to the greatest possible degree.

The following guidelines are provided in respect of labour relations:

• When a participating political system has been introduced, steps should be taken to make labour relations a field of autonomous interaction between groups.

• *Bona fide* activities relating to labour relations should be free of political and state security intervention.

• The existing institutions (such as the industrial councils) for the settling of disputes should accommodate their new partners in such a way that their needs are satisfied.

• There is an urgent need for mutually acceptable conventions regarding the use of both strikes and exclusion as bargaining instruments; such conventions should be developed by organized labour together with employers.

• Both employers' and employees' organizations should be strengthened in respect of degree of representation, internal unity, co-ordination and resources available to them.

• Constructive intergroup relations will be promoted to the extent that employers' and employees' organizations can be regarded as representative of employers and employees of all groups in South African society.

SPATIAL ORDERING

In spatial ordering, in other words the procedure according to which a given inhabitant of a country is allocated a place where he may achieve self-realization, it should be borne in mind that in a human being's life space is closely and reciprocally linked to his identity; his feeling of security and safety; his lifestyle, and his loyalties.

• Spatial ordering should allow individuals, groups and institutions the greatest possible freedom of choice, while not infringing on the freedom of choice of other individuals, groups and institutions.

165

- Spatial ordering should give recognition to the required freedom of movement of all the inhabitants of the country.

- Spatial ordering should give recognition to the variety of demographic, historical, social and other relevant factors that characterize the settlement patterns of individuals and groups.

- Spatial ordering should, as far as possible, be based on decision making and management at the regional and local authority levels.

- The following guidelines are provided for the operationalization of the above:

- The authorities should encourage renewal in spatial ordering at all levels of government by means of effective communication.

- The administration of spatial ordering should be accessible and controllable.

- Accommodation of conflicting choices and preferences of different individuals/groups/institutions should be accomplished by means of positive persuasion and negotiation rather than through statutory restrictions.

JURIDICAL FIELD

As a general guideline the South African legal system must be inbued with the fundamental qualities of justice and equality through an active programme of legal reform. With a view to promoting good intergroup relations, the legal system ought to be reformed in order to carry out in letter and in spirit the injunction contained in the preamble to the Republic of South Africa Constitution Act 110 of 1983. The following goals, in particular, should be pursued in this regard:

- To uphold Christian values and civilized norms, with recognition and protection of freedom of faith and worship,

- To uphold the independence of the judiciary and the equality of all under the law,

- To further the contentment and the spiritual and material welfare of all,

- To respect and to protect human dignity, life, liberty and property of all,

- To further private initiative and effective competition.

The South African legal system is suspect among large parts of the population because, on the one hand, the administration of justice is controlled by whites and, on the other, because, as a result of various economic, language and other factors, legal processes and administration as well as penal and litigation procedures have become inaccessible and incomprehensible to many. This legitimacy crisis in the legal system will have to be resolved systematically through training, legal aid, guidance and reform, since mistrust of a legal system is one of the strongest incentives for revolution.

It is in the national interest that the security of the state be protected by the law. However, when the application of legislation aimed at ensuring the security of the state is veiled in secrecy and marred by a lack of control, thereby creating opportunities for the suppression of political freedom, the existence and application of security legislation in itself pose a threat to the security of the state. Consequently security legislation should be applied with the greatest degree of caution, control and responsibility.

RELIGION

From the basic conditions for constructive intergroup relations that were set out earlier in this chapter, it appeared that a common value system was vitally important for South African society. Insofar as one of religion's fundamental functions is to give "meaning" to man's existence, it can be expected of religious movements that they make a positive contribution in this respect. This includes the instilling of "overriding" values, extending across the boundaries of other divisions in society, and the establishment of a framework within which differences can be used creatively to accomplish reconciliation between individuals and groups. This ideal can only be achieved, however, if the demand for justice is met, as this forms the basis of such a value system.

In view of the above, more specific attention will have to be paid to the following matters:

● The legitimacy of particular group interests should frequently be tested against certain shared religious criteria, for if discrepancies arise at this level religion can contribute to an increase in tension and even become a motivating force for open and violent conflict.

● The restriction of religion to the personal sphere, and the inability to relate religious values to other fields of society, are factors that inhibit religion from making a constructive contribution towards socio-economic equity.

● Religious movements have the special task of building bridges in a polarized society and of reducing tensions in their own ranks as well as in the broader context. It is of vital importance that denominational differences and the implacable way in which differences of opinion are often articulated should not blind people to common values at a deeper level. These values on which there appears to be remarkable consensus, will have to serve as the departure point for renewed deliberation on the basic norms that should apply to any future social dispensation in South Africa.

- The above underlines the urgent need for the restitution of ecumenical relations. Contact and dialogue between churches and religious movements should be vigorously pursued at all levels and in formal as well as informal ways.

- The relation between church and state calls for urgent attention with a view to the fulfilment of the former's prophetic calling.

- Religious movements are, therefore, faced with the challenge of propagating a common vision for a new South Africa, and of playing a mediating role between the idealized future and the present reality. This can only be achieved by concentrating on hopeful signs of change rather than on the divisions existing in South African society.

Furthermore, order and stability can only be maintained on the basis of justice. All measures will have to be tested against this criterion so that they can play a role in bringing about a more just society.

EDUCATION

Disparities in the provision of education can easily result in negative intergroup relations as they can be experienced as a reflection of unequal chances for progress and self-realization. When the subsystems in the provision of education for the various population groups also largely function in isolation so that mutual understanding, sympathy and assistance fail to materialize, the results are prejudice, mistrust, competition and isolation. In a country such as the RSA with its deeply segmented and heterogeneous population, differential population growth and limited high-level manpower and resources, the provision of equal educational opportunities is a virtually unattainable goal — even countries like the USA and Britain have not yet been able to accomplish this for their minority groups. The mere realization of the universal and complex nature of this problem by all South Africans so that everybody can co-operate positively in solving the problem instead of exploiting it for political gain would contribute towards improving intergroup relations.

The HSRC Investigation into Education did not give particular attention to intergroup relations, although the proposed educational reforms will increasingly influence these relations. Viewed from an intergroup relations perspective, education has three extremely important tasks: To obtain legitimacy and acceptance, promote good intergroup relations and create interaction and co-operation between representatives of the various education subsystems.

OBTAINING LEGITIMACY AND ACCEPTANCE FOR THE PROVISION OF EDUCATION

Education for Africans in particular, is in a period of crisis. To obtain the desired legitimacy, the policy guidelines proposed in the HSRC Education Report which plead for the introduction of education of equal quality for all residents of the RSA (as discussed in chapter 4) are here again confirmed. These guidelines naturally also have a bearing on South African society at large. The new statutory framework designed for educational reforms — particularly those relating to policy, the establishment of central advisory and decision-making bodies and the introduction of mechanisms for establishing equal norms and standards (including finance) — will hopefully contribute towards eliminating disparities and giving educational decision making and provision more credibility. A question that must also receive attention is whether a single education department, (with education management at national, regional and local levels) controlled professionally rather than politically, would not offer a better long-term solution, to a great extent removing education from the political arena.

In two strategic fields (in addition to many others) the improvement of the provision of education and intergroup relations are very closely related. Firstly, the provision of education will have to make room for the establishment and government subsidizing of *private initiative,* which would expedite the expansion of services achieve, the depoliticization of intergroup co-operation and facilitate the provision of education for underprivileged groups. Secondly, the introduction of a *medium of instruction other than the mother tongue in the case of African schools is a very sensitive matter which could harm intergroup relations because of the accompanying tension, opposition and misunderstanding. It is clear that education for Africans cannot be improved qualitatively unless the use of either of the two official languages is improved. The expertise available in white education in this regard is indispensable, and should be made use of.*

THE PROMOTION OF GOOD INTERGROUP RELATIONS THROUGH EDUCATION

Next to family life, education is the main socializer of children with regard to the cultivation and inculcation of attitudes towards intergroup relations. Anything that institutionalizes, and thus perpetuates prejudice and stereotyping in education should be eliminated. Subject matter in syllabuses and learning situations that promote prejudice should be removed and terminated respectively. Behaviour by teachers that could lead to poor intergroup relations should be regarded as unprofessional and appropriate disciplinary steps should be taken.

Education should aim at cultivating better understanding between groups. In this regard, for example, there is an urgent need for a comprehensive, general history of South Africa in which the roles of all the groups (both "ethnic" and "class") and the interaction between them are reflected in an objective, balanced manner. Education should also be used to promote skills that are essential for constructive intergroup relations in a multicultural country. Next to skills and empathy, practical language abilities are needed to facilitate communication. Education should present to one group the history and cultural background of other cultural groups and at least a third language on a regional basis. The general guideline should therefore be that, in the general socializing of new generations of South Africans, attention should be given to what is universally human — in other words, what makes the groups in South Africa dependent on each other.

THE CREATION OF INTERACTION AND CO-OPERATION

Between representatives of the individual subsystems of education from the level of national administration to local and trainee level is a prerequisite for the realization of the above aims. For the sake of sound intergroup relations, education at all levels should contribute towards intersocial, intercultural and intersports activities. The following could perhaps serve as points of departure in this regard:

• Because all parents are interested in the success of their children, communication between parents' associations could contribute towards mutual understanding and assistance, especially in the field of informal educational support.

• Communication and co-operation between representatives of umbrella teachers' associations have already proved successful and should be extended.

• In the HSRC Education Report co-operative educational service centres, at national and regional level, were recommended with a view to making services and scarce, highly trained relief personnel readily available to the education community. Although this recommendation was rejected by Government, it should be reconsidered as these educational service centres could ameliorate serious problems in education and help with intergroup liaison and aid — especially with regard to assistance in the teaching of "scarce" subjects such as Mathematics and Physical Science.

• Migration of population means that schools and hostels of certain population groups will be unused or under utilized, while those of other groups in the same area will be overutilized. The making available (or sharing) of these underutilized facilities (e.g. sports facilities) for use by other groups is something that should be encouraged. It can only succeed if there is agreement among local parents' and teachers' associations.

COMMUNICATION SYSTEM

In this report it was indicated that there was limited communication between members of the different groups. This finding should be seen in relation to the fact that communication and constructive intergroup relations in certain respects are different sides of the same coin. The importance of communication can accordingly be seen in the various facets of intergroup relations discussed so far. The following specific preconditions, which are applicable to all levels and sections of society, can contribute towards the promotion of constructive intergroup relations:

● Communication channels should be created between members of all the population groups and, in cases where such channels already exist, they should be used effectively. According to this precondition interested persons should make creative use of opportunities for intergroup communication, and where such opportunities are lacking they should be created in consultation with the people concerned. This does not imply that communication is a guarantee for constructive intergroup relations: success can only be assured by the sincerity of the approach and content of what is communicated. Experience has shown, however, that the lack of or a breakdown in communication leads to a deterioration in intergroup relations.

This condition is applicable to all levels and sections of society. There can be little doubt that the need to create open communication channels should be a top priority at government and leadership level. For optimal effectiveness, however, it is essential that all those involved should have a say in the way in which such communication channels will function. The need for open communication channels is by no means limited to the government level. The indications are that such channels are beginning to function efficiently at the labour level although much still needs to be done, for example in the field of communication skills. The need for opportunities to communicate extends especially to the level of the school-going youth who will grow up isolated and insulated unless contact is promoted at this level.

● The efficient use of communication channels requires some show of willingness on the part of the participants to achieve the stated objectives. Communication involves far more than the mere conveying of views — it entails a genuine search for points of contact.

● The development of communication skills should be regarded as a priority. In view of the multicultural nature of the population it must be assumed that such communication makes considerably greater demands on the participants than would normally be the case. It is therefore essential that all persons who are regularly in negotiating situations should be optimally prepared in respect of the skills that are required.

However this precondition extends much further. On the one hand, education and the mass media should be used to promote communication skills among all groups at all levels. On the other hand, the large spectrum of languages in South Africa requires that urgent attention be paid to the recognition of a third official language on a regional basis.

● Within the context of this and the preceding condition, attention should be focused on the noticeable lack of communication specialists trained to perform a mediating function in conflict situations. This matter also requires urgent attention.

Because of their widespread use and specific nature, the mass media should strive to a greater extent to reflect the widest possible spectrum of views on groups and their mutual relations. In this respect the media indeed have a mediating role to play, provided that a conscious attempt is made to avoid stereotyped and biased representations of people, groups and intergroup relations. This also implies the need for more equitable representation of the different groups in media management.

CONCLUSION

The realities of South African intergroup relations are particularly complex. During the *Investigation* it was found that these realities accordingly could not be explained in terms of straightforward models; in fact no single comprehensive model could be found that satisfactorily included all the most important dimensions of this issue or that could be used as a guideline for the ordering of intergroup relations.

On reading the report the question may arise as to whether the politically dominant white community will be able to retain sufficient control of the situation to curb developments that may lead to black domination. The question may also arise whether revolutionary conflict is not the only way in which white and black will reach accommodation.

The potential crisis situations implied by the above questions were examined in the findings of the *Investigation,* and particularly in the relevant work committee reports. It would be both foolish and irresponsible to shrug off concern at the possibility of such crisis situations arising as paranoia — hence the attempt to outline the obstacles on the road to accommodative and co-operative intergroup relations in a democratic social order. However, there are still many positive forces in South African society that can be used as a basis for a democratic social dispensation. This will at least reduce conflict to manageable proportions and persuade the interest groups concerned of the benefits of pursuing co-operative, rather than confrontation-based, policies.

The conclusion reached in this report is therefore that the political ordering of intergroup relations according to the original apartheid model has reached an impasse and that constructive relations cannot be developed further along these lines. On the basis of the analysis in Chapters 2, 3 and 4; the interpretations in Chapter 5 and the views put forward in this chapter, it is clear that moderate forces must be mobilized if intergroup relations are to develop positively in a conciliatory and mutually accommodating way.

On several occasions it was stated that time is a vital factor in the development of constructive intergroup relations. Any plan for the ordering of such relations must include a time perspective, indicating which steps will be carried out over roughly what period. One dominant fact remains however: The relations between groups in South Africa is a crucial matter that demands the most urgent attention. Delays in addressing the issue could have catastrophic consequences.

NOTES

Africans — the Africans of South Africa (also referred to as Blacks or "Bantu") representing various ethnologically and linguistically heterogeneous groups.

African National Congress (ANC) — political organization formed in 1912 to protect and promote the interests of South African Blacks. Until 1923 it was known as the South African Native National Congress. The present (1986) leader of the ANC is Mr Oliver Tambo.

Afrikaners — the largest White group in South Africa, direct descendents of the Dutch, French and German settlers. In the 1830's many left the Cape Colony and founded two new states, the Orange Free State and Transvaal Republic. In the 19th century the Afrikaners were known as the Boers (i.e. farmers). The Afrikaans language is derived from Dutch.

Anglo Boer Wars — the Boers and the British were involved in two major clashes, from 1880 to 1881 and from 1899 to 1902.

Apartheid — originally known as segregation, apartheid became a National Party political slogan in the 1940's. In the 1950's the policy became known as separate development.

AZAPO — short for Azanian People's Organization. A Black interest group strongly opposed to apartheid and the South African Government. It is strongly associated with the Black consciousness movement in South Africa, placing strong emphasis on Black freedom, African socialism and majority rule within a unitary socialist worker state called Azania (the ancient Phoenician name for Southern Africa). The present (1986) leader of AZAPO is Mr S. Cooper.

Belhar Confession — draft confession submitted to the Dutch Reformed Mission Church (NG Sendingkerk) on their synod in Belhar (Cape Town) in which any forced segregation on racial grounds was declared a false doctrine.

Black Alliance — a loose association of Black leaders and interest groups, primarily Black homeland leaders, opposed to apartheid, particularly the fragmentation of South Africa into small Black states. The Alliance advocates full citizenship for Black South Africans in a single state.

Boer Republics — the Orange Free State (1854-1902) and the Transvaal Republic (1852-1877; 1881-1902).

Difaqane — the forced migration of great numbers of Africans in the wake of the Zulu king Shaka's wars of annihilation (the latter known as the *mfecane*).

Frontier wars — from 1779 to 1878, nine wars occurred on the eastern border of the Cape Colony between the inhabitants and the Xhosa tribes.

Homelands — the historical and traditional loci of Black settlement in South Africa. These areas form nine geographical clusters associated with the country's nine main black ethnic groups. These groups (and the names of their respective homelands) are: Zulu (KwaZulu), Xhosa (Transkei and Ciskei), Swazi (KaNgwane), Southern Sotho (Qwa-Qwa), Northern Sotho (Lebowa), Tswana (Bophuthatswana), Shangaan-Tsonga (Gazankulu), Venda (Venda), and Ndebele (KwaNdebele). Four of these homelands have attained independence — not officially recognised by other countries — since 1976: Transkei, Bophuthatswana, Venda and Ciskei.

HSRC Investigation into Education — (HSRC Education Report; De Lange Commission) an investigation commissioned by Government in June 1980. Most of the recommendations have been incorporated in subsequent legislation. The chairperson of the investigation was Prof. J.P. de Lange. Main committee of the HSRC Investigation into Education, *Provision of Education in the RSA*. Pretoria: HSRC, 1981. Eighteen subreports were also published.

HSRC Sports Investigation — an investigation commissioned by Government in October 1979; chairperson was Prof. G.L.J. Scholtz. Main Committee of the HSRC Sport Investigation, *Sport in the RSA*. Pretoria: HSRC, 1982. Twenty subreports were also published.

Inkatha — a predominantly Zulu cultural organization founded by KwaZulu Chief Minister Mangosuthu Buthelezi. With a membership of more than a million, Inkatha claims to serve as a watchdog over the socio-cultural interests of the Zulu people — South Africa's largest ethnic group.

Khoikhoi — the Khoikhoi ("men of men") were nomadic pasturalists.

Lord Scarman — was commissioned by the British government to investigate the Brixton disorders of April 1981. *The Brixton disorders 10-12 April 1981*. London: Her Majesty's Stationery Office, 1981.

Multipurpose survey — two multipurpose surveys on national samples of the African, Coloured, Indian and White population groups were undertaken for the HSRC Investigation into Intergroup Relations. Complex probability samples of a thousand respondents each were drawn. Specially trained interviewers of the same population group as the respondents undertook the field work. In addition, three smaller surveys were also commissioned.

Nkomati Accord — a bilateral agreement between the Republic of South Africa and Mozambique signed on 16 March 1984 by the two heads of state. The accord provides for co-operative relations between the signatory states in various areas of mutual interest.

"Own" versus "general affairs" — relate to the new tricameral parliament's constitutional obligation to differentiate between two broad categories of interests: firstly — matters which specially and differentially affect a population group in relation to the maintenance of its identity and the upholding of its way of life, culture, traditions and customs; and secondly — matters normally deemed to be of national import and therefore of concern to the citizenry at large. In terms of this arrangement each of the three population groups represented in Parliament (Whites, Coloureds and Indians) has the competence to legislate separately for own affairs but conjointly in the field of national affairs. Parliamentary authority over own affairs is vested in the three chambers of Parliament: the House of Assembly (Whites), the House of Representatives (Coloureds), and the House of Delegates (Indians).

Pan Africanist Congress (PAC) — political organization founded in 1959 as a militant offshoot of the ANC, exclusively for Blacks and in favour of African unity. The present (1986) leader of the PAC is Mr John Mhlambo.

Reserves — areas exclusively inhabited by Africans; later known as Black homelands.

SALDRU — South African Labour and Development Research Unit, School of Economics, University of Cape Town.

San — the San (also known as the "Bushmen"), a nomadic people who originally roamed the greater part of Southern Africa. They are a predominantly hunting and foodgathering people.

South African Plan for Research in the Human Sciences (SAPRHS) — a plan of action agreed to by universities and the HSRC for the initiation, stimulation, co-ordination and funding of human sciences research including basic and applied, free or self-initiated as well as problem-oriented research.

Steyn Commission — the Commission of Inquiry into the Mass Media, appointed in June 1980 under chairmanship of Judge M.T. Steyn. The *Report of Commission of Inquiry into the Mass Media,* was published in 1981.

SWAPO — South West African People's Organization. A predominantly

Ovambo organization, SWAPO was founded to pursue the independence of the former South African mandate. Its leader, Mr Sam Njoma, opposes the South African administration in Namibia and has committed SWAPO to an organized quest for independence including armed struggle.

Theron report — *Report of the Commission of Inquiry into matters relating to the Coloured population group.* Pretoria: Government Printer, 1976. The Commission under the chairmanship of Prof. Erika Theron was appointed in 1973 to investigate the position of the Coloured population category within the broader South African society. Published in 1976, the report recommended a greater commitment from the government towards the socio-economic upliftment of the Coloured people as well as towards the realization of their political aspirations.

Union (of South Africa) — The Union of South Africa was founded in 1910 through the unification of four British colonies: the Cape Province, Natal, and the two former Boer Republics, viz. the Orange Free State and the Transvaal. These four former colonies subsequently became the four provinces of the Union.

United Democratic Front (UDF) — A cluster of interest groups united in their opposition to the National Party Government. Claiming the support of more than two million people spread over almost 650 affiliate organizations, the UDF claims to pursue the ideal of a united, non-racial, democratic South African socio-political order. Most of the UDF's affiliate organizations have a predominantly Black membership. The presidents (1986) of the UDF are Mr Archie Gumede and Mrs Albertina Sisulu.

Van der Walt Commission of Inquiry — Prof. Tjaart van der Walt was appointed by the Government as a one-man commission shortly after a wave of riots erupted (in September 1984) in some of the Black residential areas of the Pretoria-Witwatersrand-Vereeniging region. *Report on the investigation into education for Blacks in the Vaal Triangle following upon the occurrences of 3 September 1984 and thereafter.* Pretoria: Government Printer, 1986.

Whites — the Whites of South Africa are not a homogeneous group, but consist of Afrikaans- and English-speaking people, a large Portuguese community as well as immigrants from several other Western countries.

Wiehahn Commission — Commission of Inquiry into labour legislation, appointed under the chairmanship of Prof. Nic Wiehahn in 1977 to investigate the modernization and democratization of labour relations in South Africa, with special emphasis on the position of African workers. The Wiehahn Report laid the groundwork for South Africa's current labour relations legislation including the scrapping of most of the country's race discriminatory labour practices such as job reservation. *Report of the Commission of Inquiry into Labour Legislation.* Pretoria: Government Printer, 1979.

LIST OF WORK COMMITTEE REPORTS

Work Committee: Historical aspect: *Intergroup relations as portrayed in the South African historiography* *

Work Committee: Juridical aspect: *Law and justice in intergroup relations* *

Work Committee: Social dimensions: *The structure of the South African society* *

Work Committee: Religion: *Religion, intergroup relations and social change in South Africa* •

Work Committee: Developmental aspect: *Balanced development in South Africa* •

Work Committee: Communication: *Communication in a divided society* •

Work Committee: Social Psychological aspect: *The social psychology of intergroup relations* *

Work Committee: Economics and labour: *Growth, equity and participation* *

Work Committee: Constitution and politics: *Political co-operation within a fundamental legal order* •

Work Committee: Race, ethnicity and culture: *The politics of ethnicity/race* *

* In print
• Published

LIST OF PROJECT REPORTS

Adam, H. *Technocratic liberation: Intergroup relations in South Africa.*

Appelgryn, A. & Nieuwoudt, J.M. *Relatiewe deprivasie, militantheid en etniese houdings in Suid-Afrika.*

Basson, A.F. *Reklame en tussengroepverhoudinge in Suid-Afrika.*

Baxter, L.G. *A permanent administrative law commission for South Africa.*

Bekker, J.C., Dlamini, C.R.M., Dhlodhlo, A.E.B., Paramanand, S.K., Van den Berg, N.J.C. & Kemp, K.J. *Regspleging t.o.v. Swartes (met spesiale verwysing na Natal en KwaZulu.)*

Bekker, S. *Principles for spatial arrangement*

Benjamin, P.S. *The participation of Black trade unions in the Industrial Council System.*

Beukes, T.J.N. *Die grondwetlike hantering van tussengroepverhoudinge langs die weg van polities-ruimtelike ordening.*

Beyers, E. *Sosiaal-sielkundige teorieë oor tussengroepverhoudinge.*

Boulle, L.J. *Participatory democracy and the administration — South African prospects.*

Boulle, L.J. *Spatial arrangement: Juridical perspectives.*

Coetzee, J.H. *Volkekundige perspektief op ruimtelike ordening.*

Coetzee, J.K. *Religie as inisieerder, begeleier en inhibeerder van sosiale verandering.*

Coetzee, J.K. *Tussengroepverhoudinge binne die sosiale struktuur.*

Coetzee, T.F. *Die betekenis en effek van 'n regsubjek se ras in die Suid-Afrikaanse strafreg.*

Collins, P.H.D. *The ethnic factor in South African politics.*

Cornwell, R.J. *The dependency theorists' view of South African development.*

Crafford, D. *Pluralisme as religieuse verskynsel: die onafhanklike Swart kerke en bewegings en groepsverhoudings in Suid-Afrika.*

Cumpsty, J.S., Hofmeyer, J.H. & Kruss, G. *The role of religion in motivating or inhibiting socio-political action in the lower socio-economic group and ensuing counter influences upon the religious group.*

De Beer, A.S. *Massamediakommunikatore en mediatoeganklikheid.*

De Beer, F.C. *Die uitwerking van die Administrasieraad Noord-Transvaal (ARNT) se metode van hervestiging op tussengroepverhoudinge. 'n Gevallestudie.*

De Beer, F.C. *Hervestiging en tussengroepverhoudinge: 'n Literatuurondersoek.*

Duckitt, J.H. *Psychological theories of prejudice: An empirical assessment among White South Africans.*

Dugard, C.J.R. *Intergroup conflict as a result of the discrepancy between international law and South African law.*

Du Plessis, L.M. *The law as a regulator and/or manager of conflict, particularly in ethnically plural societies.*

Du Toit, D.A. *Menseregte: 'n empiriese en teoretiese ondersoek vanuit teologies-etniese perspektief.*

Edwards, D.J.A. *Black identity in Grahamstown and Ciskei: a psychological investigation.*

Ehlers, J.H. *Attitude of a group of White artisans and technicians towards vertical job mobility of other population groups.*

Esterhuyse, W.P. *'n Monitor van politieke geweld en gehoorsaamheid — oorsake en bydraende faktore.*

Esterhuysen, R. *Persepsies van en houdings jeens misdaad, wette en komponente van die strafregstelsel: 'n tussengroepvergelyking.*

Fair, T.J.D. *The South African national spatial system — process, structure, trends and strategy.*

Finchilescu, G. *Inter-racial contact in the nursing context.*

Fourie, F.C. & Beukes, E.P. *'n Teoretiese ondersoek van aspekte van die verhouding tussen sosio-ekonomiese faktore en politieke hervorming.*

Gerryts, E.D. *Tussengroepverhoudinge in Suid-Afrika soos in 1983 in Suid-Afrikaanse koerante uitgebeeld.*

Giliomee, H. & Du Toit, A. *The history of intergroup relations and the diversity of Afrikaner political thinking until 1910.*

Gouws, A. *Ondersoek na die houding van politieke leiers (LV's) teenoor die geloofwaardigheid van die Suid-Afrikaanse pers.*

Grobbelaar, J.I., Marais, S. & Uys, T. *'n Sosio-demografiese ondersoek van die Kleurling/Griekwa-gemeenskap in Kokstad en die omliggende platteland met spesifieke klem op die moontlike bestaan van 'Griekwaskap' as 'n outonome identiteit en die bydrae van die Griekwa Nasionale Independente Kerk in dié verband.*

Grobler, J.E.H. *Etniese konflik in die politiek; die geskiedenis van die Swart politieke versetbeweging in Suid-Afrika.*

Groenewald, H.J. *Die identifisering van faktore wat konflik veroorsaak of voorkom in die interpersoonlike kommunikasie van groepe in Suid-Afrika.*

Groenewald, J.P. *Reaksies op minderheidsgroepstatus; 'n sosiologiese studie van die Kleurlinge van Kaapstad.*

Hare, A.P. *Conflict and conflict resolution in South Africa: a dramaturgical perspective.*

Herholdt, A.N.J. *'n Politieke evaluasie van die wisselwerking tussen die Republiek van Suid-Afrika en selfregerende en nasionale state, en die onafhanklike lande.*

Holden, M. *The determinants and nature of decentralized industry in South Africa.*

Holland, M. *An examination of the effects of the European community's code of conduct on intergroup relations.*

Humphries, R.G. *Aspects of administration boards.*

Humphries, R.G. *Co-operation between municipalities serving different racial groups.*

Jammine, E. *The impact of group area policy on the Coloured and Indian communities of Johannesburg.*

Janse van Rensburg, N.S. *Die belewing van etniese grense in Promosa — Potchefstroom.*

Kalis, A.C. *'n Vergelykende ondersoek na maatskaplike voorsiening aan sekere blootgestelde groepe.*

Kok, P.C. *Bevolkingsherverspreiding in die RSA: moontlike langtermynimplikasies van huidige tendense.*

Kotzé, D.A. *Administratiewe verhoudinge en tussengroepverhouding in 'n ontwikkelingskonteks, met besondere verwysing na Ciskei.*

Kotzé, D.A. & Swanepoel, H.J. *Opvattings oor ontwikkeling en tussengroepverhoudinge.*

Kritzinger, J.J. *'n Statistiese beskrywing van die godsdienstige verspreiding van die bevolking van Suid-Afrika.*

Levin, M. *Inflasie en die herverdeling van rykdom in Suid-Afrika.*

Lighton, F.K. *Conflict in the labour sphere with particular reference to the Western Cape.*

Lohann, C. & Potgieter, R. *Die moontlike beïnvloeding van tussengroepverhoudinge by kinders deur kinderlektuur met spesiale verwysing na die beeld van kinders van verskillende volksgroepe soos vergestalt in die lektuur en die oordrag van beskouinge en gesindhede deur die outeur.*

Maasdorp, G.G. *Spatial arrangement: Economic perspectives.*

Malan, C.W. *Suid-Afrikaanse literatuur en die tipering van rasseverhoudinge.*

Marcus, G. *An examination of the restrictions imposed on the press and other publications which appear in practice to affect members of the Black group more severely than other groups.*

Mathews, A.S. *Internal security policy for a changing society.*

Mentz, J.C.N. *Die invloed van lokalisering op tussengroepverhoudinge in Afrikalande.*

McGrath, M.D. *Trends in die distribution of personal incomes in South Africa.*

Möller, P.H. & Strauss, J. *Aspekte van tussengroepverhouding binne die werksituasie in die Bloemfontein-Boshabelo-gebied.*

Mostert, W.P. & Van Zyl, J.A. *Demografiese tendense en tussengroepver-houdinge.*

Muller, A.D. *Sosiaal-psigologiese perspektiewe op konflik.*

Müller, B.A. *Die openbare verkondiging van die kerk as medium van ver-andering van tussengroepverhoudinge.*

Muntingh, L.M. *Selfhandhawing deur Jode en Moslems as minderheidsgods-dienstige groepe in 'n oorwegend Christelike Suid-Afrikaanse gemeenskap.*

Nel, E.M. *The views of the different cultural groups on the future of South Africa.*

Nel, E.M. & Rademan, W.B. *Die effek van gelyke status-kontak op Kleur-linge se houdings teenoor Blankes.*

Nel, E.M. & Spangenberg, J. *The relationship between equal-status contact at work and interracial frienships.*

Nel, E.M., Rademan, W.B., Schnetler, F. & Venier G. *Die invloed van gelyke status-kontak in die werksituasie op etniese vooroordeel.*

Nürnberger, K. *Power, beliefs and equity: economic potency structures in South Africa and their interaction with patterns of conviction in the light of a Christian ethic.*

Olivier, J.L., Scholtz, G.J.L., Heath, M.R. & Liebenberg, E.J. *Sport en tus-sengroepverhouding in Suid-Afrika.*

Olivier, N.J.J. *Instromingsbeheer as konflikreguleerder en/of -genereerder in die Suid-Afrikaanse samelewing met besondere verwysing na die invloed daar-van op tussengroepverhoudinge.*

Oosthuizen, A.J.G. *Beginsels (riglyne) vir ruimtelike ordening op plaaslike vlak in Suid-Afrika.*

Oosthuizen, G.C., Mantzaris, E.A., Pitchers, A.L.M., Saaklul, A., Nadvi, S.S. & Van Loon, L. *Religion and inter- and intragroup relations in a pluralistic religious context of a South African city.*

Pretorius, H.N. *Swartes se ervaring van die strafregpleging en die invloed daarvan op tussengroepverhoudinge.*

Pretorius, J. *Kontraksluiting en tussengroepverhoudinge.*

Pretorius, K. *Die skepping van organisatoriese strukture waardeur owerheids-dienste aan die onderskeie bevolkingsgroepe gelewer kan word.*

Prinsloo, K.P. *Die rol van taal in tussengroepverhoudinge in Suid-Afrika, met besondere verwysing na taalbeplanning.*

Ranchod, B.G. & Noor-Mahomed, J. *The right of freedom of movement —*

with particular reference to the status of South African Indians.

Reynolds, A.M. *Ruimtelike ordening: administratiewe perspektiewe.*

Rhoodie, N.J. *Intergroup conflict in deeply segmented societies. An introductory conceptual framework.*

Rhoodie, N.J. & Couper, M.P. *'n Vergelykende ontleding van drie Afrikaner-dominante gemeenskappe se perspepsies van Wit-Swart-verhoudinge in Suid-Afrika.*

Schlemmer, L. *The spatial dispensation in South Africa: an assessment and tentative principles for planning in South Africa.*

Schrire, R. *The structure and functioning of the Department of Co-operation and Development.*

Schuring, G.K. *Kosmopolitiese Swart gemeenskappe.*

Schutte, C.D. *Politieke deelname onder Indiërs en Kleurlinge in sekere stedelike gebiede in Suid-Afrika met spesiale verwysing na die eerste verkiesings onder die nuwe grondwetlike bedeling.*

Smit, P., Booysen, J.J. & Cornelius, I. *Bevolkingsverspreiding in die RSA, Transkei, Bophuthatswana, Venda en Ciskei. Verklarende aantekeninge by die 1980-bevolkingsverpredingskaart.*

Smit, P. & Kok, P.C. *Bevolkingsherverspreiding in die RSA, 1970 — 1980: ontledings van die voorlopige 1980-sensusgegewens.*

Song, A. *The effects of South African Chinese religious trends in a pluralistic society.*

Steenekamp, J.J.A. *Die omvang en aard van kulturele konflik in die bestuurstrukture van die vervaardigingsektor in die Grensstreek (1984).*

Steytler, N.C. *Black undefended accused and the extension of legal aid as a means of improving group relations and diminishing conflict.*

Strauss, D.F.M. *'n Teoretiese analise van staatkundige teorieë en modelle soos van toepassing op die huidige konstitusionele bestel en sy moontlikhede om in 'n breër deelnemende regering te ontwikkel.*

Strijdom, H.G. *Leefwêreld met spesiale verwysing na behuising, buurmanskap, gemeenskapsheid en buurt: 'n vergelykende ondersoek in stedelike areas.*

Swanepoel, H.J. *Die ontwikkeling van streeks- en plaaslike owerhede met die oog op verbeterde tussengroepverhoudinge.*

Tomaselli, K.G., Williams, A., Steenveld, L. & Tomaselli, R. *An investiga-*

184

tion into the ethnographic myths encoded into South African film and television.

Tomaselli, K.G. *Intergroup relations and the South African progressive press.*

Tyson, G.A. *Children's racial attitudes.*

Uys, R. & Schutte, P.C. *Die arbeidsgesteldheid in die Vaaldriehoek met besondere klem op die invloed daarvan op tussengroepverhoudinge.*

Van Aswegen, H.J., Kapp, P.H., Stals, E.L.P. & Verhoef, G. *Die belang van historiografiese ontwikkelinge vir die historiese perspektief op tussengroepverhoudinge.*

Van Niekerk, P.J. *Kulturele identiteit en politieke verandering.*

Van Tonder, J.L. & Mostert, W.P. *Bevolkingsprojeksies vir Suidelike Afrika vir die tydperk 1970 — 2020.*

Van Vuuren, D.P. & De Waal, M. *Vraagstukke in verband met die referendum 1983.*

Van Wyk, D.H. *'n Ondersoek na die bronne, agtergrond en toepassing van bestaande regsreëls wat bevolkingsregistrasie, immigrasie, burgerskap, ontug en gemengde huwelike in Suid-Afrika beheers.*

Van Wyk, J. & Van Vuuren, A.J. *'n Onderwerpsontleding van die literatuur oor tussengroepverhoudinge aan die hand van die RGN-TGV/INTR-Databasis.*

Van Zyl Smit, D. *Structural ambiguity of evidence as a determinant evidence credibility: a comparative study of the evaluation of different groups in the administration of justice.*

Venter, F. *Die publiekregtelike verhouding.*

Venter, F., Du Plessis, L., Olivier, N., Coetzee, T., Pretorius, J. *Die aard en inhoud van die regsverhoudings tussen die staatsowerheid en ander regsubjekte en tussen regsubjekte onderling, regsteoreties en -filosofies beskou en met besondere verwysing na konflikregulering en -generering in die Suid-Afrikaanse reg — gesamentlike oorsigverslag.*

Venter, J.F. *Ruimtelike ordening: volkeregtelike oorwegings.*

Vergnani, T. *Social distance attitudes among White, Coloured, Indian and Blank population groups in South Africa.*

Vorster, J. *Houdings van Indiërs en Kleurlinge teenoor Afrikaans- en Engelssprekendes.*

Wellings, P.A. *Core-periphery relations in the Southern Africa space-*

economy with specific reference to their influence on intergroup relations.

Wiechers, M. *Ruimtelike ordening: voorgestelde juridiese beginsels.*
Woodward, C.A. *Reform and revolution in South Africa.*

Zulu, P.M. *An enquiry into attitudes to and perceptions of amenities and resources in Black townships — Durban and the Witwatersrand.*

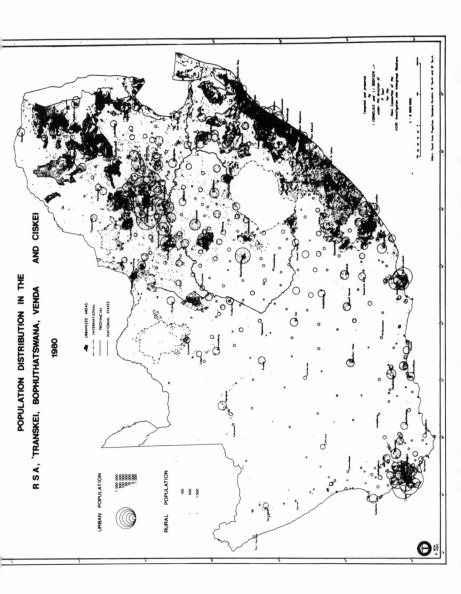

POPULATION DISTRIBUTION IN THE
R S A, TRANSKEI, BOPHUTHATSWANA, VENDA AND CISKEI

1980

URBAN POPULATION

RURAL POPULATION

187

Dr H.C. Marais (Chairman)

Prof. M. Bopape

Dr C.V. Bothma

Dr W.J. Breytenbach

Prof. S.P. Cilliers

Dr H.P. Fourie

Dr J.G. Garbers

Mr R.M. Godsell

Prof. W.D. Hammond-Tooke

Prof. E. Higgins

Prof. D.A. Kotzé

Dr J.M. Lötter

Rev. J.J.F. Mettler

Prof. J.C. Moll

Prof. C.J. Nel

Dr G.K. Nelson

Prof. G.C. Oosthuizen

Dr K.P. Prinsloo

Prof. B.G. Ranchod

Prof. L. Schlemmer

Prof. A.F. Steyn *(signature)*

Mr G.A. Thiele *(signature)*

Mr J. Tshabalala *(signature)*

Prof. H.W. van der Merwe *(signature)*

Dr J.D. Venter *(signature)*

Prof. H.G. Viljoen *(signature)*

Prof. M. Wiechers *(signature)*

Prof. N.E. Wiehahn *(signature)*

Co-ordinators

(signatures)

Prof. B.C. Lategan   Mr J.L. Olivier   Dr N.J. Rhoodie

190

State President's Office

Union Buildings
Private bag X 1000
0001 Pretoria

<u>EMBARGO</u> : For immediate release

<u>MEDIA RELEASE BY STATE PRESIDENT P W BOTHA</u>

REACTION OF THE GOVERNMENT ON THE HSRC REPORT ON
INTERGROUP RELATIONS

Issued by the Directorate : Liaison and Information
State President's Office
Union Buildings
Pretoria

12 September 1985

REACTION OF THE GOVERNMENT TO THE HSRC REPORT ON INTER-GROUP RELATIONS

1. The Government has a special calling and responsibility to promote sound intergroup relations and thereby ensure peaceful co-existence in South Africa. The Government therefore welcomes the HSRC investigation in this regard and has noted the recently published Report with appreciation, because it once again underlines the necessity of sound intergroup relations in South Africa. The Report is in the same tenor as a series of investigations and reports such as those of the Theron, Wiehahn and Riekert Commissions, the De Lange Committee and the President's Council, all of which have to a greater or lesser extent yielded practical results. The Report will undoubtedly contribute to the efforts of all involved in fostering good relations, and every responsible South African should take due note of its contents.

2. In its reaction the Government recognises that the Report concentrates mainly on one specific aspect of intergroup relations, namely their potential for conflict. Since the Report gives an overall perspective, the Government does not intend to react in detail to every aspect. However, the Government undertakes to refer the various committee and project reports on which the Report is based to the responsible authorities for their attention and for action to be taken, where necessary, as soon as these reports are available.

3. It is noted with appreciation that the Report acknowledges the complexity of conditions in South Africa and the fact that there is no single, simplistic and all-embracing solution to South Africa's social and political problems. The Government is sensitive to the delicate nature of issues that have to be dealt with daily in all spheres of life and of their potential for conflict. In many fields, therefore, the Government is engaged in planning and actions that can defuse conflict and ease tension. The Government's view continues to be that the realities of South African society preclude a single instant solution and require sustained practical and practicable action in every sphere of life.

4. The emphasis placed in the Report on the central problem of ethnicity highlights this prominent feature of South African society, and the Government endorses the recognition given in the Report to the group basis on which this society rests.

There is one particular aspect in this connection to which it is necessary to react. The consistent emphasis the Report places on the role of Government policy over the past 37 years creates the impression that the National Party in 1948 was the author of the principle that segregation can be the basis of a political solution in South Africa. This, moreover, contributes to an impression that the policy of the present Government is the main cause of relations problems in our country.

The Government deplores the lack of a correct historical perspective in the Report as regards the policy of segregation and wishes to clear this aspect up for the sake of correct diagnosis and subsequent appropriate handling of relations questions. There is ample authority, even in the works of English historians, for the fact that apartheid was already enforced in the colonial era and that the policy followed with regard to Blacks after 1910 had already taken shape in earliest times. Particularly relevant here is the work done by the largely English-speaking South African Native Affairs Commission appointed by Lord Milner in 1903. In the report of that Commission, published in 1905, domination by the Whites and race and colour as distinguishing factors in the apportionment of political rights and separate representation for Blacks in order to prevent domination, are accepted as fundamental principles.

From history it is clear, firstly, that an approach whereby ethnic groups are accepted as a basis for political accommodation is as old as South Africa itself. Secondly, it shows that the Afrikaner and the National Party, although following this approach in 1948, were not its creators or the only ones to apply it.

The Government remains convinced that it should take the ethnic group basis of the South African society into account in carrying out its task of ordering the country to ensure peaceful co-existence and to promote and protect the rights and interests of all. In this respect, comparison with the results obtained with other approaches and models in other segmented societies, especially in the Third World, convinces the Government that in South Africa rights and interests can best be protected and promoted on an equal basis within a group context. Recognition of such groups also contributes to the full development of groups in accordance with their own needs, aspirations and potential.

At the same time, however — and here the Government is in agreement with the Report — the group basis must not be emphasised at the expense of the individual or applied at the expense of groups.

Both differences and the similarities between people should be taken into account. For this reason distinction between groups is not an end in itself, but a means for protecting groups in a heterogeneous society. If such distinction affects the human dignity of some, gives rise to discrimination and causes friction instead of preventing it, separation is not in the interests of peaceful co-existence and group protection, and the measures concerned should be adjusted or done away with. For this reason the Government is prepared to accept, in the interests of sound intergroup relations, the free association of individuals and groups in certain respects.

That the Government is firmly committed to this approach is clear from the abolition of measures such as the Prohibition of Mixed Marriages Act, section 16 of the Immorality Act and the Prohibition of Political Interference Act. It likewise appears from the autonomy granted to sports and recreation bodies, from the continuing revision of measures such as those relating to the use of amenities and public transport and from the greater recognition given to the autonomy of the governing bodies of institutions of tertiary education in the composition of their student communities.

In this regard it should also be pointed out that there is an ongoing programme for the elimination of discriminatory measures and that the Cabinet regularly receives reports in this connection. Furthermore, matters that give rise to friction, uncertainty and frustration are given priority so that genuine grievances can be redressed.

As regards this matter, the Government has noted the finding that the feeling of privation in people, the phenomenon of relative deprivation as it is called, is an important cause of intergroup conflict and that steps taken or contemplated should take account of this fact. Naturally, the realities of the country's capacity for satisfying expectations should also be taken into account.

5. The Government is committed to the protection of the individual and the promotion of individual interests. The recognition of the human dignity, life, liberty and property of all, the furtherance of the contentment and spiritual and material welfare of all, and the equality of all under the law, as expressed in the Preamble to the Constitution, inequivocally testifies to this. Accordingly, the creation of equal opportunities at all levels is being given priority.

6. The Government has noted the real problems that were identified in a variety of spheres and has already undertaken, as far as lies within its responsibility, to take action to remove obstacles in the way of sound intergroup relations.

The Government would like to mention certain matters and steps in this regard that are already enjoying attention in certain spheres.

The Economy

The Government identifies itself with the idea of an economic system that provides for growth and development in order to satisfy the reasonable needs of a growing population, equal opportunities for all and to ensure maximum entry to the market. The system should also accommodate the Third World conditions that are characteristic of a large part of the national economy of South Africa.

The Government is aware that the country's limited capacity to fulfil high expectations is causing tension, and the problem is receiving attention. Due account is also being taken of the interdependence of reforms in different spheres and the fact that reform can be successful only if it is economically feasible.

The view that the market system is the most effective welfare-generating system, is supported. In a developing society, however, the absolute application of the system gives rise to inequalities, and guidance by the Government is therefore necessary.

As far as economic growth is concerned, it must be emphasised that the full potential of the economy is not being realised at present, for various reasons. Whereas a growth rate of more than 5% is needed to address unemployment effectively, it is apparent that it will hardly be possible to maintain an average growth rate of even 3,6% in the medium term. In addition to steps to stimulate sustained and balanced growth, therefore, a strategy for creating employment has been adopted. The desired market-orientation is being achieved by correcting those measures that distort the market; by promoting the formal and informal small business sector, especially through the Small Business Development Corporation; by ensuring optimum regional development; and by providing for better education, training and utilisation of the work force.

As regards backlogs in satisfying the elementary needs of certain communities, everything possible should be done to counter the perception among some groups that they are being excluded from economic benefits. The reduction of inequalities and the elimination of absolute poverty by supplying basic human needs are therefore priorities, and in these respects progress is already being made. An example of the positive steps taken in this regard is the R1 000 million that has been made available for the development of Black townships in particular.

As regards greater participation in the economy through more equal opportunities and greater occupational mobility, the Government is in agreement with the Report that access to key economic resources should not be determined by prescribed group membership. The opening of industrial areas and central business districts to all groups falls within the ambit of this goal. The Government has already adopted the view that it is necessary to abolish measures that limit the posibility of greater numbers of entrepreneurs and professional persons of all groups availing themselves of opportunities in the market system.

Labour

The guide-lines contained in the Report are already largely being implemented in the Government's present manpower policy as evolved along the lines of the Wiehahn Commission's Report and the Government's response to it. The Government is of the opinion that all the various developments that have taken place recently in the field of labour are making a significant contribution to the fostering of sound intergroup relations.

As far as job reservation is concerned, all forms of statutory job reservation have been abolished in accordance with the Government's declared policy, while the principle of abolishing job reservation in the mining industry was accepted in 1981 already. In the Public Service, too, it is found that trained persons of all population groups are increasingly being appointed to positions previously held exclusively by Whites.

Education

The Government has accepted the principle of providing, and has repeatedly confirmed its intention to provide, equal educational opportunities, including equal standards of education, for all. However, the Government agrees with the finding that "In a country such as the RSA with its deeply segmented and heterogeneous population, differential population growth and limited high-level manpower and resources, the provision of equal educational opportunities is a virtually unattainable goal — even countries like the USA and Britain have not yet been able to accomplish this for their minority groups." None the less, as the Report points out with regard to education for Blacks, rigorous efforts to achieve this ideal are continuing.

The findings on education in the Report emphasise the inequalities of the provision of education between the various population groups as inferred from the unit cost per pupil, the pupil/teacher ratio, the qualifications of teachers and the pass rate in the final school examination. Disparities such as those in expenditure per pupil should not be regarded as the only norm for the quality of education. The differences are, for example, partly to be explained by the differences in the qualifications of teachers and the resultant differences in salaries and expenditure, as well as by the unfavourable pupil/teacher ratio in certain groups. Phenomena peculiar to developing countries, such as a high growth rate of new entrants, a high drop-out rate and the fact that education has no great hold on people, are also factors that make it all the more difficult to effect significant improvement in education within a short period. Efforts to eliminate these factors continue.

While finding that the new statutory framework for education will contribute towards eliminating inequalities and lending greater credibility to decision-making and the provision of education, the Report also poses the question whether a single education department will not offer a possible long-term solution and remove education from the political arena to a greater extent. The Government is aware of expectations among certain groups that a single education department will enhance the credibility of education. However, the Government is also alive to the political sensitivity of education. The Government accordingly continues to subscribe to the views adopted in the White Paper on the Provision of Education 1983, of which the creation of a single Education Ministry to determine the national education policy that will apply to all, is part. The new Ministry of National Education, which has been functioning since September 1984, is already succeeding in promoting co-operation within the system of education provision as a whole and in obtaining consensus on various aspects of national education policy. When several of these national policy measures are announced early in 1986, it will be clear that significant progress has been made towards the provision of equal education opportunities.

The Government agrees that good intergroup and interpersonal relations can and should be fostered through education. Education, and teachers in particular, have the task of improving the image that groups have of one another and not impairing relations through their actions. Negative attitudes and negative stereotyping are unacceptable, and teachers should actively endeavour to improve attitudes and to created mutual respect among all groups.

In concurrence with what is said in the Report in this regard, it should be pointed out that history written on a basis of prejudice and presenting groups as stereotypes or portraying past events from a certain angle only, is harmful to intergroup relations. The scientific validity of all prescribed study material is therefore subject to constant critical evaluation.

Welfare

Social upliftment programmes and health and welfare services undoubtedly also have an effect on intergroup relations. In this regard the population development programme and the national health services facilities plan should be regarded as important instruments for guiding all sections of the South African population towards optimum development and realising their reasonable aspirations. Mention should also be made of the comprehensive investigation of the socio-economic position of all population groups that is being conducted at present to ensure systematic and co-ordinated action.

Social problems that result from the unstable married and family life of urban populations in particular are receiving serious attention. Acceptance, by all interested sectors, of responsibility for the provision and improvement of welfare and support services is essential in this regard.

Rapid urbanisation and associated problems as regards housing, squatting and the provision of services are receiving priority treatement. The Government is working on a strategy to ensure orderly urbanisation and to provide for more informal types of housing. Current influx control measures are also being reconsidered.

Spatial ordering

The Government acknowledges the importance of suitable living space for all and, although extensive statutory provision exists for the involvement of all interested parties in the planning and administration of spatial ordering, note is taken of proposals for the further improvement of this process.

Law

In the Preamble of the Constitution, South Africa is committed to maintaining an independent judiciary and to equality before the law. The Government also endorses the principle of the rule of law which requires that the actions of both the Government and the individual be tested against legal norms. The goals aimed at and the methods used must satisfy the requirements of a civilised legal system. In the pursuit of these principles, therefore, the law and the application of the law in South Africa are constantly being revised and adopted.

Examples in this regard are the steps that have resulted from the work done by the Rabie Commission on security legislation , the Hoexter Commission on the structure and functioning of the courts, and the South African Law Commission on law reform in general. However, certain critical findings are made in the Report regarding, for example, the law enforcement agencies, which, in the Government's view, cannot be scientifically validated.

Of particular importance for South African society is also the recognition and application of the various indigenous legal systems.

Constitutional affairs

The Government is committed to democracy as the only acceptable way in which substance can be given to every South African's political aspirations. Accordingly it is the Government's aim, by maintaining security and stability and by recognising groups' claims to authority over their own affairs, to give a political voice to all in all the decision-making processes that affect their lives.

In South Africa's plural society, however, democracy means, among other things, that the rights of minorities will have to be protected, that groups will have to be protected from being dominated by others and that a system in which groups do not enjoy such protection, cannot ensure justice and fairness.

Moreover, South African circumstances are such that enduring solutions can be found only if all concerned are prepared to arrive at a compromise through dialogue and negotiation.

Steps taken by the Government are aimed at making mutually acceptable progress towards realising the democratic ideal. The new Constitution, the recent measures relating to new local government arrangements, especially those concerning the proposed regional services councils, the structures for multilateral co-operation with the independent states, and the principle of devolution of power are all instruments that do not offer final solutions in themselves but form part of a continuing process of development to improve everyone's participation in decision-making in a democratic manner.

Furthermore to these steps, the Government has already stated that the constitutional development of Blacks and their participation in political decision-making to the highest constitutional level is now being given priority. In co-operation with Black leaders, deliberations are being continued regarding the way or ways in which progress can be made in this connection.

Intergroup communication

The Goverment is in agreement with the Report that intergroup communication is defective and that both the Government and the individual should take positive steps to bridge the gap. Note is taken of the finding that communication is hampered by social distance between groups and by stereotyped perceptions of and negative attitudes to one another. The Government, too, would therefore like to see prejudices being broken down and positive attitudes being consciously fostered, also at the interpersonal level.

In this regard reference may be made to the valuable role played by relations committees in improving communication, mutual understanding and acceptance at the local level. It is intended to extend this to all population groups so that the public can be involved in dialogue on a much wider front. Wider and wider dialogue involving all South Africans at all levels is the best way to reduce friction between groups.

Another programme is also under way in terms of which the authorities are endeavouring to maintain and foster healthy attitudes in day-to-day contact with the public.

It should also be emphasised that the Government does not wish to act prescriptively and that all development, including that in the constitutional sphere, should take place through dialogue and negotiation with those concerned. Progress is possible only if it is the result of negotiation.

Our youth are certainly not to be excluded from the fostering of sound intergroup relations. Therefore young South Africans should not grow up in isolation from one another, and the idea that there should be more contact at school level is supported. Proposals for the creation of points of constructive contact at the level of parents' associations and teachers' associations and in the provision of specialised services at regional level are therefore supported. A responsibility undoubtedly rests on the various communities — especially at the local level, where there are many opportunities for contact — to promote constructive contact between parents, teachers and pupils.

7. The Government considers it necessary to point out, and to emphasise, that it is not the only authority responsible for sound intergroup relations. Equally important and far-reaching are the involvement and responsibility of the

private sector, churches, other organisations and particularly every individual. Undue emphasis on the Government's responsibility poses the danger of the contribution made by these bodies, as well as by individuals, being under-estimated. An appeal is therefore made to all sectors and to every individual to give serious attention to their contribution towards fostering and maintaining good relations. In the final analysis, relations are primarily interpersonal; and for this reason no South African can or may distance himself or evade his responsibility in this regard.

As far as the role of other sectors is concerned, the Government believes, in the first place, that churches are specially called to bring people closer to one another, to help build a shared vision and thus to play a role of reconciliation in South African society. The Government therefore appeals to churches to be, in their own field and within their own sphere of responsibility, true instruments for justice and reconciliation through responsible action, by countering alienation and by fostering positive attitudes among their members. Secondly, the Government supports the finding that the media could fulful a more important function of mediation between groups and should endeavour to avoid projecting a stereotyped image of people. The media can therefore also make an invaluable contribution to the promotion of sound intergroup relations.

8. The Government is convinced that in general the findings and suggested guide-lines in the Report accord with its policy and actions in each of the spheres referred to. At the same time it should be pointed out that the Report does not properly spell out the steps and processes in which the Government is already engaged. This disturbs the balance in the Report somewhat.

9. None the less, the Government is satisfied that the Report as a whole supports and confirms the need for the comprehensive, balanced and sustained process of reform in which the Government is engaged to establish peaceful, secure and prosperous communities in South Africa.

10. The Report refers to the large number of common interests that bind the various groups together, and the Government whishes to associate itself with this. It is the Government's conviction that that which unites South Africans, namely their common loyalty to South Africa, is far greater than the differences between them. These common interests, this common loyalty, together with recognition and protection of group interests, are the basis on which all can live together and work together in peace in South Africa. In consonance with this is the conclusion reached in the Report that it is necessary to foster a common system of values that binds South Africans

together. If every responsible body and individual is committed to this, the ideal of sound intergroup relations can be realised. The value of the Report lies mainly in this: it has shown that, although there are obstacles, it is possible to achieve this ideal.

NEWSPAPER REPORTS

In the first three weeks after the release of the main committee's report on Intergroup Relations at least 290 newspaper reports and 29 editorials appeared in the South African and international press.

KORTOM
Willem de Klerk

Agenda op die spoor van die RGN

DIÉ vraag wat gedurende die week gevra is, is: "Wat gaan die Regering doen met die RGN se Verslag oor Tussengroepverhoudinge?"

Die Staatspresident antwoord só: "Ek het kennis geneem van die verslag. Die Regering bestudeer die inhoud daarvan en sal op 'n gepaste tydstip daarop reageer."

Intussen beteken dit nie dat ons op die Regering moet wag nie. In die demokrasie moet elkeen sy eie menings vorm en mag elkeen sy menings uitspreek.

My standpunt is onder meer: Dit is 'n deeglike stuk werk; dit bevestig deur empiriese ondersoek wat almal wat oë en ore en gewete en verstand het, reeds weet (ook die Regering weet dit); die Regering sal, by dit wat hy reeds gedoen het om groepverhoudinge te verbeter, nog baie meer, ja baie meer moet doen (ook dit weet die Regering); en die onus val op baie mense en instansies om iets te doen — nie net op die Regering of die blankes nie.

Besiel

Ongetwyfeld is reeds heelwat gedoen om rasse-konflik te temper. Die Botha-regering het 'n indrukwekkende lys van deurbrake, weg van die ou apartheid en op pad na billikheid, regverdigheid en gemeenskaplikheid. Ek tel 26 ingrypende verskuiwings van die Regering, weg van die tradisie van apartheid.

Hierdie Regering is besiel met die gees van die RGN-verslag.

Maar goed is nog nie beter en beste nie. Die pad terug sal van A tot Z geloop moet word. Vergeet maar om hier rondom K te begin watertrap. En om te sê dis maklik vir die RGN om dinge te bevind, maar dis 'n ander saak om dit uit te voer, gaan ook nie op nie. Politiek moet op die werklikheid gerig wees en nie op wensdinkery nie.

Ek is nie voorskriftelik nie, maar dis ons goeie reg om van die Regering 'n agenda te vra. Ek meen ek praat namens 'n beduidende groep kiesers, en ook namens 'n skare ondersteuners van die NP, as ek aspekte van dié agenda só verwoord:

● Dat duidelik gesê word dat die apartheidsbeleid geen basis is waarop die toekoms gebou kan word nie. Daar word met dié idee gebreek en 'n nuwe filosofie moet nou gesamentlik verwerklik word. Die grondgedagte van dié filosofie is eiese-genskap en medeseggenskap.

● Medeseggenskap beteken politieke magsdeling tussen die rasgroepe op al die vlakke van regering. Dit help nie om dit met ander slim woorde te probeer versluier of te versag nie. Die stelsel wat hiervoor ontwerp moet word, moet eiese-genskap van groepe ewe sterk waarborg.

● Alle raswette sal herroep word en groepsregte sal gesamentlik in 'n nuwe stel geformuleer word.

● Bevolkingsgroepe en swart state bly 'n bousteen in 'n staatkundige bestel (dit is deel van die kompromie), maar vrye assosiasies, grys gebiede en ander vorme van vryheid en gemeenskaplikheid word gevestig.

● Al die ander brandende kwessies soos 'n enkele onderwysdepartement, instromingsbeheer, burgerskap en nog baie wat by name genoem moet word, is op die agenda van die rondetafel wat vir dié beraad gestruktureer sal word.

● Hierdie beraad oor al die voorgenoemde word aan 'n tydskaal gebind.

Hoop

Die onus rus nie alleen op die Regering vir die ontwerp van 'n nuwe gemeenskaplike Suid-Afrika nie.

Die RGN-verslag gee duidelike aanwysings vir die algemene publiek, die kerke, die sakewêreld, die media, die regstoepassing en die onderwys om hul dinge te doen om groepverhoudings te verbeter.

Ek wil onderstreep dat dit nie net van die blanke groep geyra word nie. Swart leiers, swart instellings en ander organisasies onder ons mense van kleur moet ook sterk aangespreek word. Hul wraak, vergelding, vrees, rassisme en negativiteit sal ook aangespreek moet word.

On sal *almal* die wa uit die drif moet trek.

In Suid-Afrika sal daar altyd groepspannings bly, maar as ons dit nie verskraal nie, is daar geen hoop nie.

ꝔBeeld

Johannesburg ☎ 402-1460, Pretoria ☎ 28-6954

Woensdag, 3 Julie 1985

Bevestiging

DIE verslag van die RGN wat pas gepubliseer is, is getitel *Die Suid-Afrikaanse Samelewing: Werklikhede en Toekomsmoontlikhede*. Wat die werklikhede betref, bevestig die verslag basies wat veral blankes die afgelope dekade pynlik besef het. Dit is dat apartheid nie die oplossings gebring het waarop gehoop is nie, en dat dit baie bitterheid, verdeeldheid en konflik in die hand gewerk het.

Juis dié besef het die groot politieke verskuiwing van die jare tagtig gebring, met blankes wat ingesien het dat magsdeling met anderskleuriges 'n noodwendigheid is en dat konsensus en faktore van saambinding nagejaag moet word.

In dié opsig is die RGN-verslag dus 'n bevestiging van wat die blankes en ander groepe in die land intuïtief aangevoel het. Hier is ook nou wetenskaplike stawing dat wat reeds in Suid-Afrika aan die gang is — en spesifiek kan verwys word na die "groeipunte" van hoop wat in die verslag uitgelig word — nie maar die onverantwoorde denke van 'n paar politici of 'n party is nie. Dit verteenwoordig 'n dapper poging om werklikhede wat skeef gegroei het weer reg te kry.

Oor die toekomsmoontlikhede is die verslag minder spesifiek. Sieninge word aangebied wat as beginsels vir 'n toekomstige politieke, maatskaplike, juridiese en ekonomiese orde kan geld. Sommige daarvan is nogal ingrypend binne die raamwerk van Suid-Afrikaanse denke, soos die vryheid van assosiasie met individue en groepe (dus ook vryheid van nie-assosiasie).

As die verslag basiese denke kan stimuleer oor wat ons toekomseise en -verwagtinge moet wees, kan dit net verwelkom word. Terselfdertyd moet besef word dat dit die moeilike taak van die politiek is om die groeiende konsensus oor gemeenskaplikheid in die praktyk te vergestalt, en dat die RGN-verslag hoogstens 'n gespreksfokuspunt, 'n bevestiger en 'n wegbereider kan wees. Dit is egter nie moontlik om 'n toestand te behandel voordat daar duidelikheid oor die simptome is nie.

204

DIE BURGER

WOENSDAG 3 JULIE 1985

Saamstaan in SA

EEN van die vernaamste bevindinge van die RGN se ondersoek na verhoudinge tussen groepe in Suid-Afrika is dat segregasie, wat groepe en mense afsonder en verdeel, een van die belangrikste oorsake van 'n besonder hoë konflikpotensiaal in die land is.

As sodanig is die bevinding nie eintlik iets nuuts nie, eerder 'n onderstreping van 'n tendensie wat geruime tyd reeds in die Suid-Afrikaanse samelewing merkbaar is. Tog het dit steeds uiters belangrike implikasies, ook in soverre as wat dit as 'n verdere aanduiding dien dat in Suid-Afrika begin is met 'n politieke proses wat al hoe meer lyk na die beste uitweg uit die land se grootste probleme.

Daar is naamlik etlike jare gelede reeds besef, ook in toonaangewende Nasionale geledere, dat die ou bloudruk van rigoristiese s' ·iding, aanvanklik ingestel en toegepas om , wing tussen groepe te voorkom, in baie opsigte nie aan daardie doelstelling voldoen nie, en inderdaad soms eerder gemoedere tussen groepe en individue gaande maak.

Dié besef het gelei tot die groter klem wat op gemeenskaplikheid begin val het. Al hoe sterker is die faktore en gemeenskaplike belan-ge benadruk wat groepe saambind. Al hoe meer het begrip toegeneem vir die eise wat spruit uit 'n kernprobleem van Suid-Afrika, dat etniese en groepsverskille getransendeer moet word sonder dat dit misken word.

Onder leiding van die Nasionale Regering is gevolglik begin met die uitbreiding van die demokrasie, 'n noodsaaklike ontwikkeling in Suid-Afrika wat nou weer deur die RGN-ondersoek beklemtoon word. Dit het beslag gekry in die nuwe grondwetlike bedeling vir blank, bruin en Indiër. Daar word beoog om dit verder uit te brei na swartmense buite die nasionale state wat, deels omdat swart leiers destyds nie aan die beoogde swart raad wou deelneem nie, nog nie in sulke demokratiese prosesse opgeneem is nie.

Die RGN-verslag omskryf die eindpunt van sodanige demokratisering as 'n deelnemende demokrasie, in die sin dat uiteindelik almal in die land aan demokratiese prosesse moet deelneem. Met devolusie van mag kan veral op plaaslike vlak en binne gemeenskapsverband aan hierdie oogmerke voldoen word, terwyl op hoër vlak waarskynlik beweeg word na 'n verteenwoordigende demokrasie, waar verkose of aangewese leiers die besluite sal neem.

SOWETAN

Report blames apartheid

A MAJOR Human Sciences Research Council report has slated South Africa's apartheid system for fuelling racial friction and violence, and has called for drastic changes in the political, social and economic order of the country.

It singles out entrenched separation, population registration, a racially bound legal system, unequal education, economic job restrictions as contributing to the mistrust and resentment in society. Classical apartheid is described as a failure and a new approach is advocated with regard to group relations.

The most important findings and recommendations made in the report are:

• '· calls for the sharing of political p(erp); and a broadening of democracy. Freedom of association with individuals and groups, as well as the right to non-association, should be guaranteed;

• South Africa has a serious communication problem in that many blacks cannot speak either official language while the other race groups cannot speak African languages. A third official language on a regional basis should be considered;

• The legality of South Africa's racial and ethnic categories has been questioned by the juridical work committee. The committee finds that "race can never be a legally relevant ground for justified differentiation"; ·

• South Africa's legal system is held in deep suspicion by many black South Africans and is in need of reform. The country's security legislation is criticised in the report.

It says when laws "are veiled in secrecy and marred by a lack of control, thereby creating opportunities for the suppression of political freedom, the existence and application of security legislation in itself poses a threat to the security of the state";

• As analysis by the HSRC's juridical work committee shows that some of the country's laws do not "in all respects ensure equal treatment for all population categories";

• There is an urgent need for a comprehensive, general history of South Africa, to which the roles of all the groups and the interaction between them are reflected in an "objective, balanced manner";

• Referring to labour and unemployment, it says at least half of South Africa's labour force — between 50 and 54 percent — could be unemployed by the year 2000 if low economic growth prevails and changes are not made to the economic system;

• Influx control must be abolished — the report says the mobility of black labourers must no longer be artificially inhibited and the integrated nature of the South African economy must be accepted.

THE CITIZEN

COMMENT

New order

SINCE apartheid is beginning to crumble, the report of the Human Sciences Research Council, concluding that apartheid has failed to resolve the racial problems of South Africa, should give further impetus to the process.

Not that the Government will necessarily accept all the views and generalised suggestions of the investigation, which lasted four years.

The De Lange Commission's report on education is not being fully implemented, although major aspects are.

The HSRC report makes no political recommendations but concludes that the political ordering of inter-group relations according to the original apartheid model has reached an impasse, and constructive relations cannot be developed further along these lines.

"It was evident from research that despite bona fide intentions, the goal of 'separate but equal' cannot be achieved."

The report suggests guidelines for the Government, calling for the establishment of a democratic political structure, negotiated and participated in by all races, a newly formed legal system which would not be suspected by certain race groups, better communication at all levels of society, and the recognition of a third official language.

It concludes that South Africa needs a new social order where equality and the rights of the individual will be guaranteed.

Apartheid has not only failed to solve the country's racial differences, but the continued enforcement of segregation could incite inter-race conflict.

Political power should be shared among all race groups in a plural society and "a broadening of the democratic base of the current power structure is a prerequisite for the development of a stable social order."

The report says South Africa needs a plural society where all group-based discrimination is removed and the rights of the individuals are reaffirmed.

The researchers highlight six basic requirements:

Freedom of association, the right to participate in decision-making processes, equal opportunities, the establishment of trusted and accepted public institutions, and the recognition both of the human dignity of all people and of group identity.

The report says there are already signs of Government actions being "conducive to the establishment of a democratic social order."

It mentions the repeal of some discriminatory laws, the recognition of residential rights for certain qualifying Blacks, and the Government's growing willingness to enter dialogue with Black leaders.

The chairman of the main committee of the investigation, Dr H C Marais, also notes there are signs of hope for better group relations. These include a willingness on the part of all groups to accommodate each other's fears and aspirations, increasing economic interdependence and common loyalty to one fatherland.

Some sections of the Press have interpreted the report as being sensational, whereas it is a sober assessment of the complexities of our society and it offers, as Dr Marais himself has pointed out, no simplistic view to the problem of group relations.

Apartheid has been in retreat for years — ever since the Verwoerdian policy of turning the Black tide back to the homelands failed.

The policy could not keep Blacks out of the towns and cities because Whites are completely dependent on their labour. There is mixing everywhere except in residential areas (and there is plenty of that in places like Hillbrow).

The permanence of Blacks in "White" South Africa is now officially recognised.

Racial laws that were pillars of apartheid, like the ban on mixed marriages and sex across the colour line, as well as the ban on mixed political parties, have been repealed.

And there are more changes on the way.

South Africa is developing a new social, economic and political dispensation, and the HSRC report makes an important contribution in signposting the way.

Cape Times

WEDNESDAY, JULY 3, 1985

Heading off conflict

A REPORT of the government-sponsored Human Sciences Research Council has identified the key underlying causes of unrest in South Africa and has called for the abolition of apartheid and the influx control system and acceptance of the reality of an integrated society.

It is to be hoped that the insights of this authoritative, non-political investigation will be absorbed by the private and public sectors alike and quickly acted upon. South Africa in mid-1985 is a society teetering on the brink of civil war. It is important to face what the report calls, "the apparently polarized negative attitudes of whites, especially Afrikaans-speaking whites, and Africans towards one another." This mutual antagonism and antipathy are central to the South African dilemma and have their roots in history. The HSRC report draws attention to the cycle of violence and confrontation between African youths and the police — seen as representing the white establishment — and warns of its disastrous effects. In more concrete terms, every sjambok charge, salvo of teargas, birdshot, rubber bullets or worse is generating a corrosive hatred rather more devastating,

ultimately, than disturbance of the peace in a protest march. Overkill seems to be the watchword of the security forces. Attitudes between police and blacks are appalling. It is a vicious cycle.

It is never too late to break the cycle and stop the spiral of hate-generating violence and counter-violence. To acquiesce in the inevitability of civil war is unthinkable. In the HSRC report the healing and hopeful insights of the social sciences are offered for consideration. There are many possible lines of approach. Why not resolve to spend as much money on bringing people together — in education, sport, music, and other fields — as has been spent in the past on keeping them apart? Why not use SABC TV to break down racial stereotypes and attitudes of bigotry and prejudice which occur in all groups? In an era of petrol bombs and grenades, efficient security forces are indispensable. Yet sole reliance on harsh policing and army muscle is illusory and will in time prove fatal. So why not try something constructive? Let the moderates and conciliators pit their skills against the apostles of hatred and the advocates of force who are dragging the country to ruin.

The Natal Witness

Wednesday, July 3, 1985

HSRC warning

THE Government has been told so by the political opposition, by the churches, by the business community. Now it is being told by the HSRC. A major report, the product of a four-year study of inter-group relations in South Africa by over 200 researchers and academics, declares that South Africa's system of racial segregation has failed to enable the different races to co-exist peacefully and should be scrapped.

The 182-page summary document does not constitute light bedside reading. Its message is not frivolous either. There has been, it says, an overemphasis on groups as against individuals. Specifically, the institutionalisation of ethnicity, compelling the individual to order his life within prescribed boundaries, the resultant isolation and insulation of people and the inequalities involved in group-based allocation of resources are at the root of the conflict. And, chillingly, "if this condition is allowed to develop further it will become increasingly difficult to transform conflict constructively". The legal system is suffering from a crisis of legitimacy in the eyes of blacks and a frighteningly high percentage of people from all race groups regard violence as an acceptable method of achieving political aims.

The report warns that there are no easy solutions to the problems that beset us. Its most significant recommendations about how the potential for racial conflict could be defused are to allow people to associate naturally by abolishing the system of population registration, and to devise a political order which would enable everyone to participate in the decision-making process at every level.

In the light of this, the Government's supposedly reformist new dispensation is little improvement on the old. Blacks are still excluded, while other groups participate on a basis of ethnicity carefully contrived to ensure continued white dominance.

Proponents of the new constitution have portrayed it as an instrument of progressive reform. Quite clearly, some speedy adaptations will have to be made. In the concluding words of the report, "the relations between groups in South Africa is a crucial matter that demands the most urgent attention. Delays in addressing the issue could have catastrophic consequences".

Exactly.

208

HSRC report hailed in UK

Dispatch Correspondent

LONDON — The Human Sciences Research Council report which call apartheid a failure was welcomed as "a voice of reason" by the British press yesterday.

The 185-page document was well-reported in the major Fleet Street papers which saw in it the voice of the verligte Afrikaner.

The report was published after a four-year investigation by more than 30 academics, 200 researchers and 12 committees.

It recommended talks with leaders of all race groups for the establishment of an open democracy in South Africa and described the government's "separate but equal" goal as unworkable.

The Human Sciences Research Council is a government funded think-tank which is dominated by Afrikaner academics, both liberal and conservative.

That influential Afrikaners who produced the report can so unequivocally warn about the dangers of implementing apartheid must be a sign of hope, the conservative Daily Telegraph said.

In an editorial yesterday the paper said it was "very interesting" that a government-backed think-tank could so publicly criticise the government's fundamental principles.

"A few years ago such people would not have criticised their government's fundamental principles even in private.

"Now they do it publicly and with the benefit of the government's financial support.

"The conclusion must be that they are playing a tune which the South African Government half wants to hear," the Telegraph said.

The liberal Guardian newspaper called the report "the most far-reaching study of its kind," which represented a rational argument against the South African system.

The report advocated the abolition of apartheid and "only those impervious to logic would be opposed to its early demolition," the Guardian said.

The paper also commended the HSRC report's criticism of South Africa's apartheid and security laws.

The laws undermined the legitimacy of the state and the security laws were used mostly to silence extra-partliamentary opponents and themselves constituted a threat to the security of the state, the report found.

The report was "an unprecedented blunt and bold critique of the elaborate apparatus of legalised repression," the Guardian said.

Both newspapers said the report could bode well for South Africa's future.

"If liberal Afrikaners can advance an argument so openly, there is perhaps cause for hope," the Telegraph said.

● The Kappie Kommando has rejected the Human Sciences Research Council's report.

"The people I represent reject with contempt this attempt to defraud the country," the leader of the organisation, Mrs Marie van Zyl said, in Pretoria yesterday.

She said the report had been initiated by people in the United States. — Sapa

Daily Dispatch

"You're right, it stinks."

Power must be shared HSRC

A major Human Sciences Research Council report on group relations has attacked the apartheid system for contributing to tension and violence in South African society. It calls for active steps to be taken to reduce conflict by guaranteeing free association of individuals and equal opportunities, while recognising group rights. The main committee report is based on 11 studies which take a critical look at all aspects of society, ranging from the legal system to the presentation of South African history. COLLEEN RYAN reports.

Apartheid has reduced opportunities for spontaneous and close contact to be made between groups in South Africa and has given rise to mistrust and suspicion.

This is the conclusion reached by the HSRC main report into group relations.

It calls for the sharing of political power and a broadening of democracy which it says is crucial for the development of a stable social order.

Classical apartheid has failed, but "it would be incorrect to infer from this that alternative policies proposed in the past would necessarily have succeeded", says the report.

A study of intergroup relations revealed that conflict was increasing, mainly due to rivalry between political and economic groups.

But the HSRC study says there are "positive" signs that a democratic social order can be established in the light of the Government's recent reforms.

Analyses of factors such as attitudes, stereotypes, communication and the ambivalent roles of religion, historiography and the mass media, confirm that South Africa is a divided and polarised society.

Polarisation, bureaucratic control and government rigidity have created much suspicion and uncertainty, and as a result group relations have become "a permanent source of conflict".

"The present pattern of differentiation of interest groups in SA is undeniably and probably the major source of conflict in SA.

"Most important, though, is the finding that attitudes have changed; that there are signs of a greater willingness among people of different groups to join forces and face the challenges together," says the report.

It says reform will "inevitably be inconvenient for whites".

The key issue "is whether the forces active in society are sufficient to ensure, separately and collectively, that SA will develop a stable social order with an inescapable but manageable minimum of social disruption and conflict".

The report says "there will not be much consolation for those who are under the illusion that the transition from an apartheid society to a broader democratically oriented social order will occur virtually overnight and without a hitch — or that the whites have such control over their own destiny that they can dictate the rate, direction and nature of change according to their own needs".

Nor will there be consolation for those who simply assume that uncontrolled violence will lead to the ideal society.

"The conclusion reached in this report is therefore that the political ordering of intergroup relations according to the original apartheid model has reached an impasse and that constructive relations cannot be developed further along these lines .... It is clear that moderate forces must be mobilised if intergroup relations are to develop positively in a conciliatory and mutually positive way."

Four specific problems which emerge from the study are those of the handling of diversity, the individual and his group association, institutionalised inequality, and isolation.

The report says race is an irrelevant concept on which to base differentiation.

Blacks, coloureds and Indians do not deny the reality of group differentiation in a plural society but object to the way that group membership of individuals is ascriptively enforced by a politically dominant group.

The study says it is possible to build constructive human relations in South Africa if general religious values are followed, civil rights in terms of the common law are accepted, the individual's right to economic freedom is guaranteed and the right to democratic participation in decision-making is accepted.

Other important recommendations include:

● The political order should enable everyone to participate in some way at local, regional and national level.
● The economic system should make provision for growth and development and should offer equal opportunities.
● The juridical system should make provision for the restitution and protection of juridical values in terms of common law.
● The educational system should make provision for the establishment and propagation of common values.

The Star

Note:

These reports have been reproduced with the permission of the newspapers concerned.

210

INDEX

212